Young Muslims and Christians in a Secular Europe

Also Available from Bloomsbury

Amplifying Islam in the European Soundscape, Pooyan Tamimi Arab
Contemporary Muslim Christian Encounters, edited by Paul Hedges
Evangelical Youth Culture, Ibrahim Abraham

Young Muslims and Christians in a Secular Europe

Pursuing Religious Commitment in the Netherlands

Daan Beekers

BLOOMSBURY ACADEMIC
LONDON • NEW YORK • OXFORD • NEW DELHI • SYDNEY

BLOOMSBURY ACADEMIC
Bloomsbury Publishing Plc
50 Bedford Square, London, WC1B 3DP, UK
1385 Broadway, New York, NY 10018, USA
29 Earlsfort Terrace, Dublin 2, Ireland

BLOOMSBURY, BLOOMSBURY ACADEMIC and the Diana logo
are trademarks of Bloomsbury Publishing Plc

First published in Great Britain 2021
This paperback edition published in 2022

Copyright © Daan Beekers, 2021

Daan Beekers has asserted his right under the Copyright,
Designs and Patents Act, 1988, to be identified as Author of this work.

For legal purposes the Acknowledgments on pp. ix–xi constitute
an extension of this copyright page.

Cover image © René van Dam / 2021

All rights reserved. No part of this publication may be reproduced or transmitted in
any form or by any means, electronic or mechanical, including photocopying,
recording, or any information storage or retrieval system, without prior
permission in writing from the publishers.

Bloomsbury Publishing Plc does not have any control over, or responsibility for,
any third-party websites referred to or in this book. All internet addresses given
in this book were correct at the time of going to press. The author and publisher
regret any inconvenience caused if addresses have changed or sites have
ceased to exist, but can accept no responsibility for any such changes.

A catalogue record for this book is available from the British Library.

Library of Congress Control Number: 2020947734

ISBN:	HB:	978-1-3501-2731-9
	PB:	978-1-3501-9931-6
	ePDF:	978-1-3501-2732-6
	eBook:	978-1-3501-2733-3

Typeset by Integra Software Services Pvt Ltd.

To find out more about our authors and books visit www.bloomsbury.com
and sign up for our newsletters.

To my parents, Herman and Ineke

Contents

Acknowledgments		ix
1	Introduction: A Comparative Anthropology of Religious Commitment	1
2	Becoming Committed	35
3	Authentic Submission and Moral Self-Scrutiny	65
4	Doubt, Community, and Conviction	93
5	Fitting God In	121
6	Distraction, Habituation, and Closeness to God	147
7	Conclusion	173
Notes		187
References		197
Index		221

Acknowledgments

Over the years of writing this book, I have worked at several academic institutions, learned from new colleagues, and gained valued friendships. I have also accumulated many debts along the way. First and foremost, I thank all of those who participated in my research. While there are many whom I would like to mention by name, I cannot do so here for the sake of anonymity. I am nonetheless deeply grateful for the willingness of my research participants to welcome me into their community spaces and to share their personal stories, feelings, and struggles. Their frankness often astonished me. It has been a privilege to partake in their religious life-worlds, which so often remain poorly understood in our normatively secular times. I hope they can recognize themselves in the ways in which I have represented their views and experiences.

The research and writing took place at the Department of Social and Cultural Anthropology of the Vrije Universiteit in Amsterdam, the Department of Philosophy and Religious Studies of Utrecht University, the Leibniz-Zentrum Moderner Orient in Berlin, the Institute for Advanced Studies in the Humanities (IASH) at the University of Edinburgh, and the Alwaleed Centre for the Study of Islam in the Contemporary World at the same university. I thank the members of these institutions for their support, advice, and collegiality. I gratefully acknowledge that my work on this book was funded by the Open MaGW Program of the Dutch Research Council (NWO), research and travel grants from the Faculty of Social Sciences of the Vrije Universiteit, and a Postdoctoral Research Fellowship at IASH. I am also thankful to the Alwaleed Centre at the University of Edinburgh for its financial contribution toward the production of this book.

This study has profited greatly from the guidance and advice of Birgit Meyer. Dedicated to the project from its start, she has been an inspiring and enthusiastic mentor. I am hugely grateful for her input, encouragement, and support, which exceed all reasonable expectations. I am also deeply indebted to Anton van Harskamp, whose meticulous scrutiny of my work, erudite knowledge, and gentle enthusiasm have been an immense support. My collaboration and numerous conversations with David Kloos have been a source of pleasure and intellectual stimulation. Markus Balkenhol and Paul Mepschen have provided extraordinary inspiration and comradery. Margreet van Es has been exceptionally generous in terms of her interest in and encouragement of my work. The ideas and questions of Pooyan Tamimi Arab have helped me think outside the box. Ernst van den Hemel has motivated me on important moments. These friends and colleagues have all read drafts of parts of the manuscript and I thank them for their insightful comments and suggestions.

The research project Religious Matters in an Entangled World, directed by Birgit Meyer at Utrecht University, and the wider "religion, media and heritage" research community in the Netherlands (and beyond) have provided inspiring and collegial intellectual environments. In Edinburgh, my fellowships at IASH and the Alwaleed Centre afforded precious time and productive conditions to complete the book. Particular thanks are due to the permanent staff at these institutions, especially Steve Yearley, Ben Fletcher-Watson, Donald Ferguson, and Pauline Clark at IASH; and Frédéric Volpi, Elvire Corboz, and Tom Lea at the Alwaleed Centre. I am also grateful to Lotte Hoek, Maya Mayblin, and Christopher Cotter, who gave helpful advice and welcomed me in the academic community of Edinburgh.

John Bowen and Giulia Liberatore kindly read the entire manuscript and provided incisive and very useful comments. Martha Frederiks, Dick Houtman, Samuli Schielke, Peter-Ben Smit, and Thijl Sunier engaged closely with my work at an earlier stage and offered perspicacious feedback. Annette Jansen, Bruno Reinhardt, Irene Stengs, Jojada Verrips, Vanessa Vroon-Najem, and Marleen de Witte read, and offered helpful comments on, draft versions of chapters. I am also grateful for stimulating conversations with numerous colleagues. I cannot mention all of them here, but I would like to name Mohammed Amer, Schirin Amir-Moazami, Edien Bartels, Stefan Binder, Nella van den Brandt, Lenie Brouwer, Scott Dalby, Islam Dayeh, Daniel Nilsson DeHanas, Hansjörg Dilger, Stefan Ecks, Nina Glick Schiller, Mieke Groeninck, Murtala Ibrahim, Marloes Janson, Timothy Jenkins, Duane Jethro, Martijn de Koning, Kai Kresse, Nina ter Laan, Peter Lambertz, Erik Meinema, Inge Melchior, Norman Saadi Nikro, Mattijs van de Port, Jasmijn Rana, Johan Roeland, Lieke Schrijvers, Anna Strhan, Markha Valenta, Peter van der Veer, Oskar Verkaaik, and Rhoda Woets.

Gerd Baumann—who sadly passed away far too early—and Peter van Rooden were outstanding mentors when I started to think about the themes explored in this study. This would have been a different book without them. Ruth Marshall stimulated me at a crucial moment to pursue this comparative project. Marjo Buitelaar, Kim Knott, and David Pratten offered much-appreciated support during different stages of the project. I am also indebted to Joel Robbins, who generously engaged with my work in its final stages and helped me navigate the intricacies of finding a home for one's book. I thank the team at Bloomsbury Academic for their efficient work in bringing this book to publication. Furthermore, I am grateful to David Menassa and Achim Rosemann for sharing the joys and challenges of academic life. Thomas van der Molen and Erik van Ommering have helped and nourished me in innumerable ways during writing. I feel privileged to have such amazing friends. I thank my family, especially my brothers Wouter and Thomas, Peter-Hans, Saskia and Rie (gran) ter Weer, and Jos Palm and Mar Oomen, for their support throughout the years.

This book owes much to my parents, Herman Beekers and Ineke Palm. They have nurtured and stimulated many of the skills and dispositions I have relied on while pursuing this project. I thank them for their unrelenting trust and encouragement. Carlijn ter Weer has been a wonderful companion on this long journey, from its first stages many years ago in Amsterdam up to its completion in Edinburgh. I am deeply grateful for her commitment, support, and love over the years. It is with much anticipation that I look forward to the next adventure that awaits us.

Parts of Chapter 4 were previously published in "Pedagogies of Piety: Comparing Young Observant Muslims and Christians in the Netherlands," *Culture and Religion* 15, no. 1 (2014), 72–99. An earlier version of Chapter 5 previously appeared as "Fitting God In: Secular Routines, Prayer and Deceleration among Young Dutch Muslims and Christians," in *Straying from the Straight Path: How Senses of Failure Invigorate Lived Religion*, edited by Daan Beekers and David Kloos (Oxford and New York: Berghahn, 2018), 72–89. I thank the publishers for permission to reproduce this material.

1

Introduction: A Comparative Anthropology of Religious Commitment

On a mild summer afternoon in Rotterdam, I met with a small group of young Muslim and Christian women. As I was conducting fieldwork on young, actively practicing Muslims and Christians, I had invited them to join in a focus group discussion and talk about their experiences of living a religious life in the Netherlands. The participants were all in their early twenties, university-trained, and actively committed to their religion. At some point during our conversation, the Muslim women mentioned they constantly had to correct widespread negative images of Islam. Reflecting on her experience as a Christian, Roos reacted to this: "I rather always have the idea that I have to correct the *dull* image, because I kind of feel responsible for that. Since, especially in the student world, a lot of people really do have a bit of a dull, boring image of being Christian and of Bible study, reading the Bible." One of her Muslim interlocutors, Amane, responded laughingly: "That's actually a very big difference. We have to explain why we kill other people and…," she paused. "And you have to explain that it's not dull!" Farida finished her sentence.

While this is a fairly extreme rendition of the contrast between stereotypes of Christians and Muslims, it is illustrative of the divergent ways in which these groups tend to be perceived in Dutch society and elsewhere in Europe. Christians—specifically white Christians—are generally considered to be part of the majority population. Although they regularly take up divergent stances on moral issues concerning sexuality, family, or popular culture, neither are they generally defined as a "religious minority" as such, nor is their belonging to the nation questioned. In much of the dominant discourse, Christian culture is rather approached as outdated, odd perhaps, but by and large harmless. By contrast, Muslims, including those born in the Netherlands, often continue to be seen as people from abroad. Pronounced anxieties about Islam and recurrent practices of "othering" have fed prevalent perspectives on Muslims as essentially different from the white majority population—both Christian and secular. This has resulted in widespread assumptions about Muslims' "incommensurable otherness" (Gilroy 2005, 8), which is seen to contribute to persistent problems of integration, religiously inspired intolerance, and even extremism.

Yet, as our conversation on that afternoon in Rotterdam unfolded, it became clear how much common ground these young women shared. They experienced very similar struggles as young believers in a society that offered little support of, and frequently limited patience for, their religious endeavors. To illustrate, after Esther remarked that when she publicly talks about her Christian beliefs people tend to react with surprise or even feel challenged, Amane said she recognized this: "Sometimes I feel like you can't really be yourself completely.... When I'm sitting around the table with people and they talk about *everything* except religion, because they want to avoid that subject.... I do find that a pity." This level of consonance was illustrative for the parallels between the young Muslims and Christians I worked with more generally. Notwithstanding their pronounced religious and cultural differences, they faced common constraints on their religious expressions and practices. It also struck me that they shared a markedly self-reflexive religious commitment.

These commonalities between religiously observant young Muslims and Christians in European societies like the Netherlands have received remarkably little attention. Not only in public debates but also in academic research these groups tend to be approached differently. Studies of Christians and Muslims in Europe (and the 'Western world' more generally) have been embedded in divergent disciplinary traditions, each characterized by their own academic communities and separate theoretical debates. Research on Christians has been mostly conducted within the sociology of religion, with an analytical emphasis on theories of secularization and religious transformation. As scholars working within this tradition have pointed out, Muslims have for a long time been disregarded in this field (Poulson and Campbell 2010; Cadge, Levitt, and Smilde 2011; Yukich 2018). This religious group is more commonly studied within the field of minority and migration studies, which focuses on issues of social integration and identity formation. Driven by political concerns about "integration" (Sunier 2014), an overarching concern in the study of Muslims in Europe has been the "compatibility" between Muslim cultures and—secular or liberal—national norms and values in Europe (Peter 2006, 105; Bowen 2010, 8–10). If secularization and religious transformation constitute the default theoretical framework for research on Christians in Europe, then integration constitutes that for work on European Muslims.

To an important extent, this disciplinary division reflects the native-immigrant divide in public discourses: Christians tend to be approached as part of—or at least closely related to—the majority culture, which has been marked by the decline of organized and institutionalized religion. Muslims are rather positioned as a minority group set apart from this majority population, representing a new religious presence in Europe. Accordingly, while current forms of religious engagement among young Christians are often understood in terms of their dissatisfaction with impersonal, institutionalized religion and by their desire for a subjectively fulfilling religiosity (see e.g. Giordan 2010), those among young Muslims are more generally seen to be characterized by identity politics and their negotiation of multiple cultural registers (see e.g. Bozorgmehr and Kasinitz 2018). These separate theoretical orientations are in important ways informed by the distinct social histories of these two religious groups. Nonetheless, they have contributed to a disregard of common pathways and potentially shared patterns underlying their particular trajectories, such as the ways in which both respond to, and accommodate, contemporary secular dynamics.

The anthropology of religion has the potential to overcome this scholarly bifurcation. Yet, while the framework of secularization is transcended in ethnographic studies of Christians in Europe (see e.g. Coleman 2000; Strhan 2015; Bakker Kellogg 2019), just as that of integration is in ethnographic work on Muslims (see e.g. Jacobsen 2011; Jouili 2015; Liberatore 2017), this field too is characterized by a separation between research on Muslims and Christians. This tendency has been strengthened by the emergence of distinct anthropologies of Islam and Christianity (Meyer 2016), which have called renewed attention to theological traditions and normative frameworks. In influential strands of the anthropology of Islam, this has fostered a focus on religious tradition and Islamic piety, which are often contrasted with liberal and secular norms (see e.g. Mahmood 2005; Jouili and Amir-Moazami 2006; Fadil 2008). In the anthropology of Christianity, scholars like Joel Robbins (2003; 2004), Webb Keane (2007), and Susan Harding (2000) have highlighted the cultural and ideological particularities of Christianity. This has inspired a body of work with a focus on Christian experiences of conversion, rupture, and discontinuity with local cultural practices. Much of this literature has drawn out the interconnections between Christianity, modernity, and secularism.

While the development of these sub-disciplines has inspired vast theoretical advancement, it has also moved the analytical lens away from cross-religious comparison (Beekers 2020). Instead, intellectual efforts at comparison have taken an intrareligious focus: scholars within the anthropology of Christianity in particular have explicitly advocated the systematic, comparative study of Christians across different parts of the world (Robbins, Schieffelin, and Vilaça 2014, 559). Ethnographic comparison of Muslims and Christians who coexist in the same geographical and social spaces, I argue, does not only have equal analytical potential, but is also all the more urgent in the light of contemporary realities of interreligious co-existence and the challenges these entail. Such work can shed light on the convergences between particular groups of Muslims and Christians as well as offer a nuanced and situated understanding of their differences.

On that basis this book offers a comparative ethnography of religious commitment among Muslim and Christian young adults in the Netherlands. It approaches these groups as young Dutch people who are pursuing their religious aspirations within a shared socio-historical context. Indeed, my research participants have all grown up in Dutch society, speak Dutch, have gone through the same school system, attend the same universities, compete on the same job market, and navigate the same (urban) landscapes. They also participate in—or are at least familiar with—the same public debates, national events, forms of popular culture and mass media. More broadly speaking, they co-exist in a predominantly secular, pluralist, and high capitalist society. This study starts from the premise that the opportunities, constraints, and challenges that this shared context entails with respect to their pursuit of religious commitment provide a productive entry point for comparatively analyzing the everyday religious lives of these young Muslims and Christians.

The Netherlands provides an important context for a study of religious dedication under prevailing secular conditions. While Western European societies have generally seen a substantial erosion of institutionalized Christianity since the 1960s, this process has been especially rapid and intense in the Netherlands (Houtman and Mascini 2002, 455; Van Rooden 2010, 175). Moreover, liberal-secular and progressive values are particularly pervasive in Dutch popular and political culture. Notions of individual freedom, sexual liberty, free speech, and the separation of church and state are central to dominant narratives about national identity (Duyvendak, Geschiere, and Tonkens 2016; Kešić and Duyvendak 2019, 447). As a result, religious communities, which may in many cases not conform to progressive and liberal norms, are routinely criticized and put under pressure. Indeed, as I will discuss below, in Dutch public debates Protestants, Catholics, and, especially, Muslims are often placed in opposition to dominant liberal and secular values. Because of the strong secular nature of Dutch public culture, an analysis of religious commitment in the Netherlands provides a sharply focused lens on the potentially tense relation between religious endeavors and the secular dynamics found more widely in Europe today.

Young Revivalist Muslims and Christians in the Netherlands

This study is based on ethnographic fieldwork conducted between 2009 and 2012 in several urban settings in the Netherlands. In this fieldwork, I focused on highly educated young adults aged between 18 and 28, who strove to actively practice their religion in their everyday lives. Specifically, I worked with Sunni Muslims of various—but mostly Moroccan—backgrounds and Calvinist Protestant Christians of Dutch descent.[1] I deliberately looked at ethnically Dutch, white Christians—rather than Christians with a migration background—so as to move the analysis beyond an exclusive focus on migrant or ethnic minority groups and to challenge taken-for-granted boundaries between (Muslim) "migrants" and (Christian) "natives." My focus was on young believers who oriented themselves on revivalist tendencies in contemporary Islam and Christianity. Most of the young Muslims I worked with attended talks and mosque classes, and visited websites, within Salafi and other reformist networks. Most of the young Christians I met had joined student associations and attended events situated within the evangelical movement and listened to evangelical worship music. Yet, while they drew inspiration from these revivalist strands, most of my interlocutors neither identified themselves explicitly with them nor ascribed fully to their ideologies or theologies.

In the Netherlands, as elsewhere in Europe, these revivalist-oriented Sunni Muslims and Protestant Christians comprise two of the most prominent groups expressing a vibrant religious commitment and fueling public and academic debates about the continuing public presence of religion (Ter Borg et al. 2008; Roeland et al. 2010; Roy 2013). This religious engagement is particularly apparent among the younger generations. Recent survey research conducted by the Netherlands Institute for Social Research (SCP) has indicated the continuing, and even renewed, vitality of religious involvement among young Sunni Muslims and Protestant Christians. With regard to the former group, the SCP observes that "the importance of faith" is increasing for "a large part of the second generation" (Huijnk 2018, 14). With respect to young Dutch Christians, it identifies a revival of the "Christian religious tradition," which is expressed in church attendance, doctrinal adherence, and the value attached to a strong faith (De Hart 2014, 87).[2]

This book focuses on these groups of actively practicing, revivalist-oriented young adults for three main reasons. First, I aim to better understand, through a grounded ethnographic approach, the remarkable religious fervor and dedication found among these young believers. What does this religious commitment look like in their everyday lives, what factors contribute to it, what modalities of understanding and living in the world does it enable, and to what extent do they succeed in inhabiting these? Second, I am interested in the ways in which religious pursuits are affected by the social context in which they take place. It can be expected that very committed believers face an especially pronounced contrast between their ambitious religious aspirations and the pluralist world in which they find themselves. This is likely even more so for young people, who participate particularly actively in that pluralist world given their close engagement with school, jobs, popular culture, consumerism, and new media (C. Smith and Snell 2009, 77).[3] I seek to explore how the pious endeavors of young Muslims and Christians are crisscrossed by these kinds of engagement, and the modes of being and acting they imply.

Finally, these revivalist-oriented groups, often labeled as "orthodox," "fundamentalist," or "radical," are at the forefront of today's public debates and anxieties about religion in the Netherlands and elsewhere. Given the prevalent stereotypes, prejudices, and suspicions of these Christians and—especially—Muslims (Borgman 2009; Bowen 2012b; Nussbaum 2012), it is my goal to contribute to these debates by providing a nuanced, empirically informed picture of precisely these religious groups. Doing so, I do not claim to offer a comprehensive overview of Christianity and Islam in the Netherlands. Rather, my goal is to examine what it means to pursue a strict religious path in a predominantly secular Europe through a comparison of religiously dedicated young Christians and Muslims in the Netherlands. While the groups I focus on take up prominent positions among young religious people, they are not necessarily representative for all young Dutch Muslims and Christians. I should therefore note from the outset that the particularities of the groups I worked with have shaped my comparative analysis. To understand why, in the Netherlands today, their pious endeavors stand out and are often met with raised eyebrows—if not outright suspicion—it is useful to take a closer look at the recent history of religious changes and the shifting discourses on religion in this country.

Religious Changes in the Netherlands

Until the second half of the twentieth century, institutionalized Christianity had been of major social, cultural, and political importance in the Netherlands. In an influential analysis of distinct "religious regimes" emerging in the course of Dutch history, Peter van Rooden (1996, 20–42) has described the central social and political place of religion ever since the institution of the Dutch Republic in the late sixteenth century. In the seventeenth and eighteenth centuries, the Reformed church became the "public church" of the Republic, which meant that Calvinist Protestants enjoyed strong social and political privileges—at the cost of Catholic and non-Calvinist Protestant denominations. In the nineteenth century, the Netherlands came to be reinvented as a "Protestant nation," in which Protestant religion—broadly defined, so no longer restricted to the Calvinist church—was seen as constitutive of individual membership to the national moral community. From the end of the nineteenth century, the socio-political order of a unified Protestant nation dissolved due to the emergence of separate moral communities of orthodox Protestants, Catholics, socialists, and, to a lesser extent, liberals.

This era of "pillarization," which lasted until the mid-twentieth century, resulted from movements of mass social and political mobilization. These started with the Calvinist movement of the theologian Abraham Kuyper, which created religious, social, and political institutions outside of the structures of the national Protestant church (Van Rooden 1996, 34–7). Catholics, who had regained rights of congregation and organization, soon followed with their own institutionalized sub-culture, as did socialists. In this period, organized religion took a central position in social, cultural, and political life in the Netherlands. The social lives of the majority of Dutch were framed by the structures of organized religion and ideology. Schooling, housing, unions, media, and associational life were to a large extent organized and regulated by orthodox Protestant, Catholic, and socialist institutions—even if these bounded "pillars" were also evaded and contested by some parts of the population (Van Dam 2011).

After the Second World War, and especially from the 1960s onward, these confessional and ideological worlds gradually lost their social prominence (Van Dam and Van Trigt 2015). Their social infrastructure slowly crumbled as confessional and ideological identity became less pertinent for civic organizations, social institutions, and cultural associations. During these decades, church affiliation decreased dramatically. Christian church membership dropped from just over 75 percent of the population in 1958 to 50 percent in 1980 and 30 percent in 2012 (De Hart 2014, 38). Meanwhile, the portion of the population that regularly—in most cases weekly—attends church services decreased from 50 percent in 1966 to 12 percent in 2015 (Bernts and Berghuijs 2016, 25). Other countries in Northwest Europe have witnessed parallel developments (McLeod 1997), even if the process of church decline has been particularly dramatic in the Netherlands (Van Rooden 2010).

This widespread decline of organized religion, in the Netherlands and elsewhere in Western Europe, has in part been triggered by socio-economic developments such as the rise of the welfare state, quick economic growth, the onset of consumer cultures, increasing personal mobility, women's emancipation, and the introduction of television (Kennedy 1995; Mazower 1999; Righart 2004). In the Netherlands, these processes increasingly undermined the notion that all Dutch citizens belonged to any one of the distinct moral communities embodied by the pillars. Instead, they contributed to a renewed conception of the nation as a single moral community (Van Rooden 1996, 44; Van Dam and Van Trigt 2015). Cultural changes also played an important role: especially from the 1960s onward, ideals of self-realization, self-expression, and authenticity transgressed the (elite) realms of philosophy, art, and literature, and entered into mass culture (Taylor 2007, chap. 13; Brown 2009; Van Rooden 2010). As people's everyday lives were increasingly influenced by heightened mobility, affluence, consumption, and ideals of autonomous self-expression, Christian religious practices were, as Van Rooden put it, "slowly pushed ... ever farther away from the core of personal life until they simply became irrelevant" (2010, 191).

For many, however, the move away from church did not mean a complete break with religion or spirituality, but rather an engagement with other, often more personalized forms of belief and spiritual practice (Van Harskamp 2000; De Hart 2011; cf. Heelas and Woodhead 2005). Recent survey research has shown that a substantial group of 17 percent of the Dutch are not—or no longer—affiliated to any church but still consider themselves to be "believers" within a broad Christian framework. Another 10 percent have little affinity with Christian faith but do see themselves as "spiritually" inclined (Bernts and Berghuijs 2016, 40ff.).

Moreover, the decline of institutionalized Christianity has not affected everyone to the same degree. Today a substantial minority of 25 percent of the Dutch consider themselves to be affiliated to a Christian church (Bernts and Berghuijs 2016, 21). This adherence is particularly strong among Calvinist Protestants, specifically among the more conservative denominations among them (De Hart and Van Houwelingen 2018). These communities, concentrated in the Dutch "Bible Belt" but present throughout the Netherlands, continue to form a self-conscious Protestant sub-culture characterized by a strong sense of identity and by a social infrastructure that includes educational institutions, media outlets, and political parties (Baars-Blom 2006; Pons 2014; Exalto 2017). In recent decades, further, evangelical and Pentecostal churches and organizations, which emphasize subjective experience and contemporary forms of worship, have gained popularity (Roeland 2009; Versteeg 2010; Klaver 2011). These include a rapidly grown number of "migrant churches" (Jansen and Stoffels 2008; Knibbe 2009; Smit 2012).[4] While the Dutch Roman Catholic Church has been especially hard-hit by declining church attendance (Bernts and Berghuijs 2016, 25), it also continues to harbor active local communities and renewal movements (Winkeler 2004; Van Dijk-Groeneboer 2010). Most of the young Christians with whom I conducted research hailed from the Calvinist Protestant sub-culture and subscribed to any one of its constitutive denominations. The great majority of them was also involved, to varying degrees, with the evangelical movement through for instance youth organizations, student associations, church activities and festivals.

The decline of church affiliation since the 1960s has coincided with a growing presence and visibility of Muslims in the Netherlands. While Islam has long been a part of the Dutch (colonial) past,[5] today's Muslim communities in the Netherlands derive mostly from a history of labor migration, especially from Turkey and Morocco, during the 1960s and 1970s. People of Turkish and Moroccan descent now constitute two-thirds of the total Dutch Muslim population of around 1 million people (6 percent of the total Dutch population) (Huijnk 2018, 21, 23). Smaller groups of Muslims include those with postcolonial backgrounds (Indonesians and Surinamese), refugee backgrounds (from Iraq, Afghanistan, Somalia, and former Yugoslavia, among other places), and converts to Islam (Huijnk 2018, 21). The great majority of Muslims in the Netherlands are Sunnis,[6] with most subscribing to either the Hanafi school of religious jurisprudence (predominant in Turkey) or the Maliki school (predominant in Morocco).

Many—though not all (Akgündüz 1993, 369–74)—of the Turkish and Moroccan labor migrants came from rural areas and had enjoyed limited education (De Jong 2008, 61). When it became clear, by the 1980s, that these migrants and their families were not just temporary visitors but staying in the country for an indefinite period of time, they started to organize themselves religiously. This process resulted in the gradual institutionalization of Islam in Dutch society (Landman 1992). Today, there are around 450 mosques in the Netherlands as well as a wider Islamic social infrastructure including representative bodies, advocacy organizations, educational institutions, and halal businesses (De Koning 2019, 484–92). Most mosques and other Islamic institutions are established and managed along ethnic lines (De Koning 2019, 484). Yet, as I have observed during my fieldwork, there is a growing number of mosques that are not (completely) defined by ethnicity and that offer their sermons, talks or classes in Dutch. These mosques, some of which ascribe to a Salafi theology, attract young Muslims particularly.

Today, more than half of the Dutch people with a Turkish or Moroccan background were born in the Netherlands.[7] Most of them take up notably stronger socio-economic positions than their parents, especially when it comes to education, employment, and income (CBS 2018). Nonetheless, there continue to be stark differences between the Moroccan and Turkish Dutch populations as a whole and the ethnic Dutch population.[8] For instance, 27 percent of the Moroccan Dutch between the ages of 25 and 45 have enjoyed higher education at (vocational or academic) universities, as compared to 41 percent of the same age group among ethnic Dutch (CBS 2018). Likewise, in 2017 unemployment rates were still significantly higher among Turkish and Moroccan Dutch (9.6 and 11.3 percent respectively) than among ethnic Dutch (3.9 percent) (CBS 2018). In relation to this, cases of discrimination against Muslims and migrants on the job market are recurrent and, more generally, experiences of discrimination and intolerance have increased in recent years among Muslims in the Netherlands (Huijnk 2018, 65).

Religious affiliation among Turkish and Moroccan Dutch has remained strong in the past decades. According to the most recent survey report on Dutch Muslims' religiosity conducted by the SCP, 94 percent of Moroccan Dutch and 86 percent of Turkish Dutch identify themselves as Muslim (Huijnk 2018, 6). For the latter, this percentage has dropped slightly from 93 percent in 2006. In both groups, around 40 percent report that they weekly attend the Friday prayers in the mosque. For men, for whom this ritual is considered to be a religious obligation, this figure is just over 50 percent (Huijnk 2018, 33). Overall, 78 percent of Moroccan Dutch and 33 percent of Turkish Dutch state that they pray five times a day (36). The majority of Dutch Muslims report that they always eat halal and fast all days during the Ramadan. Moroccan Dutch, along with the smaller group of Somali Dutch, are found to exhibit the highest levels of religiosity on average (13). The SCP further shows that various religious practices, such as prayer, mosque attendance, and, for Moroccan-Dutch women particularly, wearing a *hijab* (Islamic veil), have become more widely observed in the last ten years (14). Levels of religious practice are highest among the first generation of Muslim migrants, but continue to be substantial among the second generation. In an earlier study, the SCP had already identified a remarkable increase in mosque attendance among the second generation between 1998 and 2011 (Maliepaard and Gijsberts 2012, 16).

The young Muslims with whom I conducted research belong to this group of religiously committed young adults. While most of my research participants were of Moroccan descent, I also worked with people with Turkish and, to a lesser extent, other ethnic backgrounds (including ethnically Dutch converts to Islam). All of my Muslim interlocutors had been born in the Netherlands or moved to the country with their families when they were very young. While many attended the same mainstream Moroccan (or Turkish) mosques as their parents did, they also learned about Islam by attending talks, following classes in (often Salafi) reformist mosques, reading books, and browsing the internet. While these young Muslims were active participants of Dutch society in terms of—among other things—language fluency, educational and work experience, media use, and friendships, they often did not feel fully accepted as part of that society. Moreover, although they rejected prevalent representations of themselves as "strangers," they too occasionally reproduced discursive distinctions between the "Dutch" and themselves (as "Muslims," "Moroccans," or "Turks").

Islamophobia and Shifting Discourses on Religion

The lack of social acceptance that many of my Muslim interlocutors experienced was related to the hardening political climate toward Islam in the Netherlands—and elsewhere in the Western world. In the first couple of decades following the arrival of Moroccan and Turkish migrant workers to the Netherlands, these communities were, in social and political discourses, primarily defined by their ethnicity. They came to be framed as "ethnic minorities," which were conceptualized as bounded migrant communities characterized by particular ethnic cultures, which were not (yet) fully integrated into Dutch society and socially deprived in comparison to the majority population—and therefore construed as a "problem group" demanding targeted government policies (Rath 1991, 15–19, 40–4). In these policies, cultural "traits" were understood to be temporary obstacles to full integration and "ethnic" organizations were regarded as stepping-stones making such integration possible (Rath 1991).

This approach started to change in the course of the 1990s and 2000s. In this period, migrants and their children with an Islamic background were increasingly "discovered" *as* Muslims (Sunier 2010, 123). This occurred against the background of a number of international events that turned Islam into an issue of major political interest, including the end of the Cold War and the reorientation of NATO on Islamic fundamentalism as a major threat (Esposito 1994). At the same time, Islam became more visible in Dutch urban spaces. In a move that reflected a longer tradition of Orientalism (Said 1995, 280), "Muslim culture," often depicted as something homogenous and coherent, "increasingly became the explanatory factor, not only for specific (collective) behavior of Muslims, but also for all kinds of societal problems they faced" (Sunier 2010, 124). And these societal problems seemed to be growing, not least due to the collapse of the manufacturing industry in the 1990s, which left many former "guest-workers" unemployed (Van der Veer 2006, 116). In the wake of 9/11 and the murder of Dutch filmmaker Theo van Gogh by a radicalized Moroccan-Dutch Muslim in 2004, negative perceptions of Islam became more widespread and unequivocally voiced by right-wing populist politicians such as Pim Fortuyn (who was assassinated by an animal rights activist in 2002), Rita Verdonk, and Geert Wilders. In recent years, anxieties about Muslims have further grown due to the rise of ISIS and its appeal on small segments of the Dutch Muslim population (Berger and Rademakers 2015) and due to concerns about the promotion of segregation and intolerant attitudes within parts of the Salafi movement.[9] In this context, Islam has been depicted not only as an impediment to social integration, but also—especially when it comes to Salafism—as a security threat (Vellenga and De Groot 2019). Compared to other European countries, public criticisms of Islam have been particularly strong and, in many cases, also particularly harsh and intolerant in the Netherlands (Van der Veer 2006; Mepschen, Duyvendak, and Tonkens 2010; Brubaker 2017, 1194–7). This phenomenon, spearheaded by political actors such as Fortuyn, Wilders, Ayaan Hirsi Ali, and, more recently, Thierry Baudet, can be related to already established anti-religious sentiments in the country on the one hand and to a "primordial turn" in prevalent discourses on the other.

Indeed, the narratives about Islam built on, but also transformed, longer existing discourses on religion in the Netherlands. Ever since the 1960s "cultural revolution," which was spearheaded by young people who revolted against what they saw as a dogmatic and patriarchal culture legitimized by Christian religion (Kennedy 1995; Righart 2004), intellectual and cultural elites have regularly portrayed religion as a threat to the now normative ideals of individual autonomy, sexual freedom, and the right to personal happiness and enjoyment (Borgman 2009, 30; Schinkel 2012, 241). These discourses on religion entail a distinctly temporal dimension whereby—particularly orthodox—religious adherents are framed as "lagging behind" today's perceived progressive and libertarian culture. Through such a hierarchical politics of time (Knibbe 2018, 660), religious subjects are "denied coevalness" (Fabian 1983, 31): they are not seen as people who are shaped by, and give shape to, contemporary society as much as others. Initially directed at Christians, this temporal discourse has been increasingly adopted with reference to Muslims, whose religiosity is regularly framed as an anachronistic phenomenon in a de-churched and predominantly secular culture (Van der Veer 2006, 120–2; Mepschen, Duyvendak, and Tonkens 2010, 970ff.). In recent decades, indeed, public criticism of religion has come to focus primarily on Islam (Kennedy and Valenta 2006, 345).

This heightened preoccupation with Islam has come, I suggest, with a more fundamental shift in Dutch secularist discourses. These discourses have moved, at least in part, from a critique of religion as an *internal* force, something of our past that we have not yet rid ourselves of completely, to a critique of religion as an *external* force, which forces itself upon a Dutch nation now perceived as essentially liberal and secular. As this external force is seen to be constituted by Islam in particular, there is a tendency to locate Muslims outside of the Dutch nation and to see them as a potential threat to that nation's perceived unity and secular order (Sunier 2010, 125–6; Schinkel 2012, 249). This discursive shift has coincided with the rise of a primordial language of belonging based on the distinction between "allochthons" and "autochthons"—indicating those "from a foreign land" and those "from this land" (Geschiere 2009). Implying something of an immutable essence, these terms suggest an unchangeable and recognizable identity that marks one as being either from "here" or from "another place" (Yanow and Van der Haar 2013). In everyday discourses, the term "allochthonous" has been particularly applied to people of Moroccan and Turkish descent (Geschiere 2009, 150) and often used interchangeably with the term "Muslim." Even though the word "allochthon" has recently been barred from official policy discourse, its extensive usage—and the broader discursive frames that the term signifies—has contributed to a shift in the representation of Muslims: rather than "not yet like us," they have increasingly come to be regarded as essentially "other."

This construal of Muslims as "allochthonous" and essentially "other," even if it does not necessarily express an explicit theory of "racial" hierarchies, points to a racialization of Muslims (Tamimi Arab 2012; Yanow and Van der Haar 2013; De Koning 2016). Tariq Modood and Nasar Meer, who have written extensively on this topic, argue that Islamophobia not only entails a "potentially sedate critique of Islam as a religion" but also "traffics in stereotypes about foreignness, phenotypes and culture" (Meer and Modood 2019, 19). Racialization, Steve Garner and Saher Selod (2015, 12) explain, "entails ascribing sets of characteristics viewed as inherent to members of a group because of their physical or cultural traits. These are not limited to skin tone or pigmentation, but include a myriad of attributes including cultural traits such as language, clothing, and religious practices." Heterogeneous people are fixed into an essentialized group, which is the product not so much of their similarity as of "the unity of the 'gaze' itself" (Garner and Selod 2015, 14). As a result of this process of racialization, being Muslim is perceived as an inherited and predetermined identity, rather than an outcome of personal actions, decisions, and beliefs. This is an important point to make in the Dutch context, given the hesitancy or reluctance among public intellectuals—and to some extent also scholars—to acknowledge the pervasiveness of racializing tendencies in discourses on minority groups (Wekker 2016; cf. Tamimi Arab 2012).

The primordial turn in Dutch debates about religion may explain why today's discomfort with religion is less directed at Christians, even though there continue to be moral outcries about especially orthodox-Calvinist and Pentecostal Christians' perceived divergence from liberal norms, particularly when it comes to issues of gender, sexuality, and LGBTQ rights (Knibbe 2018; Derks 2019). While Christians' cultural and sexual morality is regularly criticized, it is generally not taken as a reason to question their belonging to Dutch society—in the way it often is for Muslims (Beekers and Schrijvers 2020). Added to this, the discourse of autochthony and its concomitant quest to define what it means to be "Dutch" have inspired a nostalgic longing for a lost national identity (Duyvendak 2011). In recent years, politicians, intellectuals, and writers have increasingly appealed to Christian tradition as a defining feature of that identity—mobilizing and reframing the religion less as a system of beliefs and ritual practices than as a source of cultural heritage and memory (Van den Hemel 2014; Beekers 2017; Brubaker 2017; Meyer 2019). In that sense, Christians are now not merely seen as "lagging behind," but also as representatives of a religion that is regarded as essential to Dutch culture.

Toward a Comparative Anthropology of Muslims and Christians

This book offers a critical perspective on these conventional public representations of Dutch Muslims and Christians through a comparative ethnographic study of religious commitment. Such comparative work with two or more groups understood to be ethnically or religiously distinct has remained underdeveloped in anthropology, notwithstanding notable efforts to revive comparative approaches (see e.g. Holy 1987; Gingrich and Fox 2002; Scheffer and Niewöhner 2010; Van der Veer 2016; Candea 2018). Anthropologists have commonly defined their discipline as intrinsically comparative and many make use of some form of implicit comparison, especially by contrasting "other" concepts and categories to those of one's own society (cf. Candea 2018, 16). Yet, although important work has been done based on fieldwork with two or more culturally "distinct" groups (I cite some examples below), such explicitly comparative research has been less common. This relative lack indicates the discipline's ambiguous relationship to comparison. As the British anthropologist E. E. Evans-Pritchard famously remarked in the 1960s: "There is only one method in social anthropology, the comparative method—and that is impossible" (cited in Niewöhner and Scheffer 2010, 8).

This methodological unease with the comparative method results for an important part from the cultural relativist approach that characterizes the discipline. After having largely dispensed with the ambitious cross-cultural ambitions that typified early anthropology, the discipline has focused more on cultural specificity than on making generalizations (Holy 1987, 8). If human reality is culturally determined, so the argument goes, then each "culture" can be found to construct its own distinct reality, making the work of "translation" and comparison across cultures highly problematic (Bloch 1977). Anthropologists' ambiguity toward comparison is also informed by their method, in which the emphasis is put on intimate knowledge of a particular cultural group based on long-term, intensive participant-observation with that group. Dividing one's attention between two or more groups and having to learn about their day-to-day concerns, rituals, languages, traditions, and histories necessarily put limits on one's intimate knowledge of any one group. This is the inevitable setback of any comparative endeavor. Anthropologists, then, tend to be "unsympathetic" to "formal comparative operations" (Barth 1999, 78) and "shy away from the challenges of comparing complex practices" (Niewöhner and Scheffer 2010, 5).

As Jörg Niewöhner and Thomas Scheffer point out, comparison has become "an exercise within ethnographic fields rather than across fields. This is why the established statistical approach to cross-national or cross-cultural comparison lacks an ethnographic counterpart of similar disciplinary standing" (2010, 8–9).

Ethnographic comparison, however, has the potential to render insights that are more likely to remain obscured in non-comparative accounts. As Matei Candea (2018, 8) puts it succinctly, comparisons offer "bundles of heuristics which get jobs done." This involves delineating, and subsequently juxtaposing, particular social groups or other units of comparison—even if we know that reality is always more complex than such categories imply (Candea 2018, 8). This analytical work of "producing comparability" makes it possible to explicate social phenomena and relations that may otherwise remain unrecognized or unconnected (Niewöhner and Scheffer 2010, 11). Such juxtaposition can shed light not only on convergences but also on situated differences. It offers, as Karin Knorr Cetina has put it, a "comparative optics" whereby patterns observed in one unit of comparison serve "as a sensor for identifying and mapping (equivalent, analog, conflicting) patterns in the other" (1999, 4). While some recent strands in anthropology move even further toward assumptions about the uniqueness and incommensurability of distinct cultural worlds, as illustrated in part by what is known as the ontological turn (cf. Van der Veer 2016, 5), I suggest that our current era of global cultural flows, local diversification, and—often tense—intercultural and interreligious encounters makes comparative ethnographies more pressing than ever.

Rich and inspiring examples of such comparative ethnographic work include Edmund Leach's (1964) classic study of Kachins and Shans in highland Burma and Gerd Baumann's (1996) work on inter-ethnic interactions in a London suburb. Both authors sought to break with the anthropological conventions—in their respective times—of focusing on supposedly bounded cultural groups. They analytically situated groups that had thus far been described as fundamentally different, and studied independently from each other, into one comparative framework. Both Leach and Baumann examined how these groups not only interacted on an everyday basis but also shared particular discursive tools in order to position themselves in relation to others. In this way, they offered a *different kind* of intimate anthropological account as compared to research focusing on a single group. They provided a detailed description of a particular, localized social field marked by inter-group convergence, co-existence, interaction, and mutual borrowing, as well as by wider social dynamics affecting different groups simultaneously. Indeed, it seems more appropriate in such contexts to speak of a single rather than multiple ethnographic fields.

When it comes to research on Muslims and Christians, ethnographic comparison has remained underdeveloped. Much of the existing comparative work is based on quantitative survey research (e.g., Mullet and Azar 2009; Grundel and Maliepaard 2012; Zulfikar 2012; Koopmans 2015; Maudet 2017). Notwithstanding the important insights that such quantitative work can offer, it often falls short of providing a multidimensional and holistic understanding of everyday religious lives. The fewer existing qualitative comparative studies often focus less on the added value of Muslim-Christian comparison (i.e., the particular insights generated by juxtaposing these religious groups) than on a cross-religious analysis of particular theoretical concerns, such as youth and sexual identity (Yip and Page 2013), women's citizenship (Nyhagen and Halsaa 2016), or gender and female agency (Franks 2001; Bracke 2004; 2008a).[10] More explicit comparative work includes larger scale, theoretical explorations of Muslim and Christian revivalism (Dorraj 1999; Hefner 2010; Roy 2013) and joint publications by scholars working on different religious groups (Roeland et al. 2010; Van Dijk-Groeneboer et al. 2010).

Important initiatives of anthropological comparison of Muslims and Christians have come from scholarship on Africa, especially West Africa, where sizable populations of Muslims and Christians often live side by side (Sanneh 1996; Larkin and Meyer 2006; Soares 2006; Dilger 2013; Dilger and Schulz 2013; Peel 2015; Janson and Meyer 2016a; Ibrahim 2017; Nolte, Ogen, and Jones 2017). A large part of this work looks at the diverse forms of contact, conflict, and mutual borrowing between these religious groups. This focus on inter-religious encounters is informed by African contexts in which either Muslims or Christians (and sometimes both) constitute dominant groups in society. The situation in the Netherlands—and elsewhere in Western Europe—is different in that religiously observant Muslims and Christians constitute minority groups (albeit with different positions of privilege) facing a predominantly secular public sphere, in contrast to the religiously infused public cultures characterizing many African societies (see e.g. Hirschkind 2006; Meyer 2006; Larkin 2014). Consequentially, Muslims and Christians in the Netherlands are prompted less to relate to one another as to the secular dynamics of mainstream culture.

A productive entry point to ethnographic comparison of Muslims and Christians in Europe, then, is precisely to study how their everyday religious pursuits are shaped and constrained within a largely secular context. Already in 2004, Olivier Roy advocated an approach that places European Islam alongside "other Western religions" by examining the potentially intersecting ways in which adherents of different religions respond to today's predicament of "globalization" and "secularization" (2004, 26–7). To the limited extent that this call has been taken up, it has tended to take the shape of sweeping sociological accounts such as Roy's (2013) own work on the nature of contemporary religious fundamentalism, which focuses on attempts to invoke a "pure" religion devoid from cultural influences. More ethnographic sociological studies include Jeffrey Guhin's (2016) research on the responses to evolution theory in American Sunni and evangelical high schools and Daniel Nilsson DeHanas's (2016) work on civic engagement among young Muslims of Bangladeshi descent and young Christians of Jamaican descent in London.

In this book, I share DeHanas's concern with transcending an exclusive focus on the integration of Muslims in Europe by developing "comparative research that sets Muslims in context with others" (DeHanas 2016, 2). Yet whereas DeHanas looks at civic integration among second-generation migrant youth (Muslim, Christian, and non-religious), my focus is not on questions of immigrant integration but rather on the everyday pursuit of religious commitment among Muslims and Christians whom I approach above all as young adults who have grown up in Europe. The goal of this book is not to draw a comparison of the religious traditions of Islam and Christianity as such (as advocated for example by Decosimo 2018), but rather to examine how specific groups of young Dutch Muslims and Christians inhabit these traditions under shared social conditions. I aim to examine how Christian and Islamic modes of self-making and world-making are shaped, challenged, and perhaps enhanced by these shared conditions—looking specifically at the ethics of authenticity, cultural pluralism, fast capitalism, and the pervasiveness of modern media.

Secular and Capitalist Conditions of Religious Commitment

Most scholars of religion today reject secularization theory, which, in its "orthodox" variation, predicts "the diminishing social significance of religion" in the modern world (Wallis and Bruce 1992, 11). It is now commonly argued that religion is rather being transformed, relocated, and expressed in new ways.[11] Scholars have in recent years increasingly theorized the notion of "the secular"—and cognate concepts such as secularity and secularism—in order to examine the particular modes through which religion is understood, conditioned, or governed (see e.g. Calhoun, Juergensmeyer, and VanAntwerpen 2011; Mahmood 2016).

Most of this work takes either one of two approaches: the first is inspired for an important part by the work of Talal Asad (2003) and perceives the secular—or *secularism*—as a mode of governance. Rather than a stable cultural entity, the secular for Asad is inextricably linked with the category of religion and emerges within contextual and power-dependent constructions of a religious-secular dichotomy. The second, in line with Charles Taylor (2007), takes the secular—or *secularity*—as a phenomenon of intellectual culture, and as part of our "social imaginary": "the way we collectively imagine, even pre-theoretically, our social life" (2007, 146). Under conditions of secularity, Taylor argues, belief in the transcendent is challenged by the inclination "to understand our lives as taking place within a self-sufficient immanent order," which "can be envisaged without reference to God" (2007, 543). This effectively leaves belief as one option among others (3). Taylor's emphasis on the optionality of belief reflects a long sociological tradition, with Peter Berger (1967; 2014) as one of its foremost proponents, that treats pluralism as the defining trait of secular society.

What Asad and Taylor share is their approach to the secular as a *lived* reality—rather than merely a political doctrine or institutional frame—and as always interrelated with the religious (cf. Van Harskamp 2010). In this book, I build on these approaches to the secular as an everyday reality that shapes the conditions of possibility and impossibility for contemporary religious engagement. As Ashley Lebner, building on Taylor, puts it: secularity can be understood as a "lived condition" in which one is inevitably confronted by pressures that "may throw into question one's lifeways and beliefs" (2015, 69).

Yet, what struck me during my fieldwork was that for my Muslim and Christian interlocutors these pressures originated not only from intellectual thought, ideology, or political modes of governing religion, but also—and at least as much—from practical, everyday experiences grounded in contemporary consumer culture and a high capitalist economy. It became clear to me that their religious lives were importantly conditioned and constrained by the embodied habits and the taken-for-granted structures of everyday life in an accelerated and media-saturated culture. These made it difficult for them to realize their ambition—informed by their revivalist approach to faith—of pursuing, and consistently prioritizing, a self-conscious religious commitment. They grappled with routine practices that effectively, and often subtly, pushed religious activity to the background of their everyday lives.

While sociological and anthropological studies of religion have in recent decades put more emphasis on the compatibility between religion and consumer capitalism than on the potential tensions between them (see e.g. Martikainen and Gauthier 2013), my findings suggest that we need to pay full attention to both aspects of the relationship. Thus, I examine how the practices, aspirations, and sensibilities grounded in religion relate to, and are both affected and constrained by, those grounded in consumer capitalism. I understand these capitalist dynamics to be entangled with the lived conditions of secularity that religious practitioners encounter in the contemporary world. Indeed, consumer capitalism and the material practices and values related to it have often been described as an important substructure of secular practices and moralities (see e.g. Eagleton 2009, 39).

Thus, this book seeks to bring the study of religion and secularity in conversation with the extensive literature on contemporary capitalism, specifically the work on post-Fordism (Harvey 1989; Sennett 1998; Bauman 2000), fast capitalism (Eriksen 2001; Agger 2004), and network society (Castells 2000). This enables a broader understanding of the conditions of contemporary religious practice, which helps to make clear that many of the challenges to projects of religious commitment are not sited outside of young believers' lives but are part and parcel of their everyday routines, sensibilities, and desires (cf. Strhan 2015). This point is often disregarded in, especially, studies of Muslims in Europe, which tend to separate their religious endeavors from the secular environments in which they live.

Situating religious practice within these everyday secular and capitalist conditions, this book highlights the precariousness of the religious pursuits of my Muslim and Christian interlocutors. I show that their pious ideals were continuously challenged by competing modes of imagining and living in the world. Although they were generally confident about the truth of their religion and the path they wanted to follow, they often found it hard to stick to that path. Their religious commitment constantly risked losing its sense of priority and urgency. However certain they felt about their religious quest, its execution tended to be challenging. In strikingly similar ways, these young Christians and Muslims struggled with living in a social reality in which the option to live a less committed, less pious, kind of life was always close at hand. In today's Dutch society, their pursuits of faith took the shape of highly reflexive, aspirational projects that were inherently unstable.

The Interplay between Pious Aspirations and Social Constraints

By approaching the people I have studied as religious groups I neither assume that their religion constitutes the only relevant marker of their identities—as if they are "walk[ing] around in a religious bubble" (Ammerman 2014b, 194)—nor do

I want to suggest that they constitute homogeneous or unitary groups, thus falling into the pitfall of what Rogers Brubaker (2004, 8) terms "groupism." Rather, I approach the young adults I have worked with as "Muslims" and "Christians" because I aim to better understand what the pursuit of a strict religious path entails for young people in the Netherlands. My emphasis is on religion as an everyday activity: not a static identity but a practical and reflexive endeavor that draws from particular moral repertoires. Similarly to what Brubaker (2004, 81) argues for such categories as ethnicity, race, and nation, I hold that religion refers to important—though not stagnant—frameworks (textual traditions, established institutions, moral authorities, doctrines, and so forth) through which people make sense of their lives and distinguish themselves from others.

Taking the differentiating categories of Muslim and Christian as my point of departure makes it possible to explore both the disparities and the convergences between the everyday experiences of my Muslim and Christian interlocutors, thereby complicating the prevalent emphasis on their differences. Moreover, far from walking around in a religious bubble, the people with whom I worked lead multidimensional lives. Their religious engagement not only competed but also became entangled with other activities, ideals, and aspirations. Indeed, a basic starting point of this book is that pursuits of religious piety have to be understood within the wider social contexts in which they are situated. Religious subjectivities are shaped not in a vacuum but in interaction with other aspects of everyday life. This multiplicity of everyday life has become an increasingly important theme in the anthropology of religion, particularly in studies of Muslims.

The development of the anthropologies of Islam and Christianity has been driven by a desire to move beyond instrumentalist approaches that explain religious practices (away) by emphasizing their political, economic, or social dimensions. Informed, in part, by the global Islamic revival and the growth of evangelical and Pentecostal Christianity since at least the 1970s, anthropologists of Islam and Christianity have sought to pay serious attention to the role of religious models and ideals in the fashioning of moral subjects (see esp. Harding 2000; Robbins 2004; 2007; Mahmood 2005; Hirschkind 2006; Keane 2007; cf. Marshall 2009). Other scholars in these fields, however, have argued that this "non-reductive" approach to religion has resulted in a disproportionate emphasis on religious norms, piety, and discipline. Anthropologists of Islam, in particular, have pointed out that religious ideals often remain unfulfilled in the context of the ambivalence, multiplicity, and contingency of everyday life (Marsden 2005; Osella and Soares 2010; Schielke 2010; 2015; Simon 2014). Scholars of Christianity have similarly analyzed how religious endeavors are constrained by cultural traditions and socio-economic circumstances (Scott 2005; McDougall 2009; Chua 2012), or by the contradictions within religious doctrine itself (Cannell 2006; Engelke and Tomlinson 2006). This increased interest within the anthropology of religion in the indeterminate and incoherent nature of everyday life resonates to some extent with a broader turn to "everyday" or "lived" religion (see e.g. Ammerman 2007; McGuire 2008; Dessing et al. 2013), which puts the emphasis on the ways in which "ordinary" people imagine and practice religion in their everyday lives, often outside religious institutions.

This book builds on this scholarship on the imperfect achievement of religious ideals by looking closely at the experiences of struggle, uncertainty, and distraction among the young Muslims and Christians with whom I worked. Yet my findings also suggest that there is more to this dynamic than merely unfulfilled aspirations. What I learned during my fieldwork was that the felt setbacks that characterize these young people's everyday lives also affected and even reinvigorated their religious engagement in important ways. This kind of interplay between contingency and religious commitment has received little attention in the anthropological study of both Muslims and Christians. Instead, this scholarship has increasingly been characterized by an opposition between analyses of piety and self-fashioning on the one hand and analyses of everyday life and moral ambivalence on the other (Kloos and Beekers 2018). This is particularly evident in the anthropology of Islam: as Nadia Fadil and Mayanthi Fernando (2015) point out, the growing body of work on everyday experiences of ambivalence has tended to depict textual norms and everyday practices as separate and even opposed realms. Writing from a sociological perspective, Nancy Ammerman (2014b, 190) similarly warns that the analysis of lived religion should not only focus on activities outside the purview of religious authorities but also include what happens within religious organizations and in line with orthodox prescriptions.

While Fadil and Fernando (2015) emphasize that religious norms are not only thwarted but also reiterated in everyday life, they pay less attention to the other side of the equation: the ways in which the ambivalences of everyday life shape the pursuit of religious norms. As I have argued elsewhere with David Kloos, a particularly fruitful way to overcome the problematic opposition between "religion proper" and "lived reality" is to examine how everyday experiences of ambivalence, uncertainty, or failure affect practices of religious self-fashioning and pursuits of moral coherence (Kloos and Beekers 2018). Apart from pointing to the multiplicity of everyday life and the limits this poses to pious pursuits, we look at the ways in which experiences of imperfection "feed back" into processes of religious formation.¹² Further developing this approach, and building on other recent work on the productive potential of self-perceived inadequacy in religious life (De Koning 2013; Liberatore 2013; Strhan 2015; Kloos 2018a; Laidlaw and Mair 2019; Fahy 2020), this book puts the dialectical relationship between religious aspirations and experiences of fragmentation center stage.

A fruitful starting point to study this dynamic across religious groups is their shared social context, which affects the possibilities of religious action and fuels experiences of fragmentation. In his influential paper on the anthropology of Islam, Talal Asad (1986) pointed to such a situational analysis of Islamic practice. While the paper is best known for its conceptualization of Islam as a "discursive tradition," inspiring ethnographic studies of pious self-fashioning based on authorized religious norms, an important part of Asad's argument was that Islamic tradition is always shaped and constrained by particular social conditions. He proposed an approach that examines "the efforts of practitioners to achieve coherence" by taking into account both the constitutive force of Islamic discursive traditions and the "historical conditions that enable the production and maintenance of [these traditions], or their transformation" (17). More specifically, Asad pointed out that "the attempt by Islamic traditions to organize memory and desire in a coherent manner is increasingly remade by the social forces of industrial capitalism, which create conditions favorable to very different patterns of desire and forgetfulness" (17).

Tanya Luhrmann's (2012a) study of the ways in which American evangelicals cope with pluralism and secular skepticism provides a useful example of this kind of analysis—although she does not refer to Asad's approach described here. Following the work on secularity by Charles Taylor and others, Luhrmann points out that the "secular-sited Christianity" of her evangelical interlocutors is infused by "the acute awareness that one can choose not to believe" (2012a, 378). These evangelicals, she argues, have responded to this predicament by cultivating a "deliberatively playful, imaginative, fantasy-filled experience of God" (372), which enables them to sidestep the prevalence of doubt in their religious lives. Luhrmann suggests that this particular interpretation of Christian faith is "a direct product" (372) of the cultural pervasiveness of secular doubt.

In a similar vein, I aim to trace particular modalities of religious commitment that result from the interplay between religious aspirations and socio-historical conditions. As in Luhrmann's case, these aspirations and conditions cannot simply be seen as either opposed to or harmonious with each other. Rather, I approach their relations in terms of "articulations" in Stuart Hall's sense of linkages between two different elements that may occur under particular conditions but that are not inevitable or unchangeable (1997, 141). Whereas Hall emphasized the role of articulation in the formation of ideologies, I focus on everyday practices. Likewise, Magnus Marsden and Konstantinos Retsikas (2013) employ the notion "articulation" to analyze how—in their case—Islam is shaped and transformed, sometimes in unexpected ways, under particular socio-historical circumstances. Articulation, they argue, refers to the enmeshments and connections between arenas of social life that have historically been construed as distinct (2013, 14). I do not, however, use "articulation" as a synonym for fit or convergence, as Marsden and Retsikas (2013, 20) appear to do when they write about articulations between "being Muslim" and "being modern," or as Daromir Rudnyckyj (2011, 133) does when he indicates the overlap between Islamic and capitalist ethics in Indonesia. Rather, I approach articulations as complex interactions that do not merely entail either conflict or harmony, but rather a productive antagonism that results in the generation of particular and perhaps unforeseen modalities of religious engagement. The argument I develop in this book is that the secular and capitalist conditions my interlocutors faced in their everyday lives contributed to recurrent religious struggles and felt inadequacies, which subsequently revitalized their religious commitment in particular ways. An approach geared toward tracing such articulations opens up productive possibilities for comparative inquiry, which start from the embeddedness of Islamic and Christian aspirations in a shared socio-historical context.

The Fieldwork

This study is based on ethnographic fieldwork conducted between September 2009 and November 2012, mainly in Rotterdam and The Hague, cities in the west of the Netherlands, and Ede, a town in the middle of the country. The largest part of data collection took place in a period of fulltime fieldwork between March 2010 and March 2011. Rotterdam was the central location for my research with both young Muslims and Christians. In The Hague, I conducted additional research with Muslims, in Ede with Christians. This latter town, where I started my fieldwork, is the home of a Christian vocational—or professional—university, the *Christelijke Hogeschool Ede*, attracting large numbers of young Protestant Christians from across the nation. During the academic year 2009–10, I was able to work with an evangelical student association connected to that university. I participated in one of its small groups (*kringen*): Bible study groups consisting of—in this case—eight people who met once a fortnight to have dinner together, sing worship songs, discuss their faith and pray. I also attended collective meetings of the student association and joined my small group for a few days at the large-scale evangelical festival *Opwekking* and for a weekend outing to the Belgian Ardennes.

Midway through my fieldwork in Ede I decided to extend my focus to Rotterdam, one of the most culturally and religiously diverse cities of the Netherlands, which harbors a large population of people with Muslim backgrounds. The city also houses a large Christian population, both of Dutch and of non-Dutch descent. At the time of my fieldwork, nearly 11 percent of the Rotterdam population self-identified as Protestant, nearly 15 percent as Catholic and just under 14 percent as Muslim.[13] In contrast to a place like Amsterdam, Rotterdam is geographically close, and well connected, to the Dutch "Bible Belt." It is a place where significant numbers of Muslims and Christians not only co-exist but are also exposed to urban routines and alternative—religious and non-religious—cultures or lifestyles. Rotterdam has, further, taken a central place in Dutch public debates about the management of cultural diversity, particularly when it comes to its Muslim population (Uitermark and Duyvendak 2008).

In Rotterdam, I established contact with various Muslim organizations and youth networks. The Muslim student association that I here call An-Nur,[14] based at the Erasmus University in Rotterdam, proved to be one of the most fruitful entry points for my fieldwork. It catered to a Muslim student audience and regularly organized events, which typically centered on talks by guest speakers about such themes as Islamic history, theology, and prescriptions for a virtuous Muslim lifestyle. Compared to other Muslim student associations in the city, An-Nur put a particularly strong emphasis on religious knowledge and piety. It drew its speakers from various places, including Islamic educational institutions and—often Salafi-oriented—mosques. Their events usually drew dozens of Muslim students, the majority of whom were of Moroccan descent.[15]

Apart from An-Nur, I participated in the activities organized by a youth committee in a mosque in a town near Rotterdam and joined the committee's formal and informal get-togethers for several months. I also attended Friday sermons and youth conferences at a Salafi-oriented mosque in South Rotterdam, visited classes at an Islamic educational institute, and established contact with young people volunteering for an association situated within the Gülen movement.[16] Many of the young Muslims I met attended classes and talks in mosques in The Hague, particularly at an important Salafi center that I here refer to as El Hijra. For that reason, I extended my fieldwork to The

Hague, where I attended religious classes taught by two particularly popular youth imams, Dawoud at El Hijra and Omar Khalil at a local neighborhood mosque.[17] Through all of these activities, I was able to build up a network of young Muslims whom I regularly met at Islamic talks, sermons, conferences, and classes, taking place in various mosques and educational institutions in Rotterdam and other cities.

In Rotterdam, I also conducted fieldwork with young Christians, acquainting myself to various churches, Christian youth clubs, and student associations. Establishing a long-term fieldwork site proved to be more challenging than it had been in Ede. While the Christian students there seemed to be happy, eager even, to accept my participation in their association, young Christians in Rotterdam seemed to be more reserved about my presence, at least within the intimate sphere of a small group. With hindsight, I relate this to the more pluralist and secular character of Rotterdam, where young Christians continuously encounter people with different convictions from theirs. Christian organizations, and especially small fellowship meetings within these, provided them with safe spaces (see Chapter 4). The young Christians in Ede, by contrast, appeared to keenly welcome the input of a non-Christian outsider like myself in the context of what many of them perceived as a relatively closed Christian world. In Rotterdam, I was finally given permission to join a small group with four young men in an evangelical student association, which I here call Pilgrim Students. This small group was part of a men's only club (*dispuut*) within the student association. I participated in the club's bi-weekly meetings and small group gatherings throughout the academic year of 2010–11, and I frequently attended the (mixed-gender) communal nights of the student association, which were held every other week.

Next to Pilgrim Students, I participated in various activities organized by churches or Christian groups in the city, including social outreach and interreligious dialogues, and I regularly attended church services of several— evangelical, Pentecostal, and Protestant Reformed—churches. I most often visited a Reformed church, affiliated to the Protestant Church in the Netherlands (PKN), that has a very high proportion of young people in its congregation, including students, starting professionals, and young families. It is one of the most frequented churches by the members of Pilgrim Students. I also participated in several of this church's catechism classes.

By focusing my fieldwork on social settings in which young believers met each other and discussed, learned about, and practiced their religion, I sought to gain a good understanding of their religious worlds. Yet I was also keenly interested in their experiences in everyday settings outside these religious institutions, as I was striving to gain a fuller picture of how they lived their religion in their day-to-day lives (cf. Schielke 2010; Dessing et al. 2013; Ammerman 2014b). So while most of my fieldwork took place in religious contexts, I also regularly met with my interlocutors in other settings, including coffee bars, public transport, universities, public parks, and their homes. Furthermore, conducting in-depth interviews proved especially helpful in learning about the ways in which these young Muslims and Christians lived their religion in the variegated contexts of their everyday lives.

Thus, I conducted qualitative, in-depth interviews with twenty-four Muslim and twenty-four Christian young adults, whom I had generally met, or contacted, through the settings in which I conducted fieldwork. Leaving the decision where to meet up to my interlocutors, almost all of my interviews with young Muslims took place at the universities or colleges they attended, except for some of the men whom I interviewed in other public places or in their homes. I met my female Christian interviewees either at their universities, in their homes or—in a couple of cases—somewhere in town. Most of the interviews with the Christian men took place in their homes, a few others at university or a coffee bar.[18] Most of my interlocutors seemed to feel comfortable to speak freely and frankly about their everyday experiences, concerns, and struggles. Some were relieved to notice this themselves: for example, Judith, a pastoral theology student in Ede, remarked that because she was going to be interviewed by someone who "didn't come from the church," she had worried that she would give a very rosy picture of her faith. But she felt she had not done so, as she had told me about the challenges she faced in living out a religious life. Apart from these young adults, I interviewed several figures with leadership positions in my Christian and Islamic fieldwork settings. I also organized a focus group with six young women, Muslim and Christian, most of whom I had got to know during my fieldwork. This group met three times.

These extensive conversations offered invaluable sources of data in terms of my interlocutors' lived experiences, everyday challenges, and personal biographies. The discussions that follow in this book are mostly based on these interviews as well as the discussions and interactions I witnessed in the religious settings I participated in, even though I also draw from fieldwork in other settings. As I have alluded to above, scholars like Samuli Schielke (2010, 2) have warned that a reliance on fieldwork within religious settings may result in an ethnographic picture that puts disproportionate emphasis on religious commitment. This is a relevant point for my study since, although religious commitment is the central topic and therefore necessary focus of this book, my interest is precisely in the ways in which religious endeavors interact with other dimensions of my interlocutors' everyday lives. I have found, however, that the discussions within the religious contexts I attended did not merely dwell on pious ideals. Much attention was devoted to the challenges to attaining these ideals in multifaceted and sometimes messy everyday lives. Furthermore, these challenges were all the more pronounced in the interviews I conducted. In this regard, I agree with scholars like Jenny Hockey (2002) and Martin Forsey (2010), who argue that conducting interviews should not be seen as a mere "second choice" in ethnographic research. Qualitative interviews, Forsey points out, yield information about people's biographies, social background, cultural influences, ambitions, views, and the reasoning behind their choices, thereby contributing crucially to ethnography's purpose of "understanding and explaining the cultural context of lived experience" (2010, 567). In relation to this, as my research experience has shown me, interviewing can provide rich insights into the complexities of people's everyday lives and the often ambiguous ways in which these are negotiated.

In terms of selection, I have aimed to enhance comparability by matching the groups of Muslims and Christians I worked with. Because indicators of religiosity can differ from one group to another, I have not set any strict criteria for levels of religious practice. Rather, I focused on Christians and Muslims who sought to actively practice their faith on a daily basis, regarded their religion as a moral guideline in their lives and adhered, to varying degrees, to literalist interpretations of their faith. The people with whom I worked typically continued to place themselves within the mainstream orthodox (Sunni or Calvinist) traditions in which they had been brought up, while they also engaged with transnational Islamic and Christian revivalist movements, particularly Salafism and evangelicalism. I came to understand that this combination of a mainstream orthodox background and a revivalist orientation represented an important trend among both young Dutch Muslims and Christians and, hence, also an important point of convergence between these groups.

Furthermore, I sought to match the young Muslims and Christians in terms of demographic and socio-economic factors. I focused on young people aged between eighteen and twenty-eight, with most being in their early twenties. In both groups, I included both men and women in my study. Among the young Muslims, I tended to encounter more men in my day-to-day fieldwork, since, in the mosque settings I attended, men and women were usually seated separately. Yet I did establish good contact with women as well, particularly in the context of the student association An-Nur. My contacts with men and women in the Christian settings were usually balanced, although at Pilgrim Students I met more men due to my participation in a men's only club. I interviewed as many men as women in both groups.

Most of my interlocutors were students, the majority at academic universities and some at vocational universities. Others had already started their first job. The shared level of education of my Muslim and Christian interlocutors meant that they were heading toward, or had already achieved, relatively well-paid jobs. This affected their relation to contemporary culture and society in terms of their (prospective) purchasing power, media consumption, the significance of study and work in their lives, and their aspiring professional careers. As we will see throughout this book, these factors are relevant for the ways in which they pursued their religious aspirations in the wider context of their everyday lives.

Yet, as already pointed out, Dutch communities with a migration background, such as the Moroccan-Dutch I worked with, continue to be disadvantaged socio-economically compared to the ethnic Dutch population. This is partly caused by differences in cultural capital and the effects of growing up in unprivileged families (Gracia, Vázquez-Quesada, and Werfhorst 2016), while ethnic boundaries and discrimination on the job market can also have a significant impact (Waldring, Crul, and Ghorashi 2014). Moreover, coming from often disadvantaged families, it is likely that many face care-taking responsibilities toward their parents or other family members, both financially and practically. Despite these challenges, research has found that the great majority of highly educated second-generation Turkish and Moroccan Dutch have secured employment, in most cases in line with their education (Waldring, Crul, and Ghorashi 2014, 72).

My decision to focus on young Moroccan-Dutch Muslims in particular was partly based on the practical circumstance that they tend to speak Dutch with each other and regularly attend religious settings in which Dutch is the main spoken language. Their Turkish counterparts, although fluent in Dutch, more generally use Turkish (which I do not master) among each other. Furthermore, the influence of transnational Islamic revivalism among young Moroccan-Dutch provided a productive point of comparison in relation to the revivalist currents among young Dutch Christians. Indeed, it has long been observed that especially young Moroccan-Dutch tend to strongly distinguish between an allegedly transcultural Islam and Moroccan cultural traditions (Buitelaar 2006, 39; De Koning 2008, 308). The resources they employ in shaping their personal religiosity—institutions, books, websites, and so on—are usually grounded in transnational revivalist movements, particularly Salafism (cf. Roex

2013, 27), rather than in particular national religious traditions (as is more generally the case among Turkish-Dutch).

Let me end this section with a brief reflection on my personal participation in the field. My subject position—especially as a white, "native" Dutch, male academic who is not religiously affiliated—has inevitably had an impact on the research. My lack of a religious affiliation, for one, may have made my position seem "neutral" in the eyes of my interlocutors, but it also meant I remained a relative outsider in both groups. Being male has facilitated my access to some spaces (the men's only student club in Rotterdam for instance), but restricted access to others, such as social gatherings of Muslim women. And my ethnicity may well have had some influence on what both my Muslim and Christian interlocutors told me with respect to issues of belonging and cultural difference.

Just as my subjectivity has influenced the research, the fieldwork has also had an impact on me. Evans-Pritchard once wrote that a fieldworker "lives in two different worlds of thought at the same time, in categories and concepts and values which often cannot easily be reconciled. One becomes, at least temporarily, a sort of double marginal man, alienated from both worlds" (1973, 3–4). Likewise, I experienced my fieldwork as an intensive period of deep engagement with the religious worlds of the young people I studied. Moving back and forth between my own familiar everyday setting and not just one but two "different worlds of thought," I became perhaps not just a double but a triple marginal person. Indeed, I frequently started my Sundays attending a church service, listening to the words of the preacher, joining in—or at least mumbling along—the singing of psalms and chatting with congregants over coffee, and subsequently moving on to a mosque to participate in a religious class, sitting on the soft carpet among dozens of young Muslim men, listening to the imam exalting the virtues of the prophet Muhammad, and sticking around after class to catch up with the attendees. Conducting fieldwork in these Christian and Islamic worlds within the same period—and, indeed, regularly within single days—demanded a continuous switching between different settings of participant observation, each of which invited different kinds of discursive engagement, embodied participation, and sensory attunement (consider the difference between listening to evangelical worship songs or recitations from the Quran).

While demanding, moving between these different religious worlds was also instructive as it sensitized me not only to the distinct modes and moods of religious engagement of my Muslim and Christian interlocutors but also to the shared intensities of conviction and religious commitment that I witnessed among them. In their own ways, these young adults were all passionately dedicated to their God. Moreover, working in two religious fields paradoxically helped me cope with the kind of epistemological in-betweenness that Evans-Pritchard described: the truth claims and aesthetic forms of either one of the religious groups I engaged with—including the "embarrassing possibility of belief" (Ewing 1994, 571) that this engagement fostered at times—for me always coincided with those of the other group. In fieldwork on religion, the balancing act between detachment and proximity, inherent to all participant observation and indeed implied in the concept itself (Robben and Sluka 2007, 6), can be particularly challenging due to the researcher's often deep engagement with religious truth claims (see e.g. Harding 2000; Orsi 2005; Van de Port 2011). I feel that my simultaneous immersion into both of these religious worlds, which spoke to me and addressed me in different ways, helped me to strike a balance between academic detachment and open receptivity in each of them.

Outline of Chapters

In structuring this book, I have aimed at a close comparison throughout. So rather than dividing the book in separate parts on Muslims and Christians, I discuss and juxtapose both groups in each of the chapters. Chapter 2 takes a closer look at the revivalist-oriented pursuits of religious commitment among the young Christians and Muslims with whom I worked. It shows that they both emphatically strove toward attaining a "conscious" faith, which they perceived to be distinct from established modes of being religious. By exploring how these religious aspirations were shaped by personal biographies, formative settings, and relevant others, I argue that these young people's relation to conventional Protestantism and Sunnism was, however, more complex than revivalist narratives of breaking with tradition suggest.

The subsequent chapters interrogate how these religious pursuits were shaped by the secular conditions in which they were situated. Chapter 3 demonstrates how my interlocutors' ideas about what it entails to be a good Muslim or Christian were simultaneously shaped by an ethics of submission (often associated with religious orthodoxy) and an ethics of authenticity (commonly understood to be prevailing in the late-modern Western world). For both, I argue, these ethical repertoires were not necessarily conflicting but rather integrated into their religious endeavors. Yet these young people's emphasis on religious commitment as a reflexive, sincere, and deliberate act did engender feelings of shortcoming, ongoing struggles, and critical introspection. Moving to an intersubjective level, Chapter 4 examines my interlocutors' ongoing encounters with alternative convictions, beliefs, and commitments in today's pluralist Dutch society. I show that that these encounters fed, in somewhat different ways for the young Muslims and Christians, doubt about the urgency of fully surrendering themselves to the tenets of their religion. Such religious surrender easily slipped into seeming optional rather than inescapable. I show that the doubts and uncertainties the young believers experienced stimulated them to regularly participate in social settings of religious pedagogy, where they attained reaffirmation of their religious convictions and encouragement to pursue a pious lifestyle.

The last two chapters focus on the practical and routine challenges to pursuing a religious path under conditions of contemporary capitalism. Chapter 5 examines a struggle that came up time and again in my conversations with young Christians and Muslims; that of devoting adequate time to their religion in their busy and hurried lives. This shared struggle, I argue, can be understood in the context of the acceleration and fragmentation of everyday life in today's fast capitalist culture. At the same time, I demonstrate that these very conditions of fast capitalism also endowed my interlocutors' practices of worship with a renewed impulse and significance. Chapter 6 focuses on the active engagement of these young Muslims and Christians with secular mass media, popular culture, and entertainment—domains that have become increasingly pervasive in the context of today's accelerated and digitalized consumer capitalism. While my interlocutors were attracted to this mass-mediated popular culture, they also felt that it drew them away from God, in terms both of content and of embodied routines and dispositions. These pervasive distractions, however, also reinvigorated their religious commitment, stimulating them to intensify their religious practices so as to bring back routine to their religious lives and restore their proximity to God.

The conclusion brings together the different lines of inquiry in this book by focusing on the precarious condition of my interlocutors' religious lives. I discuss how this condition did not only make their pursuits of faith fragile, but also stimulated active care and nourishment—a dynamic that may be characteristic for religious commitment under secular and capitalist conditions more generally. The conclusion further discusses one of the most striking differences between my Muslim and Christian interlocutors: their divergent socio-political positions in the context of the increasingly pronounced nativist politics of belonging in contemporary Europe, in which debates about Islam, radicalization, and security have become more and more central.

This book's grounded ethnographic analysis of the everyday lives of young Dutch Muslims and Christians disrupts the narratives of Muslim-Christian difference that tend to underlie such nativist politics. It shows that their pursuits of religious commitment were affected in strikingly similar ways by secular and capitalist culture, which they not merely encountered as an outside force but actively participated in themselves. This rendered their religious endeavors both highly self-reflexive and inherently vulnerable. Their stories show that religious certainty, piety, and commitment, qualities that elicit such social apprehension with regard to Islam in particular, always go together with religious doubt, struggle, and ambivalence. This book demonstrates that this precariousness of religious engagement constituted not only a drawback to the pious pursuits of young Dutch Muslims and Christians, but also a motivating force.

2

Becoming Committed

The young Muslims and Christians this book focuses on pursued a personal faith based on self-conscious engagement, self-reflection, and active commitment. Despite differences in the emphases they put in their religious endeavors, there are striking parallels in how they understood their own religious engagement and positioned themselves in their respective religious fields. Both sought to attain a reflexive or "conscious" faith, which they often contrasted with a more taken-for-granted mode of being religious they attributed to their parents or their wider religious communities. This chapter explores these religious aspirations and looks at the biographical paths and contextual factors that have led these young adults toward them, including, importantly, the influence of revivalist—especially Salafi and evangelical—currents.

By placing these revivalist-oriented pursuits of Muslim and Christian commitment alongside one another, this chapter builds on—and revisits—earlier analyses of shared features of contemporary revivalist movements. In the Dutch context, researchers of young evangelicals, Salafis, and New Agers have argued in a co-authored piece that these groups, despite the differences between them, share a quest for "pure" and "real" religious truths that "set[s] them apart from the traditional types of church-based or mosque-based religion embraced by older generations of faithful" (Roeland et al. 2010, 289). The authors suggest that these young people reject "the demands made by particularistic religious traditions and their institutions"—especially "the church and its dogmas" in the case of evangelicals and "culturalized religions" in that of Salafis. Instead, they are striving to revitalize religion through its "purification" (297, 300). This analysis resonates with Olivier Roy's (2013) argument that contemporary religious "fundamentalism" (be it Christian, Islamic, or Jewish) is characterized by a drive to disconnect religion from geographically defined cultures and identities.

In other parts of the world, too, scholars have juxtaposed Christian and Muslim revivalists. Brian Larkin and Birgit Meyer have argued that evangelical

Pentecostals and Islamic reformists in West Africa, while seeming to be "diametrically opposed" to one another, "share a great deal of common ground" (2006, 286), particularly "concerning the rejection of traditional culture, new ways of being modern in a religious idiom and a global orientation" (308).[1] Writing on Southeast Asia, Robert Hefner (2010) has addressed the "unprecedented" religious resurgence that he sees taking place across religious traditions, including Islam, Christianity, and Buddhism. He identifies a common thread in these "new varieties of religion" (1031) when it comes to a popular demand—"in the face of far-reaching social change" (1034)—for "access to heretofore restricted practices of the faith, as well as their application to everyday concerns by ordinary believers" (1042).

Similarly to these works, this chapter is concerned with young Christians and Muslims who pursue a revivalist faith that they perceive to be distinct from established institutions and modes of being religious. Yet, rather than the overarching—and therefore also rather generalized—analyses offered in these texts, I aim to take a more detailed, comparative ethnographic look at this turn to a committed, revivalist faith among young Dutch Muslims and Christians. I explore how their religious commitment has been shaped by their personal biographies, formative settings, and relevant others. By doing so, I pay particular attention to the ways in which these young Muslims and Christians position themselves in relation to established religious institutions, to their parents' modes of religiosity, and to revivalist movements.

This chapter, then, moves the analytical lens from a focus on general features of revivalist movements to an exploration of the particular paths and experiences that have directed these young believers toward their revivalist faith. On the one hand, this specifies the extent to which these processes of Christian and Muslim revivalism are characterized by parallel trajectories. On the other hand, it offers a more complex picture of these young people's relation to established religious traditions (typically represented by their parents). As the studies discussed above indicate, much of the literature on religious revivalist movements emphasizes religious innovation, change, and a break with "tradition" or "culture." While a re-working of established ways of being religious was also central to my interlocutors, their relation to conventional, or mainline, Protestantism or Sunnism was rather ambiguous. Despite the strong influence that revivalist currents exerted on them, most did not break fully with the religious traditions in which they had grown up. This partial embrace of revivalist movements characterized both the young Muslims and Christians with whom I worked, but it was particularly evident among the latter.

The question how young religious subjects relate to older generations and established religious traditions has been a central concern in the literature on religious youth (see e.g. Collins-Mayo and Dandelion 2010; Giordan 2010; Herrera and Bayat 2010; Klingenberg and Sjö 2019). Much of this work, as Peter Hopkins et al. (2011, 315–16) point out, emphasizes either the unidirectional transmission from parents to children or the conflictual relations between them, at the cost of a more nuanced analysis of the multiplicity of intergenerational relations. Studies on religious youth in Europe, particularly—but not exclusively—those on Muslims, have often focused on their conflicts with, and criticisms of, their parents and older generations (see e.g. Douwes 2001; Mandaville 2001; Roy 2004; De Koning 2008; Roeland 2009; but see Fadil 2017). This chapter shows that while my Muslim and Christian interlocutors did regularly criticize their parents, they continued to be embedded in the religious life-worlds in which they had grown up. Some also acknowledged or even admired their parents for their religious dedication or lifestyles.

The chapter further highlights the ways in which intersubjective contexts of families, friendship circles, schools, universities, and communal religious settings shaped these young people's religious pursuits. Notwithstanding their concern with a self-reflexive and personal commitment, my interlocutors' religious aspirations were—as Omri Elisha puts it regarding American evangelicals—rooted in "social networks and institutions in which standards of personhood [were] constructed" (2011, 18–19). In these social networks, they acquired repertoires of discourse and practice that were characterized by a revivalist impulse. These repertoires exposed particular differences, especially when it came to the greater emphasis on religious knowledge among my Muslim interlocutors and on a more subjective experience of developing a relationship with God among the young Christians. Before moving to my interlocutors' religious biographies and the roles of their families in them, I will first address the notion of "faith" that played a central role among both groups.

Aspiring to Faith

The term *geloof* (faith) was at the heart of the religious aspirations of both my Muslim and Christian interlocutors. While both frequently used this Dutch word, the young Muslims also regularly employed the Arabic term *iman*,[2] which they treated as the equivalent of—and consistently translated as—*geloof*. Both groups used this term in a similar, relational and practical, sense. It did not merely denote the religion or set of beliefs to which they ascribed. In different variations among my Muslim and Christian interlocutors, *geloof*, or faith, indicated the strength of their relatedness to God, determined by the extent to which they gave religion an important place in their everyday lives and lead their lives in proximity to God. Their concerns with faith, then, reflected their ideal of "being close to God." In Arabic, the word *iman* comes with precisely such implications: it denotes faith in the active sense of how one relates to, and trusts, God.[3] My Christian interlocutors regularly employed the notion of a "living faith," which similarly implied a state of being close to God. These Christians also linked "faith" to their aim of acquiring a strong "personal relationship with God." Faith, moreover, involved a decidedly practical and active component for both my Muslim and Christian interlocutors. It was not simply something one had, but something one pursued. This implied working on one's self and cultivating one's closeness to God—not just individually but also in supportive social networks. For these young people, the notion of faith indicated less a fixed state than an ongoing, long-term process (cf. Kloos 2018a).

Because *geloof* carried such active, relational, and practical connotations for my interlocutors, I translate this term, which could be rendered in English as either "faith" or "belief," as "faith." When my interlocutors used the term in a more propositional sense, I translate it as "belief." In his seminal work on the concept, Wilfred Cantwell Smith (1977; 1979) demonstrated that the modern notion of belief has come to rest on an understanding of belief as, above all, propositional (1977, 69ff.). This had not always been the case. Rather than expressing one's judgment on the question whether God exists, to say "I believe in God" used to mean: "Given the reality of God as a fact of the universe, I hereby pledge to Him my heart and soul. I committedly opt to live in loyalty to Him. I offer my life to be judged by Him, trusting His mercy" (44). Smith held that these earlier connotations of belief can today be adequately described by the term "faith" (69). More than a "state of mind," faith entails an active "engagement" (Smith 1979, 5). Anthropologists have similarly proposed to move beyond—modern, Protestant—conceptions of belief as a state of mind to analyses of religious commitment as "constituting activity in the world" (Asad 1993, 47; cf. Good 1994, chap. 1; Robbins 2007, 14–16).[4]

In the anthropology of Islam, "piety" has become a widely used concept to analyze the practices, discourses, and mindsets involved in the pursuit of religious ideals. Inspired in particular by the work of Talal Asad (1993) and Saba Mahmood (2005), analyses of piety look at the ways in which Muslims engage in practices of self-cultivation in order to acquire virtuous religious behavior, emotions, and dispositions. My interlocutors' pursuits of faith resonate with this conceptualization of piety and I do refer to this term to discuss how aspirational projects like theirs have been analyzed in the recent literature.

Yet I foreground the notion of faith, rather than piety, throughout this book. This is, first, because it is a key emic term: my interlocutors use it much more commonly than piety, or *vroomheid* in Dutch. The Christians rarely spoke about *vroomheid*, the Muslims did so only occasionally and often as an ideal type, for example, in Islamic teachings on "the pious forefathers." Second, while piety has generally come to refer to normative projects of self-discipline, my interlocutors' pursuits of faith also importantly entailed spiritual attempts at becoming closer to God. For them, faith denoted not only an aspiration to pious virtuosity but also a pursuit of experiences of peace, wholeness, and tranquility. For sure, pious pursuits do not foreclose such spiritual experiences, but the recent literature on piety has devoted limited attention to these (but see e.g. Mittermaier 2011). Finally, in the anthropology of Islam, "piety" has regularly been construed in opposition to (idealized) conceptions of "the liberal-secular" (for critiques of this tendency, see Schielke 2010; Jansen 2011). By contrast to such juxtapositions of piety and secularity, this book focuses on the *interactions* between religious pursuits and secular conditions.

The Turn to Personal Islamic Commitment

Generally, the young Muslims with whom I worked did not identify themselves explicitly with any specific Islamic movement (apart from Sunnism). Many were little concerned about what school of religious law (*madhhab*) they followed, a few did not even know. Neither did most explicitly reject following a *madhhab*, as Salafis do.[5] These young Muslims, excepting the converts, had all received an Islamic religious upbringing. Islam had been passed on to them as part of their family life. They participated in religious holidays and rituals such as Ramadan. Most had also been sent to a Quran school, where they spent a number of years learning to recite the Quran in classical Arabic. Some had also followed other religious classes. My interlocutors had generally learned how to perform the Islamic ritual prayer (*salat*) from their parents and some told me that one of their parents, usually the father, would regularly talk to them and their siblings about their religion.

Yet most of my interlocutors said that it was only later in their adolescence that they became self-consciously committed to Islam. They commonly regarded the religion of their childhood as a self-evident part of their (family) lives, to which they had not always given much thought. Looking back at their childhood religiosity, many remembered that it was more about obedience to rules than about personal conviction. While they had—generally fond—memories of the ways their parents talked to them about Islam, many were retrospectively dissatisfied with their parents' inability to discuss religious issues in more profound ways. They later came to view their religion as something of major personal significance, demanding their full attention and commitment—a turn they described with such phrases as "starting to practice" (*gaan praktiseren*) or "becoming involved with my faith" (*bezig gaan zijn met mijn geloof*).[6] These denoted an increased practice of Islam, a heightened concern with one's inner faith (*iman*), and a personal exploration of the religion.

A good illustration of such a personal turn, or "return,"[7] to Islam is the story of Naima, a 24-year-old studying for an MA degree in law at Erasmus University in Rotterdam and working part-time for the local council. Born in Morocco to an Arabic speaking family, she had moved to the Netherlands when she was three and lived in Rotterdam since then. When she was around sixteen, Naima started to try and observe her prayers, which she had learned to perform at home, more consistently. At this time, she said, she wanted to take her religion "more seriously." She felt that "if you really believe in it … then you also have to really demonstrate it." So little by little she started to practice more and, when she was eighteen, took up wearing a *hijab* (Islamic veil). When I asked her how her decision to start practicing her faith had come about, she answered that she "simply grew older" and reflected that "I call myself a Muslim but I don't practice it at all [*ik doe er niks aan*]. I only fast, but actually just because everybody does that, … not really because you know why you do it or because you have, uhm, studied it."

Like Naima, many of my Muslim interlocutors associated their turn to Islam with the moment they began to consistently try to practice the *salat*: the ritual prayers that ought to be performed five times a day on prescribed times and according to particular procedures and bodily rituals. I was often told that the *salat* is an indispensable part of what it means to be a Muslim (cf. Henkel 2005; Mahmood 2005, 123; Kloos 2018b). For the women I met, donning the *hijab* was also an important part of "starting to practice." All my female interviewees wore one. An exception was Haniya, a 28-year-old jurist who had worn it for a year when she was sixteen and decided to take it off again after she was insulted in public two times. For some of the young men I encountered, the turn to "practicing" their religion similarly coincided with the decision to grow their beards. As a convert to Islam I met at an Islamic youth conference put it to me: "The beard is the headscarf of the man." Yet while donning the *hijab* was generally understood to be an obligation for Muslim women, growing a beard was rather seen as (highly) "recommended" according to the *Sunna*, the tradition of the Prophet Muhammad.

The turn to Islam also importantly entailed engaging in religious reflection and learning. The young Muslims talked about starting to "think" about one's religion and starting to "read." Indeed, reading books was often a first important step in their personal religious exploration. These would normally be concise, introductory books on Islam, written in Dutch, bought from local Islamic bookshops or web shops. Furthermore, my interlocutors explored their religion by visiting Islamic websites and internet forums, and listening to Islamic talks, both online and offline—profiting from the large number of Islamic talks at mosques, youth conferences, and Muslim student associations. Many also followed courses with private Islamic institutions. All this responded to these young Muslims' longing for, as they put it, "acquiring knowledge about Islam," aimed at gaining religious awareness and at correctly practicing Islam. To inform oneself about one's religion was also seen as an important Islamic prescription and a crucial part of what being a Muslim entailed. As Naima pointed out, *iqra* was the first word revealed by Allah, which according to her means not only "read," but also "acquiring knowledge, being actively engaged."

My Muslim interlocutors regarded gaining knowledge as a crucial means toward strengthening their faith. When one has knowledge, "the basis is much stronger," as twenty-year-old Aisha put it. This idea reflects these young Muslims' emphasis on *informed* dedication. Rather than taking their religion for granted as a tradition they had inherited from their parents, they typically wanted to know the reasons and motivations behind Islamic practices and beliefs. They were often critical of their parents for being unable to give such explanations. This did not mean that they disagreed with the rules and restrictions their parents had set during their upbringing, but rather with the lack of a justification for these rules and restrictions with reference to religious sources.[8] Some were however more appreciative of the ways their parents explained their religion to them. Naima, for example, told me that she could always turn to her father with questions about Islam. Yet she, too, explained to me that her parents used to be illiterate and therefore had to rely on what the local imam told them. She said that this situation had drastically changed for young Muslims like her:

> You don't have to follow anyone, you don't have to rely on anyone, you can read yourself, you can interpret yourself if you want to, you can uhm decide for yourself whether you agree with something, decide whether or not you follow something.

Indeed, because of the high levels of education these young Muslims had themselves enjoyed, their access to countless religious sources in books and on the internet, and the wide offer of religious talks and courses in the Netherlands, they felt that they had far greater opportunities for independent reflection on their religion than their parents had ever had.

In Search of "True" Islam

This appreciation of independent reflection was accompanied by a longing for uncovering the tenets of "true" Islam, "untainted" by local cultural traditions (cf. De Koning 2008; Roy 2013). The young Muslims I worked with recurrently criticized their parents, and Muslim communities in the Netherlands more generally, for wrongly attributing practices, norms, or beliefs to Islam. This was especially relevant for young Muslim women when it came to the opportunities they were given as daughters and women. Yet, such critiques were not restricted to questions of gender equality. Khadija, a nineteen-year-old student in public health, who had only recently turned to "practicing" her religion, for example, criticized her father for what she regarded as a lack of knowledge regarding the Islamic rulings on listening to music:

> I listen to music. That's actually *haram* [forbidden in Islam] but I still do it. Uhm, and then [my father] comes upstairs and says "put off that music!" And then I come downstairs, like in the evening, and I find him watching *Moroccan* music [on television] as if it's nothing [*zit 'ie doodleuk gewoon Marokkááánse muziek te kijken*]. He doesn't realize, like, that that's also simply wrong. Because my music is Western, it's wrong, but because his music is part of the culture, he thinks that it's *halal* [allowed in Islam].

In part, my interlocutors' assertions about what Islam "really" said about any given issue had an empowering effect for them in relation to their parents, because it allowed them to distinguish "cultural" customs from Islamic rules, which they regarded as fairer and more universal. It also empowered them with respect to popular perceptions of Islam in wider society, which—in their view—wrongly associated Islam with women's oppression, gender inequality, and violence (cf. Van Es 2016, 133–41).

Yet while these motivations were regularly expressed by my interlocutors, their search for "true" Islam appeared to be even more importantly informed by their pursuits of personal piety. For them, acquiring knowledge about Islam, distinguishing "culture" from "religion," and uncovering the tenets of "true" Islam were all means of improving their understanding and practice of worship, enhancing their religious knowledge, and strengthening their personal relationship with God (cf. Jouili and Amir-Moazami 2006, 634–6; Jouili 2015, 37–8). The young Muslims I worked with commonly regarded perfecting their worship of God as the very core of their religion. Thus, a Quran verse that was often quoted in my fieldwork settings was "And I did not create the jinn [spirits] and mankind except to worship Me."[9] My interlocutors explained that by perfecting their worship of God they sought to fulfill the purpose of their existence and to secure a place in Paradise after death. In this context, the turn to "practicing" Islam often involved a changed relationship with God. Some of my interlocutors told me that in their childhood they had come to view God primarily as a punishing God, who sets strict rules one needs to live by. Only later did they learn to see Him (both my Muslim and Christian interlocutors consistently used male pronouns when referring to God) as a merciful God, with whom they could enter into a personal, loving relationship and whom they could please by fulfilling their religious obligations.[10]

It was especially with regard to the dimensions of spirituality and religious worship that my interlocutors did not merely criticize and challenge their parents. Many also told me that their parents had stimulated them, and continued to do so, in these respects. Although Naima took a critical distance from her parents in several ways, when I asked her about her role models when it came to practicing her religion, the sole person she pointed to was her mother. She explained that religion was very important for her mum, evidenced, for example, by her acts of voluntary fasting (practiced apart from Ramadan). An evocative illustration of such regard for one's parents was provided to me by Musa, a 27-year-old student in Rotterdam who earned his income as a professional kickboxer. He vividly remembered something his father had once said to him as a teenager:

> Imagine that everyone is sleeping and only you are getting up for the morning prayer. For who? You do that for God. And God sees that, you know. He watches. Then God sees what you are prepared to do for Him. And then it is just as if one little light starts to shine in the dark.

Several of my Muslim interlocutors similarly told me that they appreciated their parents as sources of spiritual inspiration, exemplars of religious dedication, people with a broad knowledge of Islam, or simply as the persons who had passed on the essential tenets of Islam to them. This suggests that appreciation for "the Islam of the parents" occurs not only among young Muslims who are critical of Islamic revivalist trends, as Nadia Fadil (2017) has shown, but also, to some extent, among those who are part of these trends.

It has become clear that my Muslim interlocutors had commonly experienced a shift from what they regarded as a largely non-reflexive way of being religious to a stance of informed dedication to Islam. They expressed this shift through a shared language that focused on such phrases as "acquiring religious knowledge," "following true Islam," and "distinguishing between culture and religion." Taken together, such phrases constituted a discursive framework that conveyed a particular kind of religious orientation and commitment (cf. Luhrmann 2004, 521). This framework was readily encountered by anyone entering their religious life-worlds, be they newly "practicing" Muslims or non-Muslim interested "outsiders" like myself.

It is therefore unsurprising that the notions of knowledge acquisition, "true" or "pure" Islam, and a religion/culture distinction have received much attention in the academic literature on young Dutch Muslims, particularly—but not exclusively—those of Moroccan descent (Buitelaar 2008; De Koning 2008; Ketner 2008; Roex 2013; Van Es 2016). This literature of the Dutch context is congruous to studies of young Muslims elsewhere in Western Europe, which have pointed to very similar discourses of knowledge acquisition and religious purity (e.g., Schmidt 2002; Roy 2004; Jouili and Amir-Moazami 2006; Adraoui 2009; Hamid 2009; Jacobsen 2011; Jouili 2015; Liberatore 2017). This shared language, indeed, is part of a transnational discourse of Islamic renewal that is widely shared by young Muslims across Europe (cf. Jacobsen 2011, 296) and beyond (see e.g. Bracke 2008b; Janson 2013; Kloos 2018a). The prevalence of this discursive framework suggests that it provided my Muslim interlocutors with a common language to talk about, share, and reflect upon their personal religiosities. It also suggests that they became familiar with this language via the people they socialized with and the religious contexts they participated in. For my Muslim interlocutors, as I will now show, this "field of socialization" turned out to be quite complex and diverse.

Formative Contexts

When I asked the young Muslims I interviewed to describe how their renewed religious engagement had come about, their responses varied considerably. Their parents played important roles in their initial religious formation. Yet, generally, their turn to a personal religious commitment tended to be most directly encouraged by peers: friends, schoolmates, fellow students, siblings, or cousins. Take Ali, a young, Turkish-Dutch volunteer for El Hijra, a Salafi center in The Hague. He had started to "practice" two years before we met, when he was twenty. This happened after a friend from school "began to continuously encourage" him to pray. "And at some point," Ali said, "I felt like, he is a Muslim and I'm also a Muslim. And every day I am with him and he prays every time and I don't. And once in a while I went with him to the mosque, he went inside and I just stayed outside, … I didn't even dare to go inside." Ali's parents did "not really pray" at the time. He rather learned about the significance of prayer from his friends in college and from sermons that he started to listen to. When he became convinced that he had to start praying himself, he asked his friends to teach him how to pray and he began following classes at El Hijra.

Having grown up in Rotterdam, The Hague, or smaller towns around these cities, my Muslim interlocutors were used to living in an urban, pluralist environment, amid non-Muslim people and institutions. They had commonly gone to public or Christian primary and secondary schools. In these pluralist contexts, religious encouragement could also come from less expected directions. The 24-year-old Ismael had started to actively learn about Islam and to "search knowledge" when he was 19. He had grown up in a predominantly white town in the periphery of Rotterdam and had always had mostly non-Muslim friends. His interest in Islam was sparked by one of his best friends, a "Dutch guy" he had known since kindergarten and who decided to convert to Islam: "And because of that I thought like: *Huh*? He has become Muslim, one of my best friends, but I actually can't tell him much about it at all. And because of that, yes, after that I actually really started with it. Really actively."

It was particularly in the context of their secondary schools or universities that many of my interlocutors met peers who came to stimulate their religious engagement. Several members of the student association An-Nur in Rotterdam told me that the large number of Muslim students actively practicing and expressing their religion at the university had made a big impression on them. Khadija for instance recounted that as a first-year student she noticed that one of the university buildings was "completely packed" with people. When she heard that they were waiting in front of a prayer room, her reaction was: "Get real? It's during school hours and people do their prayers on time!" This, she noted, "really was a revelation for me." These Muslim students gave shape to something of a pious youth culture that consisted of people talking with each other about the "correct" religious practices and precepts, notifying one another of Islamic conferences and classes, as well as attending Islamic talks at the university.

In relation to this, my interlocutors' turn to a greater religious commitment was also importantly shaped by their encounter with, and participation in, social settings of religious pedagogy tailored specifically to young Muslims. Particularly since around the year 2000, there has been a rapid growth and dissemination of sources of Islamic pedagogy that are accessible to young Muslims in the Netherlands, including books, websites, web forums, private institutions of Islamic education, mosque classes, religious conferences, and Muslim student associations. They are accessible because the language used is often Dutch (rather than Arabic, which many young Dutch Muslims do not master well) and because they respond to young people's immediate needs for religious learning and knowledge (De Koning, Wagemakers, and Becker 2014, 108, 149–50). Indeed, this period witnessed the emergence of an Islamic pedagogical infrastructure tailored to young Muslims, which was largely— but not exclusively—based in Salafi networks. The accounts of my Muslim interlocutors showed that, generally, once their interest in Islam was kindled they soon got involved with these kinds of religious sources. Many had favorite websites they regularly visited to find information on correct Islamic practice or to download sermons by Muslim preachers. Many would also attend religious talks and enroll in Islamic courses—on such topics as Arabic, Quranic exegesis (*tafsir*), and Islamic jurisprudence (*fiqh*)—offered by private institutions of Islamic education or by mosques.

Muslim preachers—men, and more rarely women, generally aged between thirty and fifty, who traveled around the Netherlands to deliver sermons, talks, and classes—played a major role in this pedagogical infrastructure (Beekers 2015). They had commonly grown up in the Netherlands (or in other Western countries) themselves and were familiar with the life-worlds of their young Muslim audiences. Omar Khalil,[11] a Moroccan-Dutch man of around forty who worked mainly in The Hague, was one of the most popular preachers among the young Muslims I worked with. They said they appreciated him because of his extensive knowledge about Islam and his uncompromising stance; I was often told that he did not "beat around the bush," even when it came to sensitive issues. Khalil was frequently invited by Muslim youth organizations around the country and the number of downloads of his sermons, available as podcasts online, ran into the thousands. One of the other preachers who was very popular among my interlocutors was the Surinamese-Dutch Dawoud, also around forty years old, who offered talks and courses around the country. In contrast to Khalil, he was especially liked for the rather gentle manner by which he explained Islam to his young audiences. The young Muslims I met frequently discussed these preachers and shared their video or audio clips with each other. Their decision to listen to particular preachers, and to attend particular pedagogical settings, was flexible and open to change. Because Muslim preachers could rely on few formal means to bind their audiences, they had to make sure they offered a persuasive pedagogy. This pertained to both the religious knowledge they offered and their aesthetic style, including their tone of voice, eloquence, use of Quranic recitations, dress, argumentative reasoning, and ability to emotionally "move" their audiences (Beekers 2015; Liberatore 2017, chap. 6).

The Politicization of Islam

My interlocutors frequently faced questions and criticisms about Islam in relation to such issues as integration, gender equality, and terrorism. These were articulated by classmates, teachers, and other (non-Muslim) people in their social circles, as well as recurring in the media. The people I worked with had grown up in the late 1990s and 2000s, a period in which Islam became hotly debated in the Netherlands and beyond (Sunier 2010). The comments they encountered tended to contribute to their desire to acquire knowledge about Islam, in order to learn what Islam "really" teaches and to respond to the criticisms of their religion accordingly.

For some, this entailed a trigger to engage with Islam in stronger ways than they had before. Ismael, for instance, told me about the many discussions he used to have with—both Muslim and non-Muslim—schoolmates: "You were, even if you didn't want it, simply confronted by it. ... You were simply asked questions: okay, you have four wives, or uhm, you can have as many wives as you want." This motivated him to learn more about Islam: "I usually didn't know about it and then you do try and find out, like, is that true? ... It did enrich my knowledge." As Ismael's account conveys, many of my interlocutors were not only discontented about the questions raised, which often concerned the perceived illiberal, intolerant, or violent aspects of Islam, but they also felt that they had benefited from such questions because these had stimulated them to learn more about their religion.

Numerous studies of young Muslims in Europe have pointed to the ways in which the politicization of Islam (Ivanescu 2010) has affected their religious engagement. Most scholars have examined this issue on the level of identification. They have argued that since these young people have increasingly been approached *as* Muslims, held accountable for the alleged problems and wrongdoings associated with Islam, and faced discrimination or exclusion on account of their religion, they have come to identify themselves with their religion in particularly strong terms—as a kind of "reactive identification" (Nagra 2011).[12] Other scholars have extended this line of reasoning to religious practice, arguing that the stereotyping, exclusion, and discrimination of Muslims have stimulated young people's adoption of a pious lifestyle (e.g., Connor 2010). More generally, many public commentators have interpreted the perceived "pious turn" among European Muslim youth as a reaction to an increasingly hostile environment, indeed, as a type of "reactive religiosity" (Fleischmann and Phalet 2012, 322).[13]

However, the hostile climate toward Islam was not necessarily the primary inducement of my Muslim interlocutors' renewed religious engagement. Several explicitly stated, like Ismael, that the debates about Islam and the personal questions they received stimulated them to seek out knowledge about Islam. For some, this may well have been a crucial trigger for their self-conscious religious turn. Yet, for most of the young Muslims I met, it was only one of several factors that enhanced their personal religious engagement. As we have seen, Ismael himself pointed out that his turn to "practicing" Islam was motivated above all by one of his best friends converting to Islam. For my other interlocutors, too, their increased religious commitment was influenced by such various factors as personal questions about meaning and the nature of God; experiences with misfortune, illness, or death; siblings or friends who had started to "practice"; the appeal of pious youth cultures at universities or schools; listening to Muslim revivalist preachers; reading religious books; or even, as one of my female interlocutors noted, simply being bored.

Many described their turn to personal religious commitment in terms of entering a new life-phase. When I asked my interlocutors about 9/11 and the increased public anxieties about Islam in the period in which they grew up (they often did not bring up this topic themselves), they commonly said that these did have an impact on their lives and particularly on the ways in which they engaged with, and (had to) represent, their religion. Yet they often also insisted that their interest in Islam was shaped less by public debates about the religion than by their personal development as they were growing up. Thus, when Naima told me that she started to "practice more" when she was around sixteen, I realized that this must have been around 2002, shortly after the events of 9/11. I asked her whether she thought that the ensuing debates had turned her attention to Islam and triggered her to reflect on her religion. She answered:

> Yes, perhaps in an indirect way, not really directly. Because I think that also if 9/11 hadn't happened, that I would also uhm... It simply has more to do with, uhm, yes, as an adolescent you start to think somewhat more like, you know, what am I going to do now, what is my stance, and what do I want to do with my life and so on. I simply grew older.

Naima's account was of course based on a reinterpretation of her religious development and she might underestimate the significance that 9/11 had for her. Nonetheless, it struck me that her and my other interlocutors' accounts of their personal religious biographies commonly centered on notions of life-phase (of becoming older and more "serious") (cf. Kloos 2018a), that they regularly pointed to the influence of friends and that they often did not themselves bring up the public debates about Islam in this regard.[14] Some also pointed to the influence of their parents' country of origin (Morocco for most), noting that their renewed interest in Islam had been triggered by family members there. Yet for most—if not all—of my interlocutors the social environment in which they moved in the Netherlands had been more important in this regard.

Based on my interlocutors' accounts, then, I suggest that the influence of the heated public debates about Islam on their practical religious engagement should not be overemphasized. There is little doubt that these debates had a considerable effect on their relations with non-Muslims and on the ways in which they presented and identified themselves (see Van Es 2016). Yet when they talked about their move to a greater religious commitment, they put more emphasis on their life-phase and social environment. It is notable in this regard that quantitative studies on Dutch Muslims have not been able to demonstrate a correlation between discrimination and feelings of societal exclusion on the one hand and an increase in religious identity or religious practices on the other (Fleischmann and Phalet 2012; Maliepaard and Gijsberts 2012, 159). Focusing on the hostile climate toward Islam as a factor inducing increased religiosity risks portraying the religious engagement of young Muslims as an anomaly that needs to be explained (Liberatore 2017, 11). Moreover, it seems to imply that the religious turn among Muslims should be understood as a very different process from that among young Christians.

Salafi Influences

My interlocutors' self-conscious pursuit of "true" Islam, motivated and supported by a youth-centered religious pedagogical infrastructure, reflects the influence of Islamic revivalism, particularly Salafism, among young Muslims in the Netherlands. Salafism is a heterogeneous Sunni reformist movement that draws on a long tradition in Islamic thought and that—as we know it today—crystallized in the twentieth century and became particularly widespread across the Muslim world since the 1980s (De Koning, Wagemakers, and Becker 2014, 34–6; Lauzière 2016; Wagemakers 2016). It is characterized by its aim of recuperating the alleged pristine purity of Islam by closely replicating the example set by the Prophet Muhammad and the first three generations of Muslims (*al-salaf al-salih*, or "the pious forefathers") (Wiktorowicz 2006, 207; Meijer 2009, 4).

While Sunni Muslims generally acknowledge the exemplary virtuosity of *al-salaf al-salih*, what sets Salafis apart is that they approach it as a comprehensive ideal to which they seek to comply as strictly and fully as possible, in most cases without adhering to *taqlid*, the widely accepted Islamic practice of following one of the four canonical schools of jurisprudence (Wagemakers 2016, chap. 1). Salafis commonly aim to revitalize Islam by morally improving their lifestyles and their community (De Koning 2013, 73). This is expressed in strong concerns with *da'wa* (proselytization), focused mostly on urging fellow Muslims to pursue a more virtuous lifestyle and a "purer" Islam (De Koning 2009, 379). In this regard, educational and pedagogical activities take a central place in Salafi circles (Roex 2013, 82).

Notwithstanding considerable internal variation, Salafis share an emphasis on *tawhid* (the unity of God), which results in an aversion to any practice that could be interpreted as associating others with God (idolatry or *shirk*) or as seeking intermediaries to God (Wiktorowicz 2006, 208–9). Salafis generally believe that *tawhid* can be safeguarded by emulating the Prophet Muhammad "in every detail," since he "embodied" its perfection (Wiktorowicz 2006, 209). This accounts for their strict adherence to the *Sunna*, the tradition of the Prophet, and their opposition to *bid'a*, or heretical innovation (Roex 2013, 80). In contrast to *taqlid*, most Salafis seek access to the views of the Prophet by consulting the *hadith* directly (Wagemakers 2016, 31–2). Accordingly, Salafis believe they follow, and transmit, the only true Islam, which is not adjusted to local cultures and traditions (De Koning, Wagemakers, and Becker 2014, 91–2).

In the Netherlands, the first Salafi organizations and networks emerged in the 1980s. Their influence grew considerably after the year 2000, when increasing numbers of preachers started to address their audiences in Dutch and several Islamic bookshops began to focus on disseminating Islamic books translated to Dutch (De Koning, Wagemakers, and Becker 2014, 101–8). They thereby catered to the widespread demand from young Dutch Muslims for religious knowledge in Dutch (De Koning, Wagemakers, and Becker 2014, 150). To this day, Salafis have played a leading role in the dissemination of information about Islam among—particularly young—Muslims (Roex 2013, 27). Because of their effective distribution of literature and strong representation on the internet, their influence has been larger than their numerical presence (cf. Hamid 2008, 11). Indeed, the number of Dutch Muslims who can be described as active followers of Salafism, although hard to establish, is fairly small. A study published around ten years ago reported that 8 percent of Dutch Muslims hold "strictly orthodox" religious attitudes that resemble Salafi thought. They are not necessarily Salafis but they are susceptible to Salafism (Roex, Van Stiphout, and Tillie 2010, 226). Participants in Salafi networks in the Netherlands are often young and predominantly of Moroccan descent (Buijs, Demant, and Hamdy 2006, 59), but they also include Muslims of Dutch, Somali, and to a lesser extent Turkish descent (De Koning, Wagemakers, and Becker 2014, 159–60).

In the wake of incidents with young people seeking—frequently without success—to participate in jihadi battles abroad in the 2000s, followed, in 2004, by the murder of filmmaker Theo van Gogh by a young Muslim who had participated in Salafi networks, Salafism did not only become more visible publicly, but was also increasingly associated with violence and terrorism (De Koning, Wagemakers, and Becker 2014, 142). Since I conducted my fieldwork between 2009 and 2012, these associations have only strengthened, particularly after the establishment in 2014 of a self-proclaimed caliphate by "Islamic State in Iraq and al-Sham" (ISIS). ISIS is inspired by a version of jihadi-Salafi ideology[15] and it has engaged in extremist violence around the world, including Europe. A considerable number of people from the Netherlands— around three hundred according to the Dutch intelligence service—have joined ISIS or other extremist organizations in Syria or Iraq (AIVD 2019). In this context, public concerns about Salafi—and generally pious—Muslims have increased in recent years, as have the appeals to Muslims to publicly speak out against violent extremism (Van Es 2018). At the time of my fieldwork, Salafi piety was not as closely associated with terrorism in public discourses as it is today and the participation of young Muslims in Salafi networks caused some but not as much suspicion as it does now.

By contrast to prevailing perceptions, most Salafis do not advocate violence or terrorism (Wagemakers 2016, 27), even if dominant strands of Salafi thought can yield intolerant attitudes, not least toward Shi'is (see e.g. Olsson 2017). Generally, Salafi organizations and preachers in the Netherlands, while recognizing military *jihad* as a religious obligation in particular circumstances, explicitly denounce the use of violence as propagated in jihadi-Salafi ideology. This ideology rather arises in circles outside of established Salafi organizations (Roex 2013, 217–26). The reformist aspirations of Salafis in the Netherlands generally center on the personal acquisition of a virtuous Islamic lifestyle (Roex 2013). Accordingly, the appeal of Salafi preachers among my Muslim interlocutors was grounded less in their socio-political ideas than in their accessible provision of knowledge about "true" Islam and "correct" religious practice.

Most of the young Muslims with whom I worked actively participated in Salafi networks and settings and made ample use of their resources (both online and offline). Their renewed religious engagement was inspired by Salafi thought, particularly in terms of their focus on acquiring religious knowledge. Yet they generally did not identify as Salafis, neither explicitly nor implicitly (by describing themselves as, for example, "true" Muslims or "people of the *Sunna*").[16] A few of my interlocutors also criticized Salafism, among other things for being too simplistic or too rigid. Many of these young Muslims moved quite easily between Salafi settings and contexts of Islamic pedagogy that were less characterized by a purist and scripturalist approach, including their family mosques, institutions of religious education, and particular websites. Most seemed little interested in becoming part of a specific Islamic movement, but they did readily make use of the resources the Salafi networks offered them.

Attaining a "Living" Christian Faith

My fieldwork with young Christians in Ede and Rotterdam centered on evangelical student associations and both evangelical and "mainline Protestant" (Klaver 2011, 60) churches. The young people I met there had commonly moved to Ede or Rotterdam for their studies. Most had grown up in smaller towns or villages that were typically characterized by strong local church cultures. They had been raised in mainline Protestant families that were situated in the broad, mainly Calvinist, Reformed tradition in the Netherlands. More specifically, most of my interlocutors hailed from churches that are commonly described in the Netherlands as "orthodox Protestant." These are churches—either inside or outside the Protestant Church in the Netherlands (PKN)[17]—that lean toward a conservative stance on liturgy and doctrine. When I met these Christian young adults, the majority still attended these mainline Protestant churches. Yet they commonly took a trans-denominational approach to their religion, emphasizing personal religious engagement and the perceived essence of Christian faith, as opposed to what they regarded as the liturgical and doctrinal niceties of different church denominations.

This common approach to religion among my Christian interlocutors had typically been stimulated by their participation in a range of social activities, often organized within evangelical circles. These included youth church services, Christian youth camps, religious conferences and worship festivals,[18] faith-based voluntary and evangelization work, small-scale Bible study meetings and get-togethers in the context of Christian student associations. Within these, they were encouraged to pursue an active and consciously practiced religiosity, which my Christian interlocutors described as attaining a "living faith" (*levend geloof*), "coming to personal faith" (*tot persoonlijk geloof komen*) or simply "coming to faith" (*tot geloof komen*). Much like my Muslim interlocutors, these young Christians usually contrasted this personal and dedicated faith with impersonal, passive, or non-reflexive stances on religion they ascribed to their parents and/or to the churches of their childhood.

Take Robert, a 23-year-old student in economics and member of Pilgrim Students in Rotterdam. He had grown up in Enschede, a city in the east of the Netherlands, where his father was a pastor in an orthodox Reformed church (*Nederlands Gereformeerde Kerk*). While he generally appreciated the way his parents had brought him up religiously, he said his peers in church did not engage with religion "very actively or explicitly" and he himself had never been interested much in religion. This changed in the course of his adolescent years, as he started to participate in a youth church that was attended by young people of various church denominations. This triggered him to critically reflect on his own stance on faith. At one of the services, a schoolmate invited him to join a sports evangelization project in Israel. He accepted and, eighteen-year-old at the time, participated in a five-day preparatory conference in Israel. This had a large impact on him: "Instead of it being a choice that was made for me, or was made automatically due to my upbringing, at that time it became more of a choice that I really made myself." Joining Pilgrim Students a few weeks later, Robert continued on this path and "very much grew in that respect."

Many of my Christian interlocutors told me that when they were growing up, they regarded God, church, and faith as objectively given, not as matters they could engage with personally. Later, typically around the age of sixteen to eighteen, others confronted them, and they confronted themselves, with the kinds of questions that Robert also started to pose to himself at that age: What do I believe *myself*? What does Christian faith mean to me? And what role should it play in my life? In retrospect, these young Christians pointed out that questions like these stimulated them to develop a personal religious commitment and to aim to give their faith a primary place in their everyday lives. As for Robert, it was often the combination and mutual reinforcement of different activities that increased their impact on young Christians' personal religiosities. These activities usually took place in (largely) new settings of religious sociality, often associated with the evangelical movement.

This is also illustrated by Irene, a 23-year-old student at the Christian vocational university in Ede, who was, even more than Robert, dissatisfied with what she regarded as the absence of a reflexive, living faith in her childhood. Irene had grown up in a small village to the north of Amsterdam. Her family went to the *Gereformeerde Kerk*, one of the two churches (both within the PKN) in the village. As a child, she went to a Christian primary school, Sunday school, and church. She followed catechism classes, read from a children's Bible at home, prayed with her parents, and learned prayer songs for children. Yet, she said, she never talked much with her parents about faith. Religion was done "on autopilot." Because of the way faith was presented in the church, she came to see it "simply as rules" and God as "some sort of severe man whose expectations you had to fulfill." Most of her peers, she told me, were not interested in religion. At secondary school in a neighboring village, only the minority of pupils—mostly those coming from her own village—said they believed in God. After she turned twelve, Irene "kind of said goodbye to faith." Looking back at the Christian culture of her home village, which is characterized by a substantial Protestant presence, she went as far as to say that "there are no Christians" there.

But when Irene was fifteen, a cousin gave her a flyer about a one-week Christian survival camp for youths, which she decided to join. There, she said, she encountered "a whole different side of faith." She joined others in small-group discussions and in singing evangelical praise songs, allowing her to discover "pretty hip" Christian music. There were sermons that were "really tailored for youth and really spoke to our concerns." At one point, Irene recounted, "one of the camp leaders came up to me with a Bible text, Psalm 139, which says that

God has made you and sees everything you do." This gave her "a very different image of God." In the following year, Irene accepted another cousin's invitation to join a junior, voluntary camp in Romania, which was set up by the same organization as the survival camp. This trip, too, had a huge impact on her:

> There was a song: "I want to be very close to you, as a child in the father's lap".[19] Of course it is mentioned often enough that God is a father, but only then it really sunk in that it's not some aloof man on a cloud, but that it really is a God who loves you. And I really experienced that too. And then I thought: well, now I no longer want to live without God any single day.

Irene subsequently joined a youth group of her cousin's church, which met every week at the house of a married couple who mentored the group. There she was able to "learn about faith." Soon afterward, she decided to enroll at the Christian vocational university in Ede, because she wanted to live in "a somewhat more Christian environment, as you simply need that, to have Christian youths next to you and to have Christian friends."

The stories of Robert and Irene illustrate how my Christian interlocutors' accounts of their religious life histories were at the same time individually unique and, as other studies of Christian revivalism have noted, collectively shared and socially patterned (Harding 2000, chap. 1; Luhrmann 2004, 522). By and large, these accounts followed a "standard narrative structure" (Marshall 2009, 153), which included the latent or non-reflexive religiosity of one's childhood; the encounter with different ways of being Christian in one's late teens that stimulated one to critically reflect on one's own religious engagement; and the attainment of a personally committed faith. My interlocutors generally used very similar terms to describe these different stages. Many, for example, used (varieties of) the phrase "faith became something of myself." This process of religious becoming was often talked about with a sense of wonder, joy, or good fortune—if not providence. Such shared narrative repertoires point to the influence of the social religious settings, typically situated within the evangelical movement, they came to participate in. These young Christians learned what Tanya Luhrmann (2004, 521) calls a particular Christian "syntax": a set of themes and formulas that constitute the "grammar" of a particular religious life and commitment. Yet to observe that these narratives are largely standardized is not to say that the experiences to which they refer lack in profundity. Irene's story, for instance, points to an emotional and spiritual personal process with strong effects on how she looked at herself, at others, and at God. Likewise, and similarly to my Muslim interlocutors, this process commonly entailed a changed perception of God, whom these young Christians came to see as a caring God who reaches out to them and with whom they could build a personal relationship—rather than a remote and disinterested God who sets the rules they need to live by.

In terms of relevant others, peers—friends, schoolmates, fellow students, siblings, or cousins—often played important roles in the personal religious development of my Christian interlocutors. They encouraged them to participate in—often revivalist—Christian activities. Christian student associations, in particular, provided a community of believers that supported and motivated individuals in their religious lives and struggles. Many told me that conversations, for example in small groups for Bible study (*kringen*), had "built them up" in their faith.[20] As Robert put it, discussions at Pilgrim Students triggered him to move from being able to "give the right answer" given his "good Christian background," to critically interrogating his own opinions and experiences. In these student associations, as well as in youth camps and youth churches, more senior figures played important roles as mentors or leaders, addressing young people's questions and stimulating their religious commitment and self-reflection. For several of my interlocutors, such influential senior figures also included pastors of mainline Protestant churches.

My interlocutors' relation to their parents tended to be ambiguous when it came to faith. For some, the reflexive religious commitment they were developing meant a greater leap from their upbringing than for others. Several of the young Christians I met were less critical about their parents than about their peers in their childhood churches. A small number regarded their fathers or mothers (or both) as role models of Christian dedication. Yet many described their turn to a "living" faith as a move away from their parents' modes of being religious. Even for them, however, those parents had usually played a central role in their religious formation, passing on at least basic Christian beliefs, norms, practices, and referential frames. These frames included stories and figures from the Bible, key theological concepts, and inter-church doctrinal debates. Indeed, while studies of evangelical Christianity tend to emphasize personal decision-making and radical change in the process of becoming Christian (see e.g. Klaver 2011, 363), the significance of longer processes of socialization in Christian families and communities should not be disregarded. The young Christians I met leaned on a "groundwork"—or what Pierre Bourdieu described as a "primary habitus" (see Desmond 2006, 391)—they had acquired during their upbringing. This foundation made it possible for them to develop their religious subjectivities in new directions—and often in opposition to parts of that very upbringing.

Later, they often came back to their parents to talk about their adjusted takes on Christian faith, and to reflect on their religious upbringing. Some said that at this point they actually came to appreciate their parents for their religious views, knowledge, or devotion.

Emphasizing a Trans-Denominational Christian "Essence"

My Christian interlocutors' reworked ways of being Christian were characterized by a trans-denominational outlook. Rather than the lack of a denominational affiliation, this entailed a willingness to transcend denominational differences—albeit strictly within Protestantism—despite one's specific personal affiliation. For the young Christians, achieving a "living" faith was less about joining particular churches or subscribing to specific doctrines, than about recognizing and cultivating one's personal relationship with God. This importantly involved accepting Jesus Christ as one's personal redeemer. Sarah gave a particularly strong expression of this trans-denominational position:

> God doesn't say "well, when the time is there, only all of the *vrijgemaakt-gereformeerden*[21] are allowed to enter heaven, and the others, we'll, uhm, [laughingly] we'll just leave them". That will make for a very empty heaven, I think. So I think it's not so much about, to God it's not so much about the church you come from, but about the relationship you have with Him. Whether you really know God or not. I think that in any church there are people who do know God and people who don't know God.

Sarah was a 23-year-old student in health sciences in Rotterdam. She had grown up in a town near the city and used to attend a Reformed church (which later joined PKN) with her family. At the age of nineteen she decided to leave that church because she felt that its congregants did not really have a "lively relationship with God." Through her brother and sister, she became acquainted with an evangelical church that offered accessible sermons and contemporary worship music, and that aimed to abandon fixed dogmas and liturgies. She felt at home there and decided to stay. She appreciated that it focused on what she regarded as the core of Christian faith, rather than on the doctrinal debates that have caused so many schisms in Dutch church history. Sarah described this religious approach by using the English terms *essentials* and *non-essentials*:

> What my church actually stands for is that there are essentials and non-essentials in faith. Essentials are for example the Trinity and that you believe in

Jesus Christ and accept Him [*Hem aanneemt*]. And non-essentials are things like all those little rules, uhm, well, like, baptism, or the blessing, or those kinds of things.[22] So actually all that bickering about these [issues], you know, we believe that that, well, isn't the core of your faith, so that you have to respect everyone as they are and everyone can have their own opinion about those things.

Such a trans-denominational approach, focusing on the perceived essence of Christian faith, was strongly emphasized in the Christian student associations in which I participated, in both Rotterdam and Ede. Mark, an experienced staff member at Pilgrim Students, told me that he sought to encourage the youngsters to be *Christians* rather than "mere" *Churchians* (he used those English terms). For him, this did not entail setting rules, but stimulating personal convictions. It did not mean transmitting particular dogmas, but stimulating the members to ask themselves the question "How do I live my life with God?" This, he said, would help the members of Pilgrim Students to "come to personal faith."

While this approach de-emphasizes church doctrines, it should not be mistaken for a liberal stance on Christianity. Staff members like Mark did seek to shape the convictions of the students in particular directions, which were in line with evangelicalism. And central Christian teachings, like those concerning redemption, played a paramount role among my interlocutors. Moreover, in contexts such as the student associations distinct moral norms were upheld and promoted, for example with regard to sexual conduct (Roeland 2009, chap. 8; Beekers and Schrijvers 2020).

The emphasis on the "essentials" of faith beyond the particular doctrines of individual churches appealed to—and informed—these young Christians. Nevertheless, many did not fully discard the church teachings they had grown up with. Take Sebastian, a twenty-year-old student in medicine and active member of Pilgrim Students. He had been raised in the *Gereformeerde Kerk vrijgemaakt* and was still a member of that church. As we discussed its doctrines, he argued that these should not be simply dismissed as obstinate tradition. At the same time, his words show that he himself took a rather detached stance toward them

> A lot of people are not so much stubbornly clinging to tradition, but very much want to hold on to reverence for God. And they have a point there, I think. ... When you talk about [my church], "covenant" really is a magic word.[23] ... So, well, they just love it. But then I wonder, like, covenant, what sort of theoretical concept is that? But apparently there are people who get all emotional when they hear the term, as in: "wow, covenant!"

Such an ambiguous stance on Calvinist Protestantism, marked by a tension between detachment and respect, was shared by most of my Christian interlocutors. It exposes their deep rootedness in a conventional Protestant upbringing and at the same time their socialization into reworked ways of being Christian that de-emphasize church doctrines.

Evangelical Influences

It has become clear that my Christian interlocutors' pursuit of a personal, "living" faith was strongly influenced by their participation in evangelical settings. Evangelicalism is an internally diverse renewal movement that is rooted in various Puritan, Pietist, and revivalist currents, which have formed an undercurrent in the history of Protestantism since the Reformation. Contemporary manifestations of evangelicalism are strongly shaped by the American evangelical movement that emerged after the Second World War.[24] Globally, the face of evangelicalism is marked by the explosive growth of Pentecostal and charismatic churches in recent decades, particularly in Africa, Latin America, and Asia (see e.g. Anderson 2004).[25]

The different strands of evangelicalism typically share a number of "common features" (Bebbington 1989, 2). These include a focus on personal spiritual change and transformation, a high regard for the Bible as the infallible Word of God that provides guidelines for everyday life, an emphasis on Christ's redemptive work on the cross and a commitment to evangelism or promulgation of the gospel.[26] Evangelicals emphasize their personal relationship with Jesus Christ and—most particularly for Pentecostals and charismatics—the actual presence of, and work performed by, the Holy Spirit in their everyday lives (Van Harskamp 2000, 139ff.; Klaver 2008, 147). They have sought to revitalize orthodox Protestantism by returning to "original" Christianity, untainted by the perceived corruptive influences of institutions, dogmas, and power (Miller 1997, 11; Van Harskamp 2000, 140).

The new evangelical, or neo-evangelical, movement that emerged after the Second World War has been described as both theologically orthodox and world-affirming (Shibley 1996; Miller 1997). Opposed to the defensive and disapproving stance on the secular world among earlier evangelicals, new evangelicals have adopted an open stance on society, willingly appropriating contemporary cultural styles and youth-oriented popular culture (Shibley 1996, chap. 6). Rather than world-avoiding, they became "at ease in the world" (Shibley

1998, 72)—albeit within certain limits. New evangelical churches emphasize experience (often over and above knowledge transmission) and make use of contemporary forms of worship, characterized by pop music, video projections, and in some cases also stage lighting (Miller 1997).

This new evangelical movement has increasingly influenced Dutch Protestantism since the 1950s (Stoffels 1990, 23-9; Roeland 2009, 32; Klaver 2011, 55). It grew and consolidated in the Netherlands during the 1970s and 1980s, with the creation of Dutch evangelical organizations such as the *Evangelische Omroep* (an evangelical broadcasting company) and *Opwekking* ("Revival") (Klaver 2011, 55-7). *Opwekking* distributes a growing collection of *Opwekkingsliederen*, contemporary worship songs, mostly written in—or translated to—Dutch, which have become widely popular in Dutch Christian circles, including the Christian student associations I worked with. They are also widely used in mainline Protestant churches (Klaver 2011, 192).

The growth of evangelicalism since the 1950s has been remarkable in the light of ongoing church decline in the same period (Roeland 2009, 25). This growth is not primarily expressed by evangelical church membership: while it has increased from around 60,000 in 1970 to 142,000 in 2006 (De Hart 2011, 44), this number is still relatively small. Evangelicalism rather exerts much of its influence through evangelical organizations and events that operate outside the field of mainline churches and the control of clergies (Klaver 2011, 55-6). These include voluntary organizations like Youth for Christ, student associations, and Christian youth festivals (attracting up to tens of thousands of people). Furthermore, the evangelical movement has developed a repertoire of Christian resources, practices, and activities that is now used in a variety of Christian spaces, including mainline Protestant churches (De Roest and Stoppels 2007; Klaver 2011, 58-60). These include contemporary worship songs, introductory courses on Christianity (the "Alpha course"), "small group" Bible-study meetings (*kringen*), and personal prayer sessions (ministry) (Roeland 2009, 36). This repertoire introduces—especially young—Christians to ways of being together and expressing faith that are new and often strongly appealing to them (Roeland 2009). Indeed, similarly to the role of Salafism among Dutch Muslims, the evangelical movement provides a religious infrastructure that caters to young people in particular.

Generally, this evangelical repertoire has significantly shaped my interlocutors' religious development. Nonetheless, most of them neither explicitly identified themselves as evangelicals nor joined evangelical churches. Rather, they often continued to identify themselves with the church traditions in which they had been raised and they remained members of their parents' church communities. In many cases, they sought to contribute to an evangelical type of revival *within* these church communities. Many were also quite critical of some elements of evangelicalism. For instance, while singing evangelical worship songs was common practice among all of my Christian interlocutors, several criticized these songs for being too "simplistic" compared to the psalms conventionally sung in mainline Protestant churches. Many were also wary of what they saw as the invocation of, and focus on, feelings within evangelical settings (an issue to which I return in the next chapter). Thus while evangelicalism strongly appealed to these young Christians and shaped their religious paths in major ways, most did not embrace it fully or uncritically. Nor did their engagement with evangelicalism entail a complete break from the Christian traditions and orientations they knew from home.

In Conclusion: Revivalist Commitments and Their Ambiguities

This chapter has exposed striking parallels between my Christian and Muslim interlocutors' processes of religious becoming. Both developed a decidedly self-conscious, reflexive, and active approach to their faith, which was characterized by a search for the core of their religion beyond cultural or denominational boundaries. They typically contrasted this new religious orientation with the religious environments in which they had grown up. For the young Muslims and Christians alike, it was nurtured by revivalist settings they became acquainted with during their adolescence, which were typically oriented toward Salafism and evangelicalism respectively. While their parents, and older generations more generally, usually played important roles in their religious development, their turn to a self-conscious religious commitment was often more strongly instigated by friends, schoolmates, siblings, cousins, and other peers. A core characteristic of their religious approach, shared by both groups, was the felt shift from a taken-for-granted to a reflexive faith. Indeed, what stands out in the accounts of both my Muslim and Christian interlocutors is that they regarded a reflexive, or "conscious," faith as a basic requirement of religious commitment. In the next chapter, I will further explore this emphasis on reflexivity and its connections to a wider ethics of authenticity that prevails in contemporary culture.

These concerns with religious renewal did not, however, entail a complete disembedding from the religious environments in which my interlocutors had grown up. Their search for a "pure" Islam and for the "essentials" of Christianity, respectively, built upon the religious habits and know-how they had acquired at home and within their parents' religious communities. Their upbringing had prepared them—imbued them with the knowledge and dispositions—to learn and adopt a revivalist approach to their religion. In the process, many of their basic religious convictions and practices remained largely unaltered, while the orientation and emphasis changed. Bourdieu's concept of habitus, already mentioned above, is helpful here. It can be argued that these young believers' "primary habitus," which had been constituted early in their lives, transformed into a "specific habitus," which involved discipline and training within particular settings (Desmond 2006, 391). In relation to this, most of my interlocutors did not unambiguously embrace, or identify themselves with, evangelicalism or Salafism respectively. This was particularly apparent among the young Christians, who, despite their criticisms of aspects of their religious background, often continued to identify themselves with their family's church traditions.

My Muslim interlocutors commonly took more distance from their parents' religious traditions, even if they too often continued to attend their "family mosques" and celebrate religious feasts with their families. The considerable social differences between the two Muslim generations seem to play an important role here. The young Muslims' parents had generally enjoyed substantially lower levels of education and they had commonly grown up in Morocco or other Muslim majority societies. For the younger generation, living in a highly pluralist society, having acquired a high level of education, mastering Dutch and English, and having access to endless digital resources meant that they were well equipped to make self-conscious choices in the religious directions they wanted to follow.

Apart from these intergenerational relations, the most notable difference in my Christian and Muslim interlocutors' religious pursuits concerned the emphasis they put in their revived religious commitment. Whereas the young Muslims stressed knowledge acquisition and following the "correct" religious teachings, the young Christians were somewhat less concerned with doctrines than with developing and cultivating a personal relationship with God (yet, as I show below, the two sides of this contrast were not mutually exclusive). To some extent, the focus on religious knowledge among my Muslim interlocutors was informed by a desire to empower themselves by being able to counter both "culturalized" ideas about Islam and stereotypes held in wider society. At least as importantly, the contrast between my Muslim and Christian interlocutors reflects the divergent orientations of Salafism and evangelicalism, with the former emphasizing knowledge, doctrinal purity, and religious practice and the latter focusing on the personal relationship with God, experience, and contemporary forms of worship. As I have shown, these revivalist strands are highly influential among young Dutch Muslims and Christians, respectively. Nonetheless, it is important to point out that the difference described here results from my comparison of these specific revivalist-oriented groups. A study of, for instance, Sufi Muslims and Pietist Christians would produce at least partly different results.

Even for the groups I worked with, the contrast between acquiring knowledge and cultivating a relationship with God did not hold up completely. While the young Christians did not emphasize knowledge acquisition as much as the young Muslims, they did find it important to learn about their religion and to study the Bible. They also continued to engage with Christian doctrines. Furthermore, as I discuss in the next chapter, many were wary of prioritizing subjective experiences and feelings, and they emphasized the importance of basing oneself on the Bible. In this regard, many of my Christian interlocutors had reservations about the evangelical movement. Not only did they have doubts about its emphasis on subjective feeling, but they also felt that they had more opportunities to learn about Christianity within the mainline Protestant contexts in which they had been raised. What comes into play here, I suggest, is their upbringing in Calvinist worlds in which they had learned to value long-term, cognitive engagement with "God's Word." As I discuss later on in this book, they also seemed to feel that subjective feelings were not sufficiently resilient to the challenges of living in a predominantly secular society in which religious concerns constantly risked moving to the background.

The young Muslims, in turn, were not exclusively concerned with the rational pursuit of religious knowledge and "correct" teachings. They also emphasized personal experiences of being in contact with God. Many talked about the ways in which religious worship enabled them to experience peace, tranquility, and closeness to God (I will elaborate on this theme in Chapters 5 and 6). With regard to these kinds of spiritual experiences, my Muslim interlocutors regularly drew inspiration from, and admired, their parents or other older family members, as opposed to Salafi preachers. Although most expressed fewer reservations about Salafism than my Christian interlocutors did about evangelicalism, this Islamic current did not seem to fully meet their desires for spiritual experiences. Some of these young Muslims, moreover, were critical of what they regarded as the movement's rigid, black-and-white approach to religion.

To some extent, then, the revivalist trajectories of my Muslim and Christian interlocutors appeared to constitute each other's mirror images. While the Islamic revivalism with which the young Muslims engaged emphasized religious knowledge and doctrinal purity, it offered less in the way of stimulating personal spirituality, or closeness to God. By contrast, whereas the Christian revivalism with which the young Christians were involved emphasized the experiential relation with God, many turned elsewhere to fulfill their desires for a more knowledge-based engagement with their religion. Thus, this chapter's close investigation of my interlocutors' pathways toward a revivalist faith has not only brought into focus the similarities and differences between these young Muslims and Christians. It has also exposed some of the ambiguities in their engagement with revivalist movements. In the next chapter, I turn to my interlocutors' revivalist-inspired aspirations to religious submission and interrogate how these coincided with a typically late-modern ethics of authenticity.

3

Authentic Submission and Moral Self-Scrutiny

> I very often hear my colleagues ask, like, is the headscarf actually obligatory? And some say it isn't obligatory at all. And then I say: it's very clearly obligatory. It's simply clearly stated in the Quran, in *surat* [chapter] Maryam: you have to wear a headscarf. It is even explained *how* you have to wear a headscarf. So you can't go and beat around the bush [*je kunt er niet omheen gaan draaien*]. But the most important is, as I also always say, you have to do it yourself, you have to start doing it of your own free will. You shouldn't do it for your husband, not for your father, not for anyone here. The only one you do it for is your God. If you do it of your own free will, you also do it in the right way. If you don't do that, without motivation, without [your] own choice, then it doesn't have a value. Then you do wear it, but, well, no added value.

These words are taken from my interview with Farida, a 23-year-old committee member of the student association An-Nur and pedagogical consultant to people with a migration background. Like most of my female Muslim interlocutors, she not only held that wearing a headscarf (*hijab*) is obligatory, but also articulated a line of reasoning in which obedience to the prescriptions of Islam and an emphasis on personal choice are closely intertwined. This combination of, on the one hand, pronounced ideals of obedience and subordination and, on the other hand, personal choice and individual deliberation characterized the religious pursuits of both my Muslim and Christian interlocutors more generally. These young believers voiced unequivocal aspirations to submission, to forsaking their personal desires and doing God's will. At the same time, these aspirations typically coincided with strong concerns with personal freedom, choice, and self-realization. These moral orientations built on longstanding theological doctrines in which submission to God is perceived as a privileged route to self-realization and freedom. Yet my interlocutors complemented these teachings with what appears to be a characteristically late-modern perspective by taking personal choice and reflection as preconditions for "true" submission.

In this chapter, I explore this remarkable commonality between my Muslim and Christian interlocutors: their incorporation, in different ways, of both of these ethical ideals within their moral religious subjectivities. By moral religious subjectivities I refer to their ideas about what it entailed to be good Muslims or Christians and the ways in which they sought to fashion their selves accordingly. Thus, I look at the ethical endeavors of my interlocutors and the kind of moral work on the self that these involved (Foucault 2000, 263). However, in contrast to some of the most prominent Foucault-inspired studies on religious ethics (Mahmood 2005; Marshall 2009), I show that my Muslim and Christian interlocutors drew from different ethical sources simultaneously, specifically those described here as an "ethics of submission" and "an ethics of authenticity."

Others have already signaled the coexistence of these ethical realms in contemporary religious subjectivities. For instance, Anton van Harskamp (2014, 182), building on Wade Clark Roof (2001) and Stewart Hoover (2006), points to two "simultaneously acting orientations" in many contemporary religions: an orientation toward "human autonomy" and one toward "heteronomy," or, in other words, a desire for "self-determination" and one for "bonding with a determining Other." Young Muslims and Christians in Europe (and beyond) have similarly been described as "balancing between" such ideals of submission and authenticity (e.g., Fadil 2008; Roeland 2009) or as suspended in a predicament of moral ambivalence between different ethical ideals (e.g., Schielke 2015). In this chapter, by contrast, I argue that the revivalist-oriented young believers with whom I worked did not so much balance between these moral ideals, but rather integrated both in their religious endeavors.

Yet this ethical orientation toward both submission and authenticity, or what can be called "an ethics of authentic submission," entailed high demands in terms of personal sincerity and self-conscious commitment, contributing to recurrent feelings of shortcoming and imperfection. Thus, in the second part of the chapter, I examine how the reliance on the volition and activity of the self rendered my interlocutors' ethical endeavors vulnerable in important ways. The paradox that emerges is that the submission of the self to God, implying the renunciation of that (desiring) self, required a particularly strong effort by, and reflection upon, that very self.

My discussion here resonates with the rapidly growing anthropology of ethics.[1] This body of work focuses on the ways in which social groups conceptualize and seek to achieve such qualities as the good, freedom, and virtue (see e.g. Robbins 2013; Fassin 2014; Laidlaw 2014)—and the ways they engage in everyday moral deliberations and judgments (see e.g. Lambek 2010). The inquiry in this chapter particularly builds on the anthropological study of virtue ethics, which draws from Foucauldian and Aristotelian thought (Mattingly and Throop 2018, 480–2). Yet rather than contributing to a theory of virtue, I am concerned with the articulation between, on the one hand, religiously informed ethical repertoires and, on the other, an ethics of authenticity that prevails in late-modern culture. My interest, then, is in the ways my interlocutors understand what it means to be a "good" believer within an ethically pluralist environment. Before moving on to my ethnographic material, I will elaborate on the notions of an ethics of authenticity and an ethics of submission as these are used in this chapter.

The Ethics of Authenticity and Submission

The ethical orientations I observed among my interlocutors bring to mind two separate frameworks for the analysis of moral religious subjectivity that have emerged in the literature. The first is concerned with the "subjective turn" and an associated "ethics of authenticity" as analyzed by the cultural philosopher Charles Taylor (1991; 2002; 2007) and other theorists of contemporary culture in the West. The second framework is concerned with the deliberate pursuit of pious self-cultivation through practices and discourses of submission to God and conformity to external authorities, as theorized, among others, by Saba Mahmood (2005) in her influential contribution to the anthropology of Islam. The first framework stresses the congruence between contemporary religious expressions and the concerns of authenticity, sincerity, and autonomy that are understood to characterize late-modern culture more generally. The second framework points to the ways in which religious pursuits may depart from such widespread cultural ideals and offer alternative conceptions of human flourishing.

Many scholars now agree that contemporary religion in the West is characterized by an unmistakably subjective orientation. Prominently among them, Charles Taylor has pointed out that recent decades have seen the proliferation, throughout Western society, of "expressive individualism:" the idea that one should find one's authentic way of living and expressing oneself (Taylor 2002, 80). Like other authors (see e.g. Brown 2009, 193-6; Van Rooden 2010, 190; Houtman, Aupers, and De Koster 2011, 16-22), Taylor identifies the 1960s as a "hinge moment" in which the expressivist ideals of late eighteenth-century Romantic elites "began to shape the outlook of society in general" (2002, 80-4). This expressive individualism was most conspicuously manifested in, and driven by, the new consumer culture made possible by postwar prosperity (Taylor 2002, 80–2, 102–4; cf. Campbell 1987). Taylor points to the emergence of a "culture" or "ethic" of authenticity (2002, 83–4), which he defines as

> the understanding of life ... that each of us has his or her own way of realizing one's own humanity, and that it is important to find and live out one's own, as against surrendering to conformity with a model imposed from outside, by society, or the previous generation, or religious or political authority.
>
> (Taylor 2002, 83)

This "ideal of authentic self-fulfillment" (2002, 92), Taylor argues, has also penetrated religious life and practice. Thus, today, any particular religious path taken "must speak to me; it must make sense in terms of my spiritual development as I understand this" (2002, 94).

Many sociologists of religion agree that what Taylor calls the "massive subjective turn of modern culture" (1991, 26) has increasingly come to define contemporary forms of religious and spiritual practice. Thus, Paul Heelas and Linda Woodhead have claimed that the subjective turn entails a "major cultural shift" from life lived in "conformity to external authority" toward life lived "by reference to one's own subjective experiences," whereby the subjective life-world comes to constitute "a, if not the, unique source of significance, meaning and authority" (2005, 2–4). They describe this process as the "subjectivization" of religion (2005, 7). In the 1960s, Thomas Luckmann already argued that religion in modern society becomes a private affair that is mainly concerned with "self-realization," "self-expression," and the individual's life-long quest for his or her inner self (1967, 110). This body of work has been largely characterized by a distinction between religion/conformity/obligation on the one hand and spirituality/authenticity/self-realization on the other. Later scholarship has criticized such dichotomies between institutionalized religion and individualized spirituality (Bender 2010; Ammerman 2014a). Building on this line of argument, I show in this chapter that "external" conformity and "internal" cultivation are not necessarily opposed to one another.

The subjective turn is not, as much of the earlier work in the sociology of religion seemed to assume, restricted to New Age or new spiritualties. Studies of Christians and Muslims in Western societies have also discerned trends toward an increased subjective orientation. Research on Christians, particularly evangelicals and Pentecostals, has pointed to the emphasis they often put on personal choice, inner feelings, emotional experience, and the personal relationship with God. It has been suggested that these Christians tend to play down institutions and traditions, while they highlight the personal and intimate relationship with God.[2] Similarly, research on—especially young—Muslims in Western Europe has indicated widespread concerns with self-determination, personal choice, subjective experience, and authenticity.[3] Going from this literature, it appears that these groups are shaping their religious lives in ways that converge with "the ideal of authentic self-fulfillment" (Taylor 2002, 92).

Other authors have however argued that Christians and Muslims in Europe, especially those described as "orthodox" or (strictly) observant, are less concerned with authentic self-fulfillment than with a desire to subordinate themselves to God, community, and authority. Thus, Abby Day (2008), writing about Baptist women in the UK, and Sarah Bracke (2008a), looking at young evangelical and Islamic women in the Netherlands, identify modes of religious agency and subjectivity that are above all characterized by the subordination of the self to a superior—outside—force (including male power in the case of Day). Such "willful disempowerment," Day (2008, 274) asserts, "is a self-conscious act on the part of women who desire to maintain a worldview where a higher power is in control and in relationship with them." This analysis of an "ethics of submission" (Marshall 2009, 142–3) has been developed most elaborately in anthropological studies of "pious" or "orthodox" Muslims in various European contexts (Fadil 2008; Amir-Moazami et al. 2011; Jacobsen 2011; Jouili 2015).

This work is strongly influenced by Saba Mahmood's (2005) path-breaking study of the pious endeavors of female participants of an Islamic movement in Cairo. These women's "main concern," Mahmood writes, was "the cultivation of submission to what its members interpret to be God's will" (2012, xi). They thereby gave shape to "concepts of human flourishing" (2005, 195) that diverged from liberal ideas about freedom and agency. These women did not seek to resist socially authorized practices and doctrines, but rather to put these practices and doctrines to work in their everyday lives, appropriating them as means of self-realization. Mahmood emphasizes that the ultimate goal of her interlocutors was not to discover the "true I" but rather to transcend "the 'I' that is invested in ephemeral pleasures and pursuits" (2005, 148). In what follows, I investigate what role these ethical ideas of submission and authenticity played in my interlocutor's moral religious subjectivities.

Doing God's Will

During one of our Bible study, or "small group," meetings in Ede, Irene shared a dilemma. She was finishing her degree to become a primary school teacher but felt unsure about what she wanted to do next. She actually didn't really like teaching and worried that she would apply for a job that "wouldn't be God's will" for her. Stefan, a 24-year-old student in pastoral theology who had taken a leading position in the group due to his knowledge of and passion about faith, laughingly remarked that God always asked those things from him that he actually did *not* want to do himself. So, he suggested, perhaps Irene should become a teacher after all.

In our small group meetings, we had many such discussions on doing God's will and following God's guidance. In these, my interlocutors typically distinguished between their own will—referring to their desires, wishes, urges, preferences, and so on—and God's will. More generally, the young Christians I met believed that the human self was prone to wrongdoing. In their Protestant Christian understanding, based on the (Augustinian) teaching of original sin, all of humankind inherits Adam and Eve's trespassing of God's command and is therefore unable to abstain from sin (Den Hertog 2005). This propensity to sin is understood to come particularly from "the flesh," the physical body, or in the words of the Apostle Paul: "the law of sin which is in my members" (Rom 7:23).[4] Because of their sinful nature, humans can only attain salvation through God's mercy, epitomized by Christ's redemption on the cross (Van Geest 2005). In line with these doctrines, my Christian interlocutors entertained a conception of the self as inherently imperfect. Their selves could only be sanctified by accepting Christ's sacrifice, which involved attaining a new "identity," as they often put it, as "children of God." And central to being a "child of God" was trying to do His will.

These young Christians regarded "God's will" as given and absolute, even if it was not always unambiguously clear to them. It was expressed on the one hand in the universal teachings and guidelines of the Bible and, on the other, in the very personal guidance that God provided in their day-to-day lives. The phrase "doing God's will" was generally used in relation to the choices my interlocutors had to make. This concerned not only such mundane matters as making time for personal prayer and reflection in the morning, studying for one's exams, or deciding not to drink too many beers on a student social night, but also the choices they had to make with regard to study, work, internships, and (romantic) relationships. In these matters, they felt that their own wishes, desires, and feelings did not necessarily correspond to what God expected or wanted from them. Stefan, for instance, told me that he had always had a passion for cattle farming and wanted to become a farmer. Yet at some point during his studies at an agricultural college he experienced a calling to put his life at the service of God. He decided to divert from his aspired career in farming and enrolled in the course in pastoral theology in Ede. While Stefan's sense and experience of being called to "work for the Lord" were exceptionally strong, his aspiration to follow God's plan for him and to put God's will before his own was widely shared among my interlocutors.

For these young Christians, talk about "God's will" signaled the idea that God alone had sovereignty over determining the good in one's life. At Pilgrim Students in Rotterdam, the staff member Mark once quoted the line in David's psalms "I have no good above You"[5] as an archetype of this outlook. For my Christian interlocutors, human flourishing was to be achieved by finding, not so much "[one's] own way of realizing one's own humanity" (Taylor 2002, 83), as the path that they believed God wanted them to follow. For them, living according to God's will was a moral end in and of itself, rather than a means toward "being one's true self." Yet, as will become clear below, it was nonetheless understood to entail a privileged route to self-fulfillment.

Doing God's will was strongly connected to the sense of relying on a higher force outside of oneself. As Bram at Pilgrim Students in Rotterdam put it: "I also want to be able to put my trust in something that exists outside of myself, something objective as it were, which I can fall back on." This reliance or dependence on God as a supra-subjective Being was considered to be a virtue, which some thought they ought to realize more in their lives. Thus when in a small discussion group at Pilgrim Students the question was raised what people liked to improve in their lives as Christians, one young woman responded: "I want to learn to live more in dependence on God."

Indeed, dependence on God was often described as a gift, which allowed one to flourish, to realize oneself, and, as my interlocutors sometimes put it, "to live in fullness" (*leven in volheid*). As Henk Hagoort, a Protestant Christian and at the time chairman of the board of directors of the Dutch Public Broadcasting Company, put it at a symposium on Christianity and organized at the Erasmus University Rotterdam: "You can only be yourself when you have a source outside of yourself." This statement strikingly combines the language of "authentic self-fulfillment" with its pivotal injunction to "be yourself" (Taylor 2002, 84-92) with the Christian teaching that human-beings are ultimately dependent on God and His grace, not only for their happiness but also for their salvation (Runia 2005). While the discourse of "being oneself" is typical for our times, the link between personal fulfillment and reliance on a divine power is not entirely new. As Terry Eagleton (2009, 16-17) writes with reference to Thomas Aquinas: "For orthodox Christian doctrine, it is our dependence on God that allows us to be self-determining."

Hagoort related this Christian teaching to the particular challenges that come with a successful career. He spoke about the tendencies to try and derive one's identity from one's work, to be dependent on one's success or to ask too much from oneself in order to prove oneself. These are familiar issues among successful entrepreneurs and employees in today's capitalist culture. For Hagoort, the recognition of a divine source outside of himself provided a counterweight to these tendencies.

Freedom and Fulfillment

The young Christians with whom I worked held that while submitting oneself to God's will entailed discipline and a degree of constraint, it was ultimately an enabling act that resulted in personal freedom. As it was phrased in an evangelical praise song we once sang in our small group in Ede: "By doing Your will/I learn to be free."[6] When I asked the participants of the small group what this line meant for them, Jantine said that following Jesus frees her from her everyday worries. She remarked that her recurrent anxieties about her internship dissolved when she took the step of saying "Jesus, I know that you want to carry this burden for me." Freedom through God's will was also understood in terms of being liberated from one's impulses and inclinations. Thus, Alwin pointed out that by "making a choice for Jesus" one can free oneself from things that appear to be "very normal in our world," for example when it comes to sexuality. When I discussed this issue with a couple of young men in an evangelical youth church in Rotterdam, they pointed out that while in "our culture" freedom means doing whatever you want, in their Christian perspective freedom also means being able to *refrain* from doing certain things.

Linked to the discussion above on reliance on God, this notion of freedom was based on the idea that "our freedom thrives only within the context of a more fundamental dependency" (Eagleton 2009, 16). As Nicky Gumbel puts it in *Questions of Life*, the widely used handbook in the Alpha introductory course to Christianity: "Rules and regulations can in fact create freedom and increase enjoyment" (2006, 91). Just as clear rules can help kids to enjoy a game of football, Gumbel writes, so too God's rules in the Bible enable us to be free (2006, 91–2). This faith-based freedom was however difficult to achieve and demanded practice. Several of my Christian interlocutors, for instance, told me that they were struggling not to be guided by their sexual desires. The use of the term "learn" in the song line quoted above implies precisely that freedom is not a self-evident or natural situation but a capacity that needs to be acquired and *can* be acquired through submission to God's will.

Freedom through faith also carried a more particular theological meaning for my interlocutors. In their understanding, it was above all Christ's redemptive work on the cross that set them free. This was expressed time and again in songs, conversations, and talks in the context of the Christian student associations in Ede and Rotterdam. When the phrase "By doing God's will, I learn to be free" was brought up again in the last meeting of Ede's small group, Lisa said it meant that one is free because one's sins have been forgiven—yet, she also noted that she still found it difficult to feel this. Through his death on the cross, my interlocutors believed, Jesus Christ paid a "ransom" in order to free mankind. While all people continue to be sinful by nature, they can receive forgiveness of their sins by virtue of Christ's sacrifice.

The young Christians I encountered often contrasted this redemption through Christ with the religious world described in the Old Testament, where people sought to be reconciled with God by obeying His commands and offering sacrifices to Him (cf. Muis 2005). My interlocutors explained that these people always fell short in this regard and therefore continued to be removed from God. As Julian, one of the people in my small group in Rotterdam, once put it to me, Christ has undone this separation between people and God by dying on the cross and "taking on our sins." In this understanding, He is the ultimate sacrifice reconciling believers to God (Muis 2005). My interlocutors often described this in terms of a space of potentiality being opened up: they felt that they did not have to prove themselves, to demonstrate their virtue, or to fight against their nature. Christ's redemption meant that God accepted them unconditionally. This allowed them to come to self-fulfillment and—to reiterate a phrase that was sometimes used—to "live in fullness."

This was clearly expressed by Isabel, a 25-year-old business consultant living in Rotterdam who had converted to Christianity two years earlier and frequented an evangelical church. When she had converted, she said, a "burden was lifted from my shoulders," because she felt she no longer had to achieve or prove anything and she could simply be at ease with who she was. For her, freedom meant that she did not have to carry the weight of her mistakes, did not have to become a better person, because she believed God accepted her for the person she was, with all of her shortcomings. Similarly to Hagoort, Isabel's words reflected the ethical ideals of both authenticity and submission: on the one hand she emphasized being herself and being happy about who she was; on the other, she pointed out that she was able to be herself by "doing what God wants" and "following His guidelines." Neither Isabel nor my other Christian interlocutors felt that they were able to fully realize this particular experience of freedom. Isabel said she was still grappling with feelings of guilt and bitterness in relation to her siblings and parents, which kept her from "really living freely." For her, too, becoming free was a process of learning, and more particularly a process of—as she put it, again echoing the discourse of authenticity—becoming aware of her true "identity" as a "child of God."

Submitting to God

During my fieldwork with young Muslims I regularly attended classes on the *sira*, the biography of the Prophet Muhammad, which were taught each Sunday in a modestly sized mosque in one of The Hague's multi-ethnic neighborhoods. The mosque is housed in an inconspicuous, repurposed site that has reputedly served as a Hindu temple before. On a typical visit, I entered the mosque while dozens of men were making their way to the spacious prayer room on the second floor for the *dhuhr* or noon prayer. I sat down on the soft carpet in a corner of the prayer room, taking in the atmosphere of the space, the sight and sound of visitors warmly greeting one another, the people praying, and the utterances of the imam guiding the prayer. After the prayer finished, a varying number of men (ranging between around fifteen and fifty), most of them in their twenties, stayed in the mosque to attend the class. In a separate women's prayer room, female attendees were able to follow the class through a loudspeaker. Notes with questions from the female attendees would sometimes be handed over at the door of the men's prayer room. The classes were taught by Omar Khalil, the popular Salafi youth imam and preacher whom I introduced in the previous chapter. In these classes, which he had already been giving for seven years at the time of my fieldwork, Omar Khalil talked in detail about the life of the Prophet, the ascent of Islam, the behavior of the *sahaba* (the Prophet's companions), and the battles these first Muslims fought.

Khalil's plea to obey the prescriptions and regulations of Islam ran like a red thread through these classes. He used the stories about the life of the Prophet and his companions to remind the young people in his audience of the importance of obeying the Quran and following the model passed on by the Prophet, regularly pointing out the shortcomings of today's Muslims. "The difference between the companions of the Prophet and us," he once said, "is that they were always obedient, not only when it suited them." Most of the questions put to Khalil in the Q&A sessions following his classes focused on what is permitted, recommended, or forbidden in Islam, for example with regard to playing music, marrying a non-Muslim, or living in a non-Muslim society.

This emphasis on prescriptions and regulations characterized the—often Salafi-oriented—socio-religious activities in which my Muslim interlocutors engaged more generally. These centered on learning the "correct" tenets of Islam from knowledgeable teachers or preachers, who based themselves on the Quran and the *hadith*. As is common among Muslims, my interlocutors regarded the Quran as the literal, unchanged, and unchangeable word of God, which contains His revelation to mankind conveying divine guidelines as to how people are to live and worship God (Saeed, Ayoub, and Cornell 2005; Bowen 2012a, 18). The *hadith* are accounts of "what the Prophet said or did or of his tacit approval of something said or done in his presence" (Robson 2012). Khalil and other preachers would generally only refer to *hadith* that are recognized as "reliable" or "authentic" (*sahih*) and that are taken up in authoritative collections (particularly those of the classical Islamic scholars Imam Bukhari and Imam Muslim). My interlocutors believed that the Quran and the *hadith* exposed God's will. They sought to submit to this divine revelation and thereby, as it was sometimes put, "please God," with the goal of achieving what they often described as "closeness to God" and, ultimately, a place in Paradise after their deaths.

Submitting to God entailed subordinating one's self—one's personal opinions, needs, and desires—to the will of God as expressed in His revelation. The young Muslims I worked with regularly pointed out that they put more value on what they regarded as the objective regulations of Islam and the ways these were explained by authoritative scholars, than on their personal interpretations and interests. As Naima, whom I introduced in the previous chapter, put it: "Look, you accept the Quran in its entirety. You can't say like, I accept this bit but not that bit, or I change this bit a little, because it doesn't fit the way I live today." Because of the value accorded to the religious sources, both the Quran and *hadith*, my interlocutors attached much weight to examining the textual "evidence" underlying any Islamic statement or judgment, a practice that is characteristic for the Salafi approach to Islam (Haykel 2009, 44). This did not mean that the Islamic prescriptions themselves had to be fully understood on rational grounds necessarily. In the end, my interlocutors regularly pointed out, God knows best what is good for you. Aisha, for example, told me that she wore her *hijab* "for God." Regardless of what the reasons for wearing one could be, she said she did so primarily because God, who is "the All-Knowing," has "decreed it to us." Submission to God, in this view, ultimately entailed accepting the limits of individual reasoning in the face of God's omniscience.

Subordinating one's personal desires, wants, or lusts to the will of God was seen as an important part of living an Islamic life. In Islamic teachings, lusts and desires are understood to originate from the *nafs*, a term that refers to the self or soul and especially to its lower, carnal, or "animal" faculties, that is, those faculties that tend toward evil (Metcalf 1984, 377). A distinction is commonly made between the carnal self (*nafs*), reason/intellect (*'aql*), and spirit/soul (*ruh*).[7] A helpful explanation of the relation between these dimensions of personhood in important strands of classical Islamic thought has been offered by Ira Lapidus:

> Man, constituted of body and soul, is an imperfect being, but … he holds within himself the potential for union with God and for the realization of his highest nature. His soul is a spiritual substance, created by God before the birth of the person and destined to live, beyond the death of the body, everlastingly. The soul is composed of several faculties—especially the faculties of reason (*'aql*) and of anger and desire (together called *nafs*). The soul merges faculties that are spiritual and material, angelic and bestial, divine and satanic. The true goal of life is to perfect the soul so that the spiritual and the divine elements prevail over the material and the satanic. *'Aql* has to prevail over *nafs*.
>
> (Lapidus 1984, 56)

When I talked about these concepts with Idris, a 22-year-old master student in Islamic Spiritual Care living in Amsterdam, he said that because of its connection with the body, the *nafs* tends "toward desires, toward lusts, all those things you like—and the things you like are not always good, they *can* often be good, but usually they are bad." In this meaning of the term, it has similar connotations to what is described as the "flesh" in the New Testament (Calverley and Netton 2012). Yet the *nafs* is not understood to be inherently evil; it can be corrected and disciplined. In this regard, my Muslim interlocutors occasionally spoke about the "battle against one's *nafs*" (*jihad an-nafs*).

Idris was particularly fighting his desires in the context of his, as he put it, "daily contact with the other sex." He said: "Sometimes girls are just sticking to you, because you have, yeah, a good career, a good education, and, yes, they are not always the ugliest. So, that's very difficult in fact." Idris tried to restrain from practices that he deemed Islamically "unlawful" (*ongeoorloofd*), such as pre-marital relationships and sex before marriage. Yet he did sometimes cross what he saw as the boundaries of the permissible, by flirting or looking at "certain body parts of a woman." The prohibition of sexual and romantic relationships outside of marriage was emphasized in several Islamic talks I attended on the subject, which, I observed, received particular attention in the summer. Several of the young Muslim men and women I got acquainted with told me that they had had—and sometimes still had—girlfriends or boyfriends. Many of them thought they thereby went against Islamic regulations and most sought to restrict their "wrongdoing" by, as it was often phrased, "setting boundaries" in their relationship by limiting—or altogether avoiding—sexual contact with their partners. Some decided to refrain from having romantic relationships altogether (cf. Beekers and Schrijvers 2020).

Freedom and Free Will

It was occasionally put forward during my fieldwork among young Muslims that it was through renunciation of one's desires, by following God's guidance and submitting oneself to His will, that true freedom could be achieved. In this perspective, people are "prisoners" of their desires and lusts, and Islam provides a privileged path toward "liberation." As it was put by a convert to Islam: "This is for me the ultimate definition of freedom: learning to master your own urges."[8] Similarly to what I observed among my Christian interlocutors, this notion of freedom was sometimes contrasted with what was taken to be the Western understanding of freedom, particularly the idea that freedom entailed being able to fulfill the desires of oneself or those of others.

The freedom offered in Islam was also understood to entail freedom from constraints by others. Amane, a 22-year-old law student whom I came to know in the context of the student association An-Nur, reflected on this aspect of freedom in relation to recurrent debates about Islam and women's rights. Observing that "[the issue of] women is so sensitive in this society, as in: 'she shouldn't be oppressed, she has to emancipate, yadi-yadi-ya,'" she remarked that she doubted whether women could be free when, for instance, the fashion industry pressured them into wearing very revealing clothes. Amane perceived this as a form of oppression, because she did not believe that that these women "choose for it themselves." Conversely, she did not regard wearing a headscarf, like she did, as oppression, because "I choose for it myself" (yet she reflexively added that other people might not agree that she makes this choice freely.) When I asked her about the distinction one might make between wearing revealing clothes as a norm based on social expectations and wearing a headscarf as a religious obligation, Amane responded:

> Yes, but uhm that's rather a difference for me between a divine law and a law that is imposed by society. I think that it is *precisely* as soon as you listen to others that you are being oppressed. ... If you could, uhm, regard the Quran as divine, then you say that it knows ... what is best for you, so... [brief silence]. Yes, but this is the kind of discussion that you can't have of course with someone who doesn't believe that.

Strikingly, Amane re-signified the difference between obligations and social expectations by distinguishing between divine laws and societal laws. In her view, only the latter could be oppressive. For Amane, it was her dependence on God that allowed her to be independent of others. "You're actually not dependent on anything except God," she said. Interestingly, she was acutely aware that this was a particular form of religious reasoning that may be difficult to accept by people who do not share her beliefs.

The idea that Islam afforded social independence was widely shared among my Muslim interlocutors as well as the Muslim preachers and teachers I encountered during my fieldwork. It can be seen as an expression of what philosophers have termed "negative" freedom, which refers to the absence of interference, coercion, or constraint by others (Berlin 2002, 169). While this concept of freedom resonates with Christian views on dependence on God, my Muslim interlocutors tended to put more emphasis than the young Christians on the particular aspect of freedom from constraint by other people.

The notion of "free will" also played an important role for my Muslim interlocutors. It was regularly pointed out during my fieldwork that God created human beings with a free will and that, consequently, it was up to individuals themselves to decide whether or not they obeyed God's commands. As Naima told me: "Look, uhm the Islamic rules are fixed [*vastgesteld*]. That's God's will, that alcohol is simply prohibited for example. So your will, that's your choice, as in, are you going to comply to those [rules] or not." In this context, obeying God's commands is understood to be for your own good. As Naima put it, it is something "you do for yourself," because "in the end you will receive the reward or the punishment."[9]

My Muslim interlocutors frequently referred to this notion of free will to give substance to their argument that their compliance to Islamic regulations was the result of their own choice, rather than a form of oppression. Naima, for example, told me about an "atheist" colleague who saw religion as an impediment to freedom and who used to tell Naima that she didn't know what she was missing out on, by not going out nor drinking alcohol. Reflecting on this, Naima told me: "I don't *need* to know, because it's my conscious choice. So that's my freedom, to choose not to follow that." Being conscious about one's choice was important for Naima. In her view, one was "really free" when one could think for oneself, read and interpret for oneself, independently of others: "freedom is when you have the opportunity yourself to really acquire knowledge, find out things for yourself and so on."

This strong emphasis on free will signals a notable difference between my Muslim and Christian interlocutors. Ideas about personal responsibility took a central place in the narratives of the young Muslims: in the end, it was up to individuals themselves whether or not they decided to obey God's prescriptions. In the narratives of the young Christians, by contrast, individual responsibility and individual deeds were de-emphasized because Jesus's redemptive work on the cross was ultimately understood to mean that one's salvation did not depend on one's personal thoughts and deeds. Nonetheless, the Christians also stressed individual volition, particularly in terms of the strong emphasis they put on one's deliberate decision to accept Jesus as one's personal Redeemer and on the continuing critical introspection this entailed—an issue to which I will return below.

Practicing Faith Sincerely

In sum, while my Muslim interlocutors emphasized obedience to "objective" Islamic regulations, the Christians adhered to a somewhat more abstract, and perhaps more subjective, sense of following God's guidance (even if they also gave much weight to following the word of God in the Bible). Yet both groups shared the ideals of putting God's will before one's own and of relying on God as an external, higher Being. In this regard, both gave shape to notions of the good and the good life that differed from the ethical ideals of authentic self-fulfillment. At the same time, both interpreted submission to God as a route to personal freedom and both related this to a particular conception of self-realization. For the young Muslims and Christians alike, freedom through faith entailed being liberated from one's worries, urges, and lusts. In addition, my Muslim interlocutors also emphasized freedom from social constraints, whereas the young Christians focused on the redemption from one's sins and shortcomings as well as on the ability to "be oneself." If this already suggests a convergence with the ethics of authenticity, my interlocutors' strong concerns with personal sincerity make this link with the ethics of authenticity even more apparent.

As the previous chapter already started to show, my Muslim and Christian interlocutors stressed the importance of sincerity, awareness, and reflexivity in their religious practices. The young Christians were concerned about what they regarded as a risk of slipping into a non-reflexive religious engagement. Thus, Elise, a 23-year-old student in pastoral theology in Ede, was dissatisfied about the ways in which prayer tended to be conducted in a taken-for-granted way among her friends. "I just find it important," she said, "that it is a conscious choice and that it is not self-evident, that it really is a *conviction* in fact, not something that's simply part of the game [*wat er gewoon bij hoort*]." Many of my Christian interlocutors shared this concern with deliberate and self-conscious religious practice. At times, this manifested itself in an uncertainty about one's inner convictions. In one of the meetings of our small group in Ede, Lisa remarked that she doubted whether she could regard herself as a "child of God." She explained that she wondered to what extent she was unreflexively following the paths that had already been laid out for her as opposed to "really" having faith and experiencing God's reality herself.

My Muslim interlocutors put much stress on achieving personal awareness of the meaning of their worship practices. This concern with awareness is linked to the emphasis that Muslims, and notably Salafi Muslims, put on worshipping with the correct, sincere intentions (De Koning 2018, 41; cf. Mahmood 2005). Ismael's account offers a good illustration. He told me that he regarded wearing a beard, like he did himself, not as an obligation but as "strongly recommended." Yet once one had a beard one shouldn't shave it off:

> If you [wear a beard] with that intention, really do it for faith, and after that you shave it off, then you have committed a kind of, uhm... well, not unbelief, but uhm..., you actually commit a sin as it were. ... You have to, when you get into it, you also have to think about it carefully. It's not something that you should take lightly. ... You also have to stand by it.

Thus, while for Ismael wearing a beard was not a religious obligation according to religious law, it effectively became an obligation after one had made the deliberate decision to grow one. It was the very intention of the religious act that gave it a higher, perhaps even sanctified, character. This combined emphasis on obedience to the religious prescriptions and intention also characterizes Farida's statement about wearing a headscarf, quoted at the beginning of this chapter. In her perspective, making a personal and informed choice was even a prerequisite for valid religious obedience.

These concerns with sincerity index the appropriation of a particular ethics of authenticity, one that centers not on the imperative to follow one's allegedly unique spiritual path, but rather on the requirement that one's inner convictions correspond to one's outward expressions. Without such correspondence, religious acts were seen as less valid or even devoid of value. As Aisha put it with respect to wearing a headscarf: "I do this for God, but it also has to make sense from the inside [*het moet ook van binnen kloppen*]." Like the young British women of Somali descent studied by Giulia Liberatore, my Muslim interlocutors regarded personal reflection, deliberation, and conscious choice as important preconditions of religious practice, thereby diverting to some extent from Islamic reformist teachings that rather emphasize the cultivation of interior dispositions through outward practices (Liberatore 2017, chap. 7).[10] For Liberatore, this prioritization of inner convictions signals less an appropriation of "a liberal tradition" (what I here term an ethics of authenticity) than a shift within Islamic discursive traditions that is occasioned, in part, by a hostile political climate toward Islam. I argue, by contrast, that the moral narratives of my Muslim interlocutors do point to their incorporation of a contemporary ethics of authenticity. The comparative approach taken here demonstrates that this is not a particularistic characteristic of young Muslims facing negative representations of Islam, but a religious orientation that is shared by young Christians. My data suggest that both my Muslim and Christian interlocutors have internalized a norm of sincerity that, as Webb Keane has argued, plays a pivotal role in "the moral narrative of modernity" (2007, chap. 7). Keane builds on the work of Lionel Trilling, who writes that the concept of sincerity, as it developed within European moral discourses, "refers primarily to a congruence between avowal and actual feeling" (1971, 2). Because it involves avoiding falsehood toward others by being true to one's self, it requires "arduous effort" (1971, 6).[11] As I will discuss in a moment, this was also the case for my interlocutors.

Convergent Ethics of Submission and Authenticity

The coexistence of ethical ideals of submission and authenticity has been observed in earlier studies of young Muslims or Christians in Europe. Johan Roeland (2009) describes the religiosity of young Dutch evangelical Christians as situated "between subjectivization and subjection." He asks how, in our era of self-fulfillment, evangelicalism can be so successful despite its prevalent norms of subjection (212). To answer this question, he suggests that these young evangelicals did not experience the discourses and practices of subjection as restricting their subjective life-worlds, but rather as conducive to their subjective desires and pursuits of personal well-being (212–13). In line with Heelas and Woodhead (2005), then, Roeland seems to assume an *a priori* opposition between subjective self-fulfillment on the one hand and subjection to external authorities on the other. By contrast, anthropological studies of Muslims in Europe have tended to be more sensitive to a Foucauldian understanding of subjectivity, which recognizes that subjection to norms or authorities can be experienced as a means toward self-realization. Several authors have described how young European Muslims combine aims of submission to God with aspirations to individual freedom and authenticity (Fadil 2008; Jacobsen 2011; Roex 2013).

One of the most elaborate explorations of this to date is provided by Nadia Fadil (2008) in her—unpublished—dissertation on "second-generation Maghrebi" in Belgium. She argues that for her "orthodox" Muslim interlocutors "being a 'good Muslim' balances between a *concern with the self* and a *concern with God*" (2008, 243, italics in original). She analyzes these separate concerns as distinct "ethical models" based respectively on a "liberal" secular tradition and a "non-liberal" Islamic one (218–19). Indeed, Fadil points out, religious agency can be "composed of different—sometimes contradicting—ethical imperatives" (251). She suggests that these ethical imperatives played out on different levels of her interlocutors' religious agency: the "discourse of autonomy" pertained to personal sovereignty in relation to other people, the "discourse of obedience" referred to subjection to God (248, 251). Yet she also shows that the matter is more complex than this. Similarly to my discussion above, she for instance observes that her interlocutors' concerns with autonomy were also informed by the Islamic notion of "exclusive subjection to God's will" (251).

Both Roeland and Fadil, then, describe the religious engagement of their interlocutors as something of a balancing act between the ethical imperative of subjection to God and the imperatives of personal authenticity and autonomy, which are linked by both to modern liberal culture.[12] Yet both authors also hint at the ways in which these ethical ideals come together in their interlocutors' religious aspirations. In line with these latter observations, the material presented in this chapter suggests that it is useful to move beyond prevalent approaches to contemporary religious subjectivities that focus either on an ethics of authenticity or on an ethics of submission, or that conceptualize submission and authenticity as intrinsically contradictory "moral registers" (Schielke 2015) that people draw from separately and depending on the context.[13] For the Muslims and Christians I worked with, concerns with submission and authenticity were not wholly separate from one another, but rather became linked in their religious pursuits.

For these young Muslims and Christians, striving toward submitting themselves to God was a way of developing themselves, finding their "true" selves, and becoming "free." They believed that the privileged path to "realizing one's own humanity" (Taylor 2002, 83) *involved* submitting the self to God. At the same time, in their eyes truthful and valid submission to God required self-conscious subjective engagement, personal choice, and sincerity. Summarily put: finding one's authentic self required submitting oneself to God, and submitting oneself to God required one's authentic personal involvement. Neither the ethical ideal of surrendering the self to God nor that of expressing one's "true" self was subordinate to the other (cf. Fadil 2008, 74). Rather, both of these ideals converged in my interlocutors' efforts at moral self-improvement.

A consequence of the convergence of these ethical ideals was that the endeavors of religious submission of my Muslim and Christian interlocutors relied strongly on the will, commitment, sincerity, and activity of their selves. These religious efforts required constant "work of the self on the self" (Foucault 2005, 16) and a continuous monitoring of the virtuosity and sincerity of one's acts. Foucault's exploration—in his later work on antiquity—of the "care of the self" is instructive here. The practices of caring of the self that he described pointed to a tending to the self and a caring for one's soul, which were directed at self-transformation, purification, and salvation (1990, 42). This, Foucault pointed out, was a demanding enterprise. In the ancient culture of Greece, the term "care" (*epimeleia*) implied labor: it takes time and requires the effort of "a whole set of occupations" (1990, 50). In the remainder of this chapter, I discuss the work on the self and vigilance of the self as central aspects of my interlocutors' practices of religious submission. What emerges in this discussion is a paradox: while my interlocutors' primary religious concern entailed the submission of their selves to God, this ambition stimulated a strong preoccupation with the condition of their very selves. This preoccupation with the self points to the struggles inherent in their religious pursuits.

Imperfection, Self-Improvement, and Salvation

The people I encountered during my fieldwork time and again emphasized the ways in which both their religious communities and they themselves fell short of the aspirations to piety they set for themselves. We have seen how the imam Omar Khalil repeatedly referred to the imperfections of today's Muslims when compared to the early community of Muhammad and his companions, how Idris felt that he fell short when it came to fully obeying God in matters of sexuality, and how young Christians like Irene, Isabel, and Lisa struggled at times with surrendering their will to God and experiencing Christ's redemption. Likewise, during *Opwekking* ("Revival"), an annual evangelical-charismatic festival with up to 50,000 visitors, which I attended in 2010, I was struck by the paramount emphasis on imperfection. While this massive outdoor festival was characterized by the joyful celebration of Christian faith, preachers and other speakers constantly reminded the people in the audience of their religious shortcomings, telling them they were not quite there yet, that they still needed to make the ultimate step of surrendering to God, and that they failed in "radically" following Jesus in their everyday lives.

Bram, the student from Rotterdam who talked about his desire to rely on a higher force, was particularly candid about these kinds of struggles. As we were having a coffee in Rotterdam one day, he told me about a talk at Pilgrim Students he had attended some time ago. Inspired and bolstered by the talk, he had subsequently prayed that he "gave his life to Jesus." He now told me that these were "very big words." While he had said them spontaneously at the time, he later realized that it was very difficult to "really give one's life to Jesus." In our small group a few months later, Bram elaborated on this point, explaining that he simply experienced a lack of time to "give his life to Jesus" (in Chapter 5, I elaborate on such time-related struggles). Moreover, he had his own ideas about where he wanted to be in life and he sometimes found it difficult to convince himself that following Jesus would get him there. He did believe this rationally, he said, but found it hard to *feel* it too.

Because of such felt inadequacies, my interlocutors experienced a continuing need to work on their behaviors, thoughts, and emotions, seeking to align these with their religious aspirations (cf. Kloos and Beekers 2018). The young Muslims sometimes literally talked about "improving themselves" and presented this as a continuous process: "You are never going to be perfect," Amane noted, "but you can strive to be so." A question I tried to ask in all of my interviews was what my interviewees found most difficult about being a Muslim or Christian. When I asked Fatima, a twenty-year-old psychology student in Rotterdam, she responded: "In the end, it would be the keeping up of your faith. Sure it is 'oh right, lectures and knowledge and…', but you do kind of have to get, to obtain actually, the energy and the will and the motivation to become sort of better."

When I brought up the frequent talks about the Day of Judgment in the Islamic lecture circles catering to young Muslims, she commented: "It's simply a kind of sign, like: listen, it's not unconditional …, you have to work for it. If you don't work for it, [laughing] this and this will indeed happen." These statements illustrate the widely felt imperative among my Muslim interlocutors to perform continuous moral work on themselves. They gave shape to what Weber (1978, 534–6) called a "methodical sanctification," whereby virtuous acts become instruments of "self-perfection," that is, of acquiring "those religious qualities the god demands in men."

The young Christians I worked with similarly expressed such an ethical imperative of "methodical sanctification." This is striking given the contrast often drawn between the need to work for one's own salvation in Islam and the "free gift" of salvation through Christ's redemption in Christianity. My Muslim and Christian interlocutors themselves frequently used this contrast to distinguish between Christianity and Islam. As the Christian convert Isabel stated when I interviewed her for the first time: "For Muslims it is never enough, but I live in a state of liberation." Nevertheless, my Christian interlocutors regularly made clear that maintaining a pious lifestyle required constant work. As Sarah, a 23-year-old member of an evangelical congregation in Rotterdam, told me:

> You can always choose yourself to do God's will or not.… So, you can always let yourself be guided by your human nature, or by God. And each day it is a battle to choose between these two, so between what I want or what God wants. These are often at odds with each other.

These words bear a striking resemblance to my Muslim interlocutors' concepts of free will and *jihad an-nafs* (the battle against the self). Indeed, the challenge of trying to live piously in everyday life was repeatedly articulated by my Christian interlocutors and their teachers and preachers. In our small group in Rotterdam, Julian put it particularly strongly: "I feel that I need to crucify my sinful self day after day."

At times, the Christian students in Ede and Rotterdam explicitly addressed the tensions between this imperative of self-improvement and the notion of unconditional salvation. They attempted to resolve these tensions by arguing that one's salvation should be visible in one's actions, or one's "works" to use the biblical term. Or they pointed out that one's gratitude for Christ's sacrifice made one *want* to do good. In other words, they pointed out that "good works" were not a condition for, but rather the fruit of, salvation. Members of Pilgrim Students sometimes referred to the words of the apostle Paul in this regard:

"Shall we continue in sin, that grace may abound? God forbid. We who died to sin, how shall we any longer live therein?" (Rom 6:1-2).

This view of moral conduct as a sign of salvation, however, also indexes a lingering uncertainty in the religious lives of these young Christians: Does one live up to the gift of salvation? And when does one live virtuously enough to know that one is really saved (cf. Van Harskamp 2000, 163–5)? This kind of self-scrutiny, which as Weber (2003) famously showed has a long history in Calvinist Protestantism, was vividly expressed by Isabel when I interviewed her for the second time:

> For me it never goes fast enough. With Islam it is very easy, because you know what you have to do and when you achieve it, it is good. With us, or "with us", with Christians, it's more like: it's actually never enough, because it can always be more.

Here, remarkably, Isabel made the exact opposite point from that in our first interview, when she contrasted her own "state of liberation" with that of Muslims for whom "it is never enough." This apparent contradiction is telling. My interlocutors experienced the doctrine of unconditional salvation in Christianity both as a relief and as a demanding challenge. Many seemed to move constantly between the sense that God accepted them with all their shortcomings and the sense that they always had to do better.

For my Muslim interlocutors, the relation between good deeds and salvation was more complex than Isabel and other young Christians made it seem. While they indeed believed that pious conduct increased their chances of entering Paradise after their death, they also stressed that one's salvation depended above all on God's mercy. They regarded Allah as a greatly merciful God, who was prepared to forgive all sins—apart from, some noted, *shirk* (idolatry)—as long as the believer showed sincere repentance. To illustrate, the popular youth imam and preacher Dawoud once emphasized in a talk to students that one of the most important names and attributes of Allah is *Al-Wadud*, the loving. He cited a *hadith* in which the Prophet Muhammad recounted that at the time of creation, Allah distributed only 1 percent of His mercy to the creatures he brought to life, both humans and animals, and saved the remaining 99 percent for the Day of Judgment. Thus, Dawoud said, nobody has reason to think "that he or she could never receive the love of Allah." Indeed, in different ways for my Muslim and Christian interlocutors, salvation entailed an intricate relation between God's mercy and the moral imperative to "do good." The somewhat simplified contrasts they themselves tended to draw between Christian and

Islamic salvation doctrines might indicate how they sought to make sense of the teachings of their own religion by contrasting these to the teachings of another.

Moral Vigilance of the Self

The ethical imperatives of moral self-improvement among both my Muslim and Christian interlocutors stimulated them to practice a constant moral vigilance of their selves. Such critical introspection was strongly encouraged within the Christian student associations in which I participated. Already in the first meeting of our small group in Ede, Jantine, who had prepared the meeting, invited the others to interrogate the quality of their personal faith. She distributed copies of a drawing of a swimming pool and asked her group members where they would place themselves in terms of their faith: in the deep or the shallow side of the pool, near the cold or warm water taps, in the whirlpool or on the superintendent's seat.[14] All of the group members present that day formulated remarkably articulate answers to that question, describing how they looked at their religious lives (*geloofsleven*) and what struggles they went through with respect to their faith. It struck me that most of them were dissatisfied with their religious lives and felt that they should, as it were, plunge themselves more deeply into the water.

Jantine saw herself swimming toward the warm water taps. She said she was too often tempted to regard herself as a good believer, while her faith could be more alive (*levend*) and conscious (*bewust*). "I do for example read a passage from the Bible every night," she said, "but afterwards I don't always give it much thought." She noted that she sometimes tended to see herself as a good person, who performed good deeds, while it was important to "remain alert." These remarks point to a particular dimension of my Christian interlocutors' self-vigilance. They found it important to realize that, as human-beings, they were inevitably imperfect and sinful, and therefore dependent on Jesus for their salvation.

My Muslim interlocutors' everyday religious lives were also characterized by a vigilance of the self. As Ahmet, a nineteen-year-old student in public administration who volunteered for a Gülen-inspired association in Rotterdam, put it: "While walking, while making assignments, while working, you continuously keep your norms and values in mind and you yourself screen the things you're going to do or to look at based on your criteria." While Ahmet said that such "screening" (he used the English term) of himself came naturally to him, some of my other interlocutors told me that this kind of moral self-vigilance required constant and self-conscious effort. When I asked Aisha what she found most difficult about being a Muslim, she responded:

> To be constantly critical of yourself. So simply faith [*het geloof*] itself. Uhm… In your daily life, … you do from time to time get angry and that kind of stuff. And then you sometimes feel sorry about it later on. And uhm… At times you think that you're really doing everything wrong.

Both Ahmet's and Aisha's words point to a dispositional state of constant critical introspection, shared by most of my Muslim as well as Christian interlocutors. Its aim, Aisha said, was "to be the best possible person."

Importantly, my Muslim interlocutors exercised such introspection on their personal feelings as well. As mentioned above, they were strongly concerned with the sincerity (*al-ikhlas*) of one's intention (cf. Mahmood 2005, 123, passim). In social religious settings and in conversations with me, it was frequently pointed out that the intention with which one performs religious practices was as important as the acts themselves. This is illustrated by a much-cited statement attributed to the Prophet, included in the *hadith* collection of Al-Bukhari (810–70): "The reward of deeds depends upon the intentions and every person will get the reward according to what he has intended" (Khan 1997, 45). Citing this *hadith* in Arabic and Dutch, Idris told me: "That's the basis. You can do anything you want. If you don't have intention, you have nothing."

Idris himself tried to follow this principle by critically asking himself whether he performed certain worship practices "to show off" or "for God." For example, he tried to avoid "reciting very beautifully" when he prayed together with his family, because he would know that *riya* (ostentation) would inevitably come into play. This would often happen unwittingly:

> Because the Prophet said: "*Riya* is just like a black ant on a black rock on a moonless night". You will never see such an ant. In such a cunning way *riya* can come into your heart; you start with a pious deed with a good intention, but afterwards your intention changes, because a pretty girl happens to look at you. Then you suddenly start to act more spontaneously, but then I think: you're just faking it [*ben je gewoon aan het faken*].

The concern with one's intention, then, signaled a monitoring of one's feelings and the way these feelings may change while performing virtuous acts.

Many were however also cautious about too great an emphasis on one's intention. They were wary of the kind of attitude exhibited by Ali B., a well-known Dutch rapper and TV-personality of Moroccan descent, during a short (unaccompanied) rap performance at the 2010 National Islam Congress in Amsterdam: speaking to a large audience of young Muslims, comprising many veiled women and a good number of bearded men, he jokingly remarked that while he may not have a beard he did have the "right intention." My interlocutors, by contrast, regularly stressed that intention alone was not adequate for being a good Muslim. Thus Idris told me that one's "heart" is an important but not the only aspect of faith. Referring to a *hadith* that emphasizes faith through one's "deeds" and "tongue," he noted that all three aspects (what one feels, does, and says) are important. If that wouldn't be the case, he said, then "Muslims would ignore *all* of the commands and prohibitions and say 'I believe in the heart', you see?" And here Idris chuckled: "But that's not how it works." Similarly, Amane told me that she found it upsetting when friends of her who did not wear a headscarf said that it is not obligatory to do so. She noted:

> You could say that [faith] is only interior [*in je innerlijk*], but how do you mean only interior? It is after all also, uhm, part of your faith, part of the religion, to, uhm, adapt your exterior [*uiterlijk*] to how you are. That seems logical to me at least.

Both Idris and Amane held that, while one's "heart" or "intention" was certainly important, this should not be used as an excuse for failing to obey the religious prescriptions.[15]

In a different way, the Christians with whom I worked were also ambivalent about personal feelings. On the one hand, they often pointed out that the "heart" was as important as the "mind": a strong faith should involve both feelings and rational thought. And most participated in religious practices that strongly appealed to the senses and emotions, particularly in the context of their student associations and large-scale evangelical gatherings, such as *Opwekking*. On the other hand, many of them exposed a remarkably critical attitude toward an emphasis on feelings, emotions, and experiences. They were suspicious of the primacy of feelings that, they felt, characterized many of today's Christian worship practices, particularly in evangelical and Pentecostal circles. Most of my interlocutors, who typically hailed from Calvinist backgrounds in which scripture and knowledge were greatly valued, held that personal feelings were not sufficiently reliable as sources of religious truth. They believed it was equally, if not more, important to strengthen one's relationship with God through Bible reading and prayer. As Jantine put it during a weekend outing of our Ede-based small group in the Ardennes: "Feeling good is not the best yardstick. In the end it is about the word of God!"

Accordingly, several of my interlocutors were critical about the altar call—a common practice in evangelical and Pentecostal services in which congregants are called upon to come forward to demonstrate their (renewed) commitment to Jesus Christ—that many of them had themselves participated in at least once. They pointed out that the strong feelings one might have during an altar call usually tended to ebb again afterward. For them, such singular moments of personal surrender were incapable of effecting a lasting personal change. In this regard, it was inadvisable and even "dangerous"—as Frank, who frequented a small evangelical congregation in Rotterdam, put it—to treat one's feelings as a measure of one's faith. "Feelings are always fluctuating," he said. It is therefore "best for you" to try and have "a constant trust in God, that you always know that God is with you, irrespective of your feeling." Similarly, Rachel recounted that when she had worriedly told her pastor in a Protestant Reformed church in Rotterdam that the "euphoric feeling" she experienced after her confirmation in church gradually abated in the months that followed, he had reassured her by saying: "You don't *have* to feel anything, that's not the most important." Many of my Christian interlocutors shared the conviction that faith could not be supported by subjective feelings alone, but had to be grounded in a long-term relationship with God, the committed practice of prayer and knowledge of the Bible. This view was informed by both their Calvinist background and their critical stance toward what they saw as the "postmodern" preoccupation with personal experience.

A major question at the back of these concerns was how and when one's feelings can be taken as an index of God's presence and will. My Christian interlocutors often grappled with and discussed this issue with one another. One night at Pilgrim Students, for instance, a discussion was started about prayer and "how to know what God asks from you." Benjamin told the group that he had been praying to God about his girlfriend, whom he was very happy about. When such prayer felt good, he said, he thought that he was also getting confirmation from God. In the same vein, Julian said that at times he felt that his prayer simply wasn't working, as if he was talking to the air. He had come to see this as an indication that whatever he was praying for at that moment didn't conform to God's will. Here, Bram intervened: he cautiously remarked that he wondered whether Julian wasn't relying too heavily on his own feelings, at the risk of getting the answers that he was himself longing for. Many of the Christians I encountered, in both Rotterdam and Ede, shared Bram's watchfulness and at times also suspicion of personal feelings. Others, particularly those actively involved in evangelical congregations, emphasized that God could be experienced in their own minds and bodies, and some were involved in learning how to identify such experiences (cf. Luhrmann 2007).

Conclusion

In their attempts at being "good" believers, the revivalist-oriented young Muslims and Christians with whom I conducted fieldwork drew simultaneously from an ethics of submission and an ethics of authenticity. Rather than contradictory imperatives "in between" which these young people balanced, these ethical ideals were interlinked in their everyday moral pursuits. In somewhat different ways, the young Muslims and Christians held not only that the privileged path to self-realization entailed submission of oneself to God but also that truthful submission to God required a sincere and deliberate engagement of the self. The interpretation of submission to God as a route to personal freedom, while appearing to draw from modern ideals of authenticity and autonomy, is part of longstanding theological traditions. Yet the notion that such submission should be based on a self-conscious, free and sincere choice appears to signal the adoption of an ethics of authenticity that has become especially widespread in the last fifty years or so. In other words, in these young people's religious subjectivities, an ethics of submission anchored in the religious traditions of Islam and Christianity articulated with an ethics of authenticity that has come to characterize late-modern culture in the Netherlands and elsewhere.

Because of the linkage of these ethical imperatives, my interlocutors' pursuits of faith relied substantially on the commitment, volition, and sincerity of their selves. They worried about their personal flaws, inadequacies, and imperfections. They sought to constantly work on their individual shortcomings in order to "improve" themselves, entailing a continuous "battle" against their own will and desires. They engaged, further, in an ongoing moral scrutiny of their behavior, thoughts, and intentions. For the young Muslims, this involved critically interrogating whether they performed religious acts with "sincere intentions"— that is, performing them for God alone and not in order to make themselves look better. For the young Christians, such moral introspection came with a wariness of their personal feelings, which were seen as more unstable than "God's Word" and which, in their view, could be wrongly taken as indices of God's will.

The religious endeavors of these young Muslims and Christians, then, were characterized by a strong orientation on the inner self. Even though they also reflected on the moral achievements and shortcomings of their religious communities, and stimulated their peers to work on themselves, they devoted much of their religious energy to evaluating and improving their personal piety. This emphasis and dependence on the self not only contributed to a pro-active and self-conscious religious commitment, but also made their pursuits of piety vulnerable. Paradoxically, while these young Christians and Muslims held that submission entailed the subordination of their selves to a supreme God, the means, method, and epistemological ground of their submission centered largely on the self—a potential source of either good or evil, virtue or sin, piety or impiety, that constantly ran the risk of succumbing to its desires and lapsing into negligence or permissiveness, and that therefore required constant scrutiny and vigilance.

These pursuits of submission were however not completely individualized endeavors. Rather, my interlocutors' work on moral self-improvement was strongly embedded in social relationships, communities, and networks. In the next chapter, I will explore in what ways social relations and communal settings provided my interlocutors with incentives, encouragement, and support when it came to maintaining a committed religious life.

4

Doubt, Community, and Conviction

On a Monday night in April, one of the lecture halls of a vocational university in Rotterdam has filled up with seventy or so young Muslims. They are attending one of their classes in the context of a semester-long course offered by a private institution of Islamic studies. This course entails a broad study of Islam through a close investigation of selected *suras* (chapters of the Quran) and *ahadith* (deeds, sayings, or tacit approvals attributed to the Prophet Muhammad), as well as a discussion of the ninety-nine Names of Allah and of the history and the different strands of Islam. It is simultaneously offered in four cities in the Netherlands. In Rotterdam alone, more than one hundred students are enrolled. Most students are aged between eighteen and twenty-five, the majority have a Moroccan background and around two-thirds of the students are women, many of whom—but not all—wearing headscarves. The men are sitting in the first few rows; the women are sitting in the rows behind them and on the balcony. They are taught in Dutch by Dawoud, a middle-aged man of Javanese-Surinamese background and a popular youth imam. Trained at the Islamic University in Medina, he is one of the most frequently asked speakers at young Muslims' events and conferences in the Netherlands.

When I enter the lecture hall, the class has already started: dozens of faces are fixed on the teacher and students are eagerly scribbling away in their notebooks. As I sit down on the front row, the young man next to me, apparently a convert to Islam of Dutch descent, greets me by saying "salaam aleikum." Behind me I hear young women animatedly engaging in hushed conversation, discussing the class and making sure they write down the right notes. The class takes three hours in total. Before going into the *ahadith* and *suras*, Dawoud plays a recitation of them from his laptop, performed in a beautiful voice against the background of the sounds of birds singing. The discussion involves a wide range of issues, including *ahadith* on "restraining oneself from anger" and the prescription of "excellence (*ihsan*) in all things"[1] as well as *sura Al-Ikhlas* ("Purity of Faith").

The students, and the women especially, frequently pose questions. Dawoud addresses those who raise their hands in a combination of Arabic and Dutch 'Na'am, zuster?' ("Yes, sister?"). He generally enriches his speech with Islamic Arabic expressions: "is it clear so far, *insha Allah*?" or "the Prophet made a nice comparison, didn't he? *Masha Allah!*" Some of the questions posed to him are very practical, such as: "is it allowed to wear leather?" Others are more theological: for example, when disbelief is discussed in relation to sins, one student asks: "when you commit sins, that doesn't have to mean that you don't believe, right? Doesn't it rather mean that you are weak?" While parts of the class are quite entertaining, much of it involves solid, formal learning. This does not seem to make the students, who have paid more than two hundred euros to register for the course, any less enthusiastic. During the break, one young man tells me that he is thrilled about the classes and about Dawoud in particular: "He really knows *a lot!*" The classes, he tells me, motivate him to continue learning more about Islam. Amane, whom I introduced in the previous chapter and who also participated in this course, told me that the classes, and particularly the discussions on the Names of God, have helped her to strengthen, as she put it, her "bond" with, and "love" for, God.

The members of the Christian student association Pilgrim Students are meeting in their establishment in the center of Rotterdam on a Tuesday night in February. The place is abuzz with the presence of around 125 chatting young adults, mostly between eighteen and twenty-three years old and divided equally between men and women. They are all students, most at the Erasmus University in Rotterdam, some at other universities. The majority have been raised in mainline Protestant churches, some others have an evangelical background. A minority are converts who have not had a Christian upbringing. A bell is rung and everybody adjourns to what is called the "lecture hall" at the back of the building, where they completely fill up the room. They are here for the bi-weekly communal night of the student association, in which they sing worship songs together and an invited speaker talks about a selected theme. Themes addressed during my fieldwork included Christian identity, responsible economic action for Christians, having doubts in one's faith, and being compassionate.

The president of the student association takes a microphone and introduces the topic of the evening: following Jesus. He then invites everyone to join him in prayer, asking God to reveal something of Himself this night and give guidance through the words of the speakers. This is followed by "worship": all students stand up from their chairs to sing evangelical praise songs, directed by the association's own band (consisting of drums, guitar, bass, keyboard, and three singers). The first couple of songs are quite energetic ("I want to cheer for You, my Lord!"), followed by a couple of more mellow and subdued ones. The people around me actively participate in the singing. One young man in front of me stretches out his hand in a gesture of worship. When the last song sets in, one of the (female) singers tells us that during this song "we may simply feel gratitude for Jesus's sacrifice."

Then two men come to the front of the assembly to give this night's talk (*praatje*). One, around thirty years old, is a "staff member" of the association, the other is a senior student member and is around twenty-three years old. Before they start, the president puts his hands on the backs of both gentlemen, praying to God to bless their talk. The men speak for around one and a half hours, sitting comfortably on stools, facing the audience, speaking easily and informally. They talk about the need to follow Jesus, even if that means making sacrifices. The second speaker says that when we think about following "Jesus number 1," who has promised to be there for us and offers warmth and security, we say "cool!" [*kicken!*]. But when it comes to following "Jesus number 2," who asks all kinds of difficult things from us, we say "shit…" [*kak*…]. The men argue that both "Jesus number 1" and "Jesus number 2" ought to be followed. "It is not up to us," they say, "to compromise either of these." After they finish their talk, they point out that there will be a "ministry team" in the lecture hall for anyone who wishes to speak or pray with someone. Tonight, this team consists of two male and two female members of the association. I do not see anyone coming up to them. Some people stay in the hall to talk. Most leave for the bar for a beer or something else to drink.

These two gatherings are illustrative of the social religious activities of the young Muslims and Christians with whom I worked. In this chapter, I examine the purposeful and often wholehearted participation of these young believers in communal and social settings. Most of my interlocutors not only attended mosques or churches,[2] but also participated in other kinds of settings of religious learning and socialization. For many of my Christian interlocutors, Christian student associations played important roles in this regard as quite close-knit communities where young believers, often from different church dominations, came together to meet fellow Christians, talk about their faith, join each other in worship, study the Bible, but also simply to socialize and have fun. Young Christians who were not at university often participated in similar youth clubs, usually organized by churches. For my Muslim interlocutors, private and mosque-affiliated religious institutions were important. Most either followed courses with private educational institutes like the one described above or attended classes organized by mosques about such topics as the biography of the Prophet (*sirah*), Quranic exegesis (*tafsir*), *ahadith*, or Arabic. Many also attended Islamic conferences, thematic youth nights organized at mosques, and talks by Islamic preachers who traveled around the country invited by Muslim student associations, youth associations, and mosques.

The evenings described above point to notable differences between these Muslim and Christian settings. The Muslim settings were often quite studious, characterized by young believers' desire to "acquire knowledge" and by the status of the teachers or imams, typically regarded as "persons of knowledge." The Christian gatherings, by contrast, tended to be more informal and to concentrate on mutual encouragement rather than being taught by an authoritative teacher. These Christian settings also more often took the character of a worship service, including prayer and songs. There was, further, an arresting difference with regard to gender, as at many Muslim events, as opposed to the Christian ones, a majority of the audience—usually around two-thirds—consisted of women, and men and women were often seated separately from one another. Other studies of observant Muslims in Europe similarly point to a strong representation of women in such settings.[3]

Apart from the gender dimension, the differences between the Muslim and Christian settings were not absolute. Learning processes characterized not only the Muslim settings but also contexts such as Christian student associations, the Sunday church services my Christian interlocutors usually attended, the catechism most followed at some point during their young adulthood, and the Alpha course. Moreover, relations of authority were not absent in Christian contexts, but often articulated in somewhat subtle ways. While the speakers at the student night portrayed above, for example, were (close to being) peers of their audience and conducted themselves informally, they did have an authoritative position as, respectively, staff and senior members of the association. It is people like themselves, as Mark, another of the staff members, explained to me in an interview, who took up the task of stimulating the students to engage deeply and personally with their religion, while ensuring the transmission of particular Christian convictions within the association. The Muslim gatherings, on the other hand, were not only studious but often involved devotional practices that contributed to a component of worship, such as recitations from the Quran and communal prayer.

Moreover, despite the differences in content, style, and orientation between these Muslim and Christian social settings, they importantly shared a strong pedagogical element. These were settings in which young believers learned about their religion, explored what it meant to be Christian or Muslim, and found encouragement to give their faith a central place in their everyday lives. These pedagogical spaces, many of which were quite new in kind, were characterized by the dynamic involvement of young people in them, their own contributions to the organization and maintenance of these spaces, and the interactive relations between these young people and religious leaders. Such spaces could be found within churches and mosques—often in reworked forms that appealed to young people, including, for example, contemporary worship songs in churches or accessible sermons in the Dutch language in mosques. These pedagogical spaces were also located in such settings as youth clubs, student associations, private institutions of religious education, conferences, festivals, small study groups, friendship networks, and in virtual settings such as internet sites, forums, and chat rooms.

A growing body of work has examined the contemporary relevance of community and sociality among young Christians and Muslims in Europe, indicating the shortcomings of theories of religious privatization that have long dominated the sociology of religion. Yet this scholarship provides limited explanation for this continuing, perhaps even revitalized, participation in communities among religious practitioners today. As Nancy Ammerman (1997, 352) pointed out already some time ago, the two commonplace understandings of contemporary forms of religious community as either "traditionalistic throwbacks to an earlier time" or "'lifestyle enclaves' of individualistic religious consumers" are inadequate. Drawing on—and revisiting—seminal work on religion in the late-modern era, I argue in this chapter that the value my Muslim and Christian interlocutors attached to religious sociality should be understood in relation to the challenges ensuing from the contemporary condition of cultural pluralism. I show that my interlocutors' everyday encounters with divergent convictions, beliefs, and behaviors—and their concomitant awareness of alternative ways of understanding, and living in, the world—induced relativist doubts among them. Their routine participation in communal spaces of religious pedagogy enabled them to cope with these doubts by finding affirmation of their religious convictions and encouragement to pursue a committed religious lifestyle. While the experiences of doubt as well as the communal settings took on different shapes among the Muslims and Christians, I argue that these "communities of conviction"[4] performed similar pedagogical work for both in the contemporary context of cultural pluralism.

Reconsidering the Social in Young People's Religion

Scholars examining the continuing, or renewed, relevance of community and sociality for young Muslims and Christians in Europe commonly point to new forms of togetherness that are particularly oriented toward young people. These community forms are described as spaces where young people find a measure of independence, particularly from their parents, to engage with their religion in ways that are appealing, appropriate, and comprehensible to them.[5] Thus, authors speak of "neo-communities" (Allievi 2003), "new forms of communal ritualization" (Vincett et al. 2012, 277), and modes of sociality "beyond church and mosque" (Roeland et al. 2010, 298). "Spaces" is an apt and often-employed term with regard to these settings because it implies both a physical locality and a metaphorical room for maneuver and possibility.[6]

Aligned with the revivalist tendencies discussed in Chapter 2, for young Muslims these new religious spaces are closely attuned to their concerns with acquiring reliable religious knowledge. It has often been noted that they tend to feel that the more "traditional" religious settings normally organized by their parents' generation, such as the Friday sermons and prayers in the mosque, fail to satisfy their search for religious knowledge and for advice on how to implement that knowledge in their everyday lives. This observation runs like a red thread through seminal works on young European Muslims such as those of Cesari (1998), Mandaville (2001), and Roy (2004). As Frank Peter has put it: "[The] theme of the declining influence of 'classical' Islamic institutions (mosques, imams, etc.) as a result of the profound generational changes has by now become an almost unquestioned truth in research on Western European Islam" (2006, 107). This body of research points to the rise in Europe of new settings of religious transmission as well as "new Muslim intellectuals" (Van Bruinessen and Allievi 2011, viii), providing ways of engaging with Islam—typically in the European languages that young Muslims often master best—that fit young Muslims' concerns, preferences, and lifestyles. Here, internet use often plays an important role, by providing new and easily accessible platforms of religious transmission and communication and by fostering trans-local ties and networks (Mandaville 2001, chap. 5; Gale and O'Toole 2009; Roeland et al. 2010, 299).[7]

For young Christians, new religious spaces have been found to meet their desire for forms of religious practice that are experiential, energetic and that emphasize personal engagement. This kind of religious practice is offered by the new, postwar, evangelical movement, characterized by contemporary forms of worship, the incorporation of popular culture, and a strong emphasis on one's personal relationship with God (Shibley 1996; Miller 1997). Scholars have pointed out that young Christians in the Netherlands often regard the conventional Protestant contexts in which they have grown up as overly intellectualist, impersonal, and oriented on cognition. Many are attracted by the more sensorial and experiential ways of practicing their religion offered in evangelical settings (Roeland 2009, 163–75; Klaver 2011). Research elsewhere in Europe has also shown that new, youth-oriented religious spaces offer forms of community that young Christians regard as more "authentic" or "real" than those found in conventional Christian settings (Vincett et al. 2012, 280).

The relevance of such (new) settings of community and sociality has been taken up to demonstrate the shortcomings of assumptions about religious "privatization" that underlie many analyses of secularization. José Casanova summarized the theory of religious privatization, referring to Thomas Luckmann's (1967) seminal work, as follows: "Individuals are on their own in their private efforts to patch together the fragments into a subjective meaningful whole" (1994, 37). Casanova argued against this position by pointing to trends toward religious "deprivatization" around the world, evidenced by religious traditions (re-)entering the public domain and striving to "renormativize" economic and political spheres (1994, 5–6ff.). Ammerman (1997) argued that the continuing salience of Christian congregations in the United States similarly contradicts assumptions about religious privatization. The "enduring character of these local religious gatherings," she stated, indicates that "the communal life that was supposed to disappear in the face of the modern world has simply not gone away, sociological theories to the contrary" (1997, 352, 350). Looking at young Christians, Muslims, and adherents of New Age in the Netherlands, Roeland et al. (2010, 298–300) criticize what they call the "Luckmann legacy" in the sociology of religion by arguing that social attachment has not disappeared among these groups, but rather transformed into new, particularly "networked," forms of sociality.

Reflecting on the relation between generation and community participation, Christian Smith and Patricia Snell (2009, 251–4) counter what they call "the myth of internal-without-external religion": the idea that as teenagers are entering adulthood, they tend to forsake religious group participation but hold on to a privatized, interior faith.[8] In their extensive, longitudinal survey and interview research among "emerging adults" between eighteen and twenty-three years old, mostly of white Christian backgrounds, Smith and Snell have found no evidence for this claim. Their data rather suggest the contrary:

> The emerging adults who do sustain strong subjective religion in their lives, it turns out, are those who also maintain strong external expressions of faith, including religious service attendance. Most emerging adults, by contrast, who significantly reduce their external religious participation also substantially reduce their subjective, private, internal religious concerns.
>
> (Smith and Snell 2009, 252)

In their research on the "post-boomer" generation of American Christians, Richard Flory and Donald Miller, too, criticize the often-made argument that people have become more interested in their individual quest for spiritual fulfillment than in participation in and commitment to communities (2008, 11). They observe a trend among post-boomers toward "expressive communalism": the quest for "spiritual experience and fulfillment in community and through various expressive forms of spirituality, both private and public" (2008, 17).

These studies, however, offer limited conceptual tools to better understand the dynamics between personal faith and community participation. Smith and Snell do not give an explanation for the close interrelation they have observed between "internal" and "external" religion, while the reasons Flory and Miller offer for the significance of religious community among their respondents seem rather conjectural.[9] A useful entry point to grasping the relevance of community in young people's religious lives is provided by a study of young Muslim women in France and Germany by Jeanette Jouili and Schirin Amir-Moazami (2006). They argue that these women's strong engagement with (social settings of) religious authority constituted a crucial means of cultivating strong personal faith and pious dispositions. They write: "For most of our interviewees, knowledge acquisition should not be carried out only as an individual initiative, but under the aegis of authorized representatives of the community, because it is in this frame that an 'authentic' Islam can be transmitted and faith can be most effectively cultivated and fortified" (Jouili and Amir-Moazami 2006, 634). In this chapter, I take up these authors' line of inquiry into what participation in social religious settings means to people in the light of their religious aspirations. Doing so, I also demonstrate how the relevance of these social settings is determined by the wider social context in which Muslims and Christians lead their lives. I will first discuss how my Christian and Muslim interlocutors themselves reflected on their participation in religious communities. I will look in detail at the accounts of two young women, Esther and Khadija, which are particularly illuminating and illustrative in this context.

Having Doubts, Affirming Faith

Esther, twenty-two years old, grew up in a small, predominantly Christian village in the countryside to the east of Rotterdam, where she and her family went to a Reformed church (now part of the unified Protestant Church in the Netherlands, or PKN). At seventeen, she started her studies in nursing at a vocational university in Rotterdam and at nineteen she moved to that city. In the interview I conducted with her, she stressed that the change in her direct environment from a small Christian village to a pluralist city strongly affected her religious life. Describing her childhood, she said:

> [I was] born in a Christian family, have always gone to church, received a Christian upbringing …, Christian primary school, and after that Christian secondary education: *reformatorisch* [strictly orthodox Protestant] even. … I think I have grown up in quite a sheltered way, when I consider: all my friends were Christian and the village was pretty Christian and, well, [the region] is quite Christian too, so uhm… Had little contact with nonbelievers.

When Esther went to university in Rotterdam while still living at home, she was still able to, as she put it, lead her "own life" next to her "school life." Although the student population was very "mixed," faith was not talked about much and her faith "was not very strongly contested" there.

This changed quite dramatically after she moved to Rotterdam and became intimately confronted with people with different approaches to religion, be they Christians, adherents of other faiths, or "nonbelievers." In her student flat, she came to live with flatmates who "didn't believe, or did believe but experienced it in a different way, looked at it very critically and had all kinds of philosophical theories about it." This "provoked" [*prikkelde*] her to "think about it more." She started to question things that she had always taken for granted. She posed herself questions like: Isn't prayer simply something psychological? What does it really mean, to believe? Who is God actually?

> Esther: I used to live more from, uhm, confidence, simply going for it. And [now] I was surrounded by people who were very much questioning and examining *everything* and uhm… Well, in principle I could do the same, but it had just never been stimulated so much in me. So now I did become stimulated in that regard …. Uhm, I don't know, that has also changed me I think. That you start to look at things more critically and to question things, rather than simply living your life.

Daan: And how did you experience approaching it more like that? That challenge they put to you, to look critically at…

Esther: Yes, of course it didn't happen very consciously, but uhm… They just believe in that way and I [believe] differently. But in fact it is challenging because it did… Suddenly I did start to have doubts about my faith and uhm… [about] how things fitted together and whether it was like I had always thought it was, to put it that way. And, well, I don't know, that made that I could no longer like—well, childlike confidence or something is a bit of a strange word perhaps—but that I could no longer believe in such a way, like, okay, it's all good and I'm going for it and it's all marvelous.

Daan: The idea that you actually don't have to ask questions about it, that was no longer possible?

Esther: No, because you could say, like, I'm going for it, but in the meantime you do of course have in mind the question of, yes… if it doesn't work that way, then I can also not believe it that way.

After she moved to Rotterdam and constantly met people with different views and beliefs from hers, Esther could no longer believe as unconditionally as she used to do. This resulted in questions and doubts about her faith. She emphasized though that she did not doubt the existence of God as such: "It is as solid as stone that I believe that there is a God and that He is the Creator and… these things. But uhm… somehow it is the passion [*bevlogenheid*] that I'm very much trying to retrieve."

When I asked Esther how she dealt with these questions and doubts, she started to talk about the evangelical student association she had joined in Rotterdam (a different one from Pilgrim Students). It helped her, she said, to have conversations with people from the student association—"with other Christians." The association also enabled her "to build a network" of "believers," so that she knew Christian people "in all kinds of professions and groups," whom she could talk to, call, or write an e-mail to whenever she was struggling with questions of faith. Esther said she also learned much from the older people in the association and from attending conferences organized by the evangelical network the student association was part of. By attending an international conference she had learned, she said, that "whether you are in Asia, where it is very difficult to have faith [*om te geloven*], or in the rich Netherlands, or in poor Rumania, they believe in God everywhere" and "they have sort of the same faith, even if they might shape it differently." It had been particularly important for her that she had a mentor who helped her cope with her doubts by pointing her to useful literature or videos and by encouraging her to ask herself particular kinds of questions. She felt, moreover, that the diversity of perspectives in her student association, which included people coming from a wide variety of churches, enriched her personal understanding of faith.

While learning about these different positions in her student association, Esther was also drawn to the familiar world of her own church. She joined a PKN church in Rotterdam that belonged to the same denomination as her home church. She liked this church not only because of its open and welcoming atmosphere, but also because of its "conservative" character. In the end, she said, she liked "a good solid sermon and some psalms." For her, a sermon was "solid" when it conveyed a "clear message that you can apply in your life," was guided by the Bible, and educative. Esther did visit other churches, including a "lighter Reformed church" and evangelical churches, but she preferred her own church, in part, she thought, "because your upbringing, your basis lies in that church and therefore it appeals to you more."

In the year before our interview, Esther had expressed her attachment to this church more explicitly by performing the confirmation [*belijdenis*] in the church, whereby she publicly confessed her belief in God and her subscription to the teachings of the church. She had prepared for her confirmation by following catechism classes and she told me that she had enjoyed going through such questions as "what is the church," "who is God," and "what is the Bible." When I asked her whether she did not feel that she already knew all that after all those years at her Christian student association, she answered:

> No, I actually found it enlightening, that you just, uhm… Since there are so many opinions [in the student association] and in the flat and all that, that you just go through, like, okay, this is how we see it in this church, this is how it is, and that you then think like: of course, that's actually how I have always learned it before and that's what we profess.

Thus, for Esther, following catechism classes felt as a kind of homecoming after a period of doubting, searching, and exploring. While she found the plurality of perspectives within her student association enriching, she implied that it also confused her and increased her desire for affirmation of the traditions and doctrines that she knew from the church in which she had grown up.

Khadija, a nineteen-year-old student in public health and committee member of the Muslim student association An-Nur in Rotterdam, similarly expressed a recurrent need for affirmation of her religious convictions. She was born in a village in the north of Morocco, and her family moved to the Netherlands when she was only two years old. Since then, she had always lived in Rotterdam. Khadija was the first in her family to go to university. During her first year as a student, she started to be more personally engaged with Islam:

> I started to practice more, in the sense that I started to acquire more knowledge, started to reflect more on faith. Something I didn't do before: [Then] it simply came by autopilot.[10] You simply performed the practices that you ought to do, the Ramadan and the prayers and… But that really was because that's what you had learned from your parents.

Khadija's shift with regard to her religious involvement was inspired, she said, by the many actively practicing young Muslims she met at university. At her Christian secondary school, in contrast, she had been one of the few Muslim pupils. She also felt that her parents had never explained much about religion. Now she started to learn more about her religion by talking to other Muslim students, participating in a religious "study group" with six other young women, attending religious talks, listening to sermons online, reading books, exploring the internet, and questioning one of her uncles, whom she described as very knowledgeable religiously and "almost an imam."

Through this quest for religious knowledge, Khadija sought to "strengthen" her *iman*—a phrase that was commonly used among my Muslim interlocutors. For her, *iman*, or (inner) faith, referred to "one's love for faith": "that I appreciate its value and that I really sincerely believe that everything that is prescribed will truly make me better as a human being." Thus, for her, *iman* refers to a condition of trust, or conviction, in the infallibility and goodness of what her religion prescribes for her. While she felt that her *iman* in this sense was getting stronger, Khadija still thought she was falling short. Like many of the young Muslims I worked with, she talked about experiencing "ups and downs" when it came to keeping her *iman* strong. She said that in the peer religious study group she sometimes started "to have doubts about the whole thing." This did not mean that she had doubts about the existence of God as such or about Islam being the right religion, but rather: "that I allow my *iman* to weaken, that I do know it, but don't want to be aware of it." She added: "to observe all these things, and always understand why, why all of it is good, that needs time."[11] She was struggling, in other words, to maintain a constant awareness of the necessity and benefits of a close adherence to the prescriptions of Islam.

Khadija noted that it was particularly by participating in social religious settings, where she experienced being part of a Muslim community and gained religious knowledge and encouragement, that she could resist these doubts and strengthen her religious awareness. She told me that when she attended a mosque or a religious talk, she was often moved (*ontroerd*) by what she heard and was stimulated to focus her attention on Islam. Thus, after following a talk on "love in Islam," delivered by the aforementioned youth imam Dawoud at a vocational university in Rotterdam, she commented in an e-mail to me: "I thought that the lecture was very good. It is things like these that remind me again why I am a Muslim. The love for your fellow human being *subhana Allah* [glory be to Allah]." And when, in our interview, we spoke about the role of *iman* in her everyday religious life, she said: "I notice that when I'm [spending little time] searching for knowledge, it weakens, when I go to the mosque less, it weakens. Because those are the things that make that I'm drawn to faith *straight away*." And she continued on an enthusiastic tone:

> The first time I went to the mosque on Friday and I sat next to a woman, and she started to talk with me straight away and to ask "how are you child?"—an older woman!— ... this directly gave me a good feeling. If only to see *such* a big group of people gathering for one and the same thing. Just like when I'm watching TV and I, you know, see images of Mecca. *Gigantic*, the amount of people that are going there. And they are all wearing the same and you don't see whether it is [laughs] an advocate or a pauper.

She found it difficult, however, to retain these feelings in her everyday life: "I'm so busy with worldly affairs. Even though that's only, as far as I'm concerned, a moment and one that passes before you know it. I'd do better to just focus on something that I can benefit from for I don't know how long."

Khadija usually attended a Moroccan mosque in West Rotterdam, but she had also started to visit a Salafi-oriented mosque in South Rotterdam that is frequented by—especially young—people of various backgrounds and where the imam often preaches in Dutch. She preferred the latter mosque because she did "not yet have command over the Arabic language" (as spoken in the Moroccan mosque) and she enjoyed its "openness" and "multicultural" character.

Like many of the young Muslims I met, Khadija regarded a supportive environment to be crucial for keeping her faith strong. When I asked her whether getting affirmation was important for her in this regard, we had the following exchange:

> Khadija: Yes it is, because I'm constantly in search of affirmation. Always. Because you, you just want to stay awake, to wake up, and constantly, uhm, feed yourself as it were. And therefore such affirmation is needed.

Daan: Also to keep on convincing yourself, would you say that too?

Khadija: I wouldn't say "convincing", but [I would say] convincing [myself] of the fact that it's important for me to acquire and hold on to knowledge and not, uhm, not allow it to move to the background [*wegzakken*], something that does happen sometimes. If I uhm… If, today, I would not go, like, to the mosque and would not go to lectures and would not associate with the friends, uhm, I now associate with, then I think I would really have that relapse, uhm, that I would suddenly start to think that it's no longer all that *important*.

Daan: So you actually really need that environment, like, to…

Khadija: I need like a good environment, one that is good in my view, to keep strong in that regard, people that support me in that regard as it were.

Elaborating on why she needed such a "good environment," Khadija said:

Khadija: There are many other possibilities that can also be *very* appealing, if they are made appealing by the people you associate with or the environment you are in. And that's, like, also a test [*beproeving*], not to allow yourself to get sucked in by these as it were. In that regard … I can very easily relapse into that process in which I found myself, to conform and uhm…

Daan: What, then, are other things you find appealing, things that are not Islamic?

Khadija: Uhm… yes, I do want that big house, uhm… Or big house… I want to buy a house for example, to furnish it as I want to, something that is mine and that I can leave to my children. But that's not possible because of interest, because you would take a mortgage. Uhm… Yes, very many people try to make it seem as if it's permitted, because it is a necessity. But I know better. Yet, if I would be in that environment, I would allow myself to be persuaded by [those people].

Khadija, then, made sure that she regularly attended religious settings and that she placed herself in a "good environment," so as to keep her religious convictions strong and not to get drawn in by alternative, in her eyes less virtuous, lifestyles. It is by participating in a religious community that she felt able to strengthen her *iman*, which for her meant strengthening her conviction of the goodness and infallibility of Islamic prescriptions.

The accounts of both Esther and Khadija point to a strong connection between community and conviction. Both Esther and Khadija made clear that it was by participating in social religious settings—where they experienced a sense of community, met fellow believers, and learned about their religion—that they found affirmation of their religious convictions. Both experienced a need for such affirmation and re-affirmation, because they found it hard to retain an unconditional religious commitment in the light of the doubts and uncertainties they experienced in their everyday lives. While Esther and Khadija explicated this relation between doubt, community, and conviction particularly well, I have observed it widely during my fieldwork among both Christian and Muslim young adults.

The dimension of routinization is important here. For my interlocutors, retaining strong personal convictions relied for an important part on repeated and habitual participation in social-pedagogical settings. Given their continuous encounter with alternative, or less rigorously pious, views and lifestyles in today's pluralist society, they felt a need for constantly recurrent input from their religious communities. This was vividly expressed by my interlocutors' anxieties about faith fading away in their everyday lives. Thus, Johan, a 21-year-old law student whom I came to know at Pilgrim Students, the Christian student association in Rotterdam, told me that his participation in Christian activities—church on Sundays, catechism class on Mondays, and the student association on Tuesdays—brought him into a "flow." That flow would however abate again as the week progressed and by the next Sunday he would feel a strong need for renewed "input" (he used the English terms "flow" and "input"). Such input did not always have to entail new forms of knowledge. At the Islamic classes I attended, for example, some of the same questions were posed to the teacher time and again. Being exposed once more to the same questions and answers seemed as important as learning something entirely new. Besides, as Anna Strhan (2015, 188–90) argues for evangelicals in London, habitual participation in religious communities also keeps people "knotted" in relations of support and accountability.

The spaces of religious pedagogy with which my interlocutors engaged cannot be easily classified as either public or private. Rather, they could be seen to occupy a cross-over space between public and private, where individual and group convictions are shaped and inculcated in collective settings. That these semi-public spaces played similar key roles for my Christian and Muslim interlocutors deserves emphasis, given the recurrent notion that Christians are more susceptible to religious privatization than Muslims, as the latter are understood to view their religion as a complete and holistic system (see e.g. Vincett et al. 2008, 8). My discussion here complicates such contrasts between a Christianity that smoothly moves into the private sphere and an Islam that sturdily resists privatization.

Much has been written about the assumed turn away from conventional religious institutions in contemporary religion (Luckmann 1967; Davie 2000; Hervieu-Léger 2000) and in young Dutch people's religion in particular (Janssen and Prins 2000; Roeland et al. 2010). As Esther's and Khadija's accounts illustrate, however, conventional religious settings such as churches and mosques continued to be important for my interlocutors, precisely, I argue, because they performed effective pedagogical work. By the same token, I suggest that the criticisms young people expressed about particular institutional settings can be seen to result from the failure of these settings to offer a persuasive and appealing pedagogy that could help them to cope with their questions and doubts.

Doubt and Pluralism

Like the other young Christians and Muslims I met, Esther and Khadija lived in an urban, pluralist context, in which having religious belief—let alone taking a strictly committed religious position—was not self-evident. While Esther explicitly talked about questioning and scrutinizing her beliefs, Khadija's statements about a lack of self-evidence were more subtle, though no less revealing. Her understanding of *iman* as the sincere belief that everything that is prescribed will "truly make me better as a human being" implied the real possibility of believing otherwise. Her remarks that a religious talk she attended "reminded" her again why she is a Muslim and that searching for knowledge or going to the mosque "draw" her to faith similarly reflect this lack of self-evidence. More explicitly, she realized that there are "many other possibilities" of leading one's life that can strongly appeal to her.

These are not the kinds of doubts about one's religious virtuosity that are cultivated within religious cultures as part of practices of moral self-improvement (see Chapter 3). Rather, the doubts of Esther and Khadija, and my interlocutors more generally, were triggered by encounters with other—religious and non-religious—ideas about what was true, good, or beneficial. These doubts resulted from their strong awareness of *alternative possibilities*. As Mathijs Pelkmans (2013, 4) points out, the sense of "wavering between one possibility and another" is inherent to the concept of "doubt," given the reference to the number two in *dubitare*, the Latin origin of the term. In this sense, the term "doubt" itself already implies pluralism.

Charles Taylor (2007) has argued that this kind of internalized cultural relativism lies at the heart of our "secular age." He points out that Western society has changed from a situation "in which it was virtually impossible not to believe in God, to one in which faith, even for the staunchest believer, is one human possibility among others," and "frequently not the easiest to embrace" (2007, 3). Taylor argues:

> We live in a condition where we cannot help but be aware that there are a number of different construals, views which intelligent, reasonably undeluded people, of good will, can and do disagree on. We cannot help looking over our shoulder from time to time, looking sideways, living our faith also in a condition of doubt and uncertainty.
>
> (Taylor 2007, 11)

Belief in God has become an option, and an "embattled option" at that (2007, 11). This argument has been foreshadowed by studies of pluralism in the sociology of religion. In his classic work *The Sacred Canopy*, Peter Berger characterized pluralism as the situation in which "the man in the street is confronted with a wide [variety] of religious and other reality-defining agencies that compete for his allegiance or at least attention, and none of which is in a position to coerce him into allegiance" (1967, 126). This pluralist condition, Berger argued, results in a diminishing of the "plausibility structure" of any one religious reality, that is, "the presence of social structures within which this reality is taken for granted and within which successive generations of individuals are socialized in such a way that this world will be real to *them*" (1967, 47, italics in original).

Different from such earlier sociological studies of pluralism, Taylor argues that this pluralist condition does not necessarily result in secularization in the sense of the decline and eventual disappearance of religion.[12] Rather, he posits that pluralism shapes the contours that religious belief takes in our society. Belief, he argues, has become a reflexive commitment pursued in the face of the realistic possibility of unbelief, in contrast with a situation where belief in a supernatural power is a fact of life and the choice is only between more or less religious devotion (Taylor 2007, 12). The "background framework" of religious belief has changed from a "naïve" to a "reflective" one (2007, 13).

Building on Taylor, Tanya Luhrmann has argued that contemporary Christianity in the United States "is entirely framed by the exquisite awareness that there are other theories, both religious and scientific, that one can use to explain the world" (2012a, 372). Likewise, Taylor's account of the proliferation of an internalized cultural relativism in the context of today's pluralist society closely relates to the everyday experiences of doubt of my Christian and Muslim interlocutors. Yet, with regard to these groups, Taylor's grand narrative of "a secular age" should be qualified and specified both in terms of its social and historical scope and in terms of the nature of my interlocutors' doubts.

In terms of scope, historical work in the Netherlands has shown that the shift to a reflexive "framework of belief," which Taylor describes as a century-long development, can be found only relatively recently among non-elite, ordinary Dutch people. Based on personal life-story interviews with elderly Dutch people of various religious and secular backgrounds, Peter van Rooden (2010) has demonstrated that up until the 1960s, these people's—religious or secular—worldviews tended to provide a background to their everyday lives that largely went without saying. In the separate Protestant and Roman Catholic moral communities that marked the era of pillarization (see the Introduction), Van Rooden argues, belief was part of "acts and rituals framing everyday life" (2010, 184). It resembled closely what Taylor describes as "naïve" belief. From the 1960s onward, these religious worlds started to lose their self-evidence. Van Rooden relates this to "the emergence within mass culture of the ideal and practices of the expressive and reflexive self" (2010, 190), linked to growing affluence and the rise of mass consumer society, the enhancement of mobility as a result of the common possession of cars, the increase of leisure time, and the introduction of television. In the context of the rise of discourses and practices of self-expression and self-reflection, collective and largely self-evident religious practices "gradually became less important in the lives of believers" (191).[13] Pluralism played a central role in this regard: after the 1960s, Dutch people increasingly familiarized themselves with social worlds different from the ones they had grown up in, and with new possibilities of organizing and directing their lives. In this context, it became less self-evident to experience religion as a taken-for-granted background to everyday life.

Yet this shift has not been all-encompassing. We have already seen that Esther had still grown up with a form of belief that could be characterized as "naïve" in Taylor's sense. Indeed, as Taylor (2007, 12) also points out, today too there are milieus in which "believing construals" tend "to show up as the overwhelmingly more plausible one." However, as we have seen in the cases of Khadija and Esther, as my interlocutors were growing into adulthood or moving to the big city, their believing frameworks tended to lose such "naturalness." Cracks appeared in their formerly unquestioned status and they moved—in Taylor's terms—to living their believing framework "reflectively."

It can be argued, then, that the onset of a highly pluralist culture, marked by a declining self-evidence of one's convictions and a heightened awareness of those of other people, has been a relatively recent and incomplete development in Dutch society, yet one that thoroughly shapes lived religion today. Thus qualified, Taylor's account of "secularity" helps to make sense of the everyday doubts people like Esther and Khadija experienced with regard to their religion. Such doubts are particularly poignant for believers in a place like the Netherlands, where secularist ideologies are strongly represented and where at least the major cities harbor a great diversity of religious and non-religious groups. In the context of an urban pluralist environment like that of Rotterdam, my Muslim and Christian interlocutors' commitment to a religious framework of truth could remain neither self-evident nor unquestioned. Rather, it necessarily became a deliberate and reflexive commitment, shaped by the awareness of alternative—religious and secular—frameworks of truth and morality.

However, in contrast to the kinds of doubt that Taylor (2007) and Luhrmann (2012a) describe, my Muslim and Christian interlocutors did not tend to doubt the ontological reality of God as such. Granted, the young Christians did occasionally ask questions about the very idea of a supernatural God. My Muslim interlocutors rarely did so; the closest that any of them came to voicing such doubts was the 28-year-old Haniya, who told me in an interview: "It has never been proven, like, that there really is a God. You just believe in it. And there are also other ways of looking at things. It's a way of looking at things, let me put it that way." Yet such statements were exceptional among both groups. Uncertainty about God's reality as such was not at the foreground of their doubts. These doubts rather pertained to their stance on their religion. The examples of Esther and Khadija illustrate this: Esther felt she could no longer accept everything she had learned about her religion unquestioningly; Khadija found it difficult to retain a constant awareness of the goodness of her religion's prescriptions. What both shared was a struggle to surrender themselves fully, and unconditionally, to the tenets of their religions. Although different from the "pull" of unbelief that Taylor and Luhrmann describe, these struggles too are shaped by the condition of pluralism that these authors identify. Indeed, my interlocutors' difficulties with pursuing an uncompromising religious surrender resulted to a large degree from their confrontations with alternative convictions, commitments, and priorities. They constantly had to resist a tendency to regard their religious beliefs and, more precisely, their rigorous surrender to those beliefs as "just" one option among others.

Degrees of Relativism

The accounts of Esther and Khadija reflect a more general difference between my Christian and Muslim interlocutors. While doubts among the former often centered on religious truth claims, those among the latter more often focused on the salience that Islamic prescriptions should be given in one's everyday life. These were differences by degree, which should not too readily be interpreted as resulting from an alleged emphasis on ortho*doxy* (correct belief) in Christianity and on ortho*praxy* (correct behavior) in Islam. Orthodoxy, as Asad (1986, 15) has reminded us, takes a central place not only in Christianity but also in Islam. Moreover, as we will see in the following chapters, both my Muslim and Christian interlocutors were strongly concerned with giving virtuous religious practices a prominent place in their everyday lives.

The difference between them pertained more specifically to the manner in which, and degree to which, they relativized their beliefs. The questioning of one's own beliefs, in the way Esther did, was rare among the young Muslims I met, but quite common among the young Christians. There can be several reasons for this, but one relevant factor could be the considerable scope for ambiguity that I have more generally detected among my Christian interlocutors, in contrast to strong disambiguating tendencies among my Muslim interlocutors. The young Christians often pointed to the limits of reason, noting that their religion was essentially a matter of believing. As noted in the previous chapter, the young Muslims likewise held that surrendering to God's will ultimately meant acknowledging the limits of individual reasoning. Yet they also regularly emphasized that Islam was a rational religion that had "answers for everything." The question of the Trinity is a case in point: Christians often found it hard to explain this dogma, although they did "believe" or "feel" that it was correct. Muslims were often dissatisfied with this, in their view, inexplicable Christian dogma and many pointed to the reasonableness of the Islamic conception of *tawhid*, the unity of God. Implied in this approach among my Muslim interlocutors was the notion that understanding prefigures religious belief, as well as practice (cf. Hirschkind 2006, 92–3). These different approaches may go some way in accounting for the divergent degrees of relativism I observed. Yet this could also work the other way round: the room for ambiguity might "harness" Christians against reasoned assaults on their faith, while the emphasis on reason might make Muslims vulnerable to such assaults, precisely by submitting their beliefs to the domain of rational debate.

A different perspective from which to approach this difference is that of my interlocutors' personal biographies. Esther's move to Rotterdam in the context of her studies meant that she was for the first time seriously confronted by people with divergent ideas about religion. By contrast, for Khadija going to university meant meeting Muslim peers who turned out to be an important influence on her personal religious engagement. As we saw in Chapter 2, during her first days at university she was astonished to see other Muslim students performing their prayers on time. It is also relevant to note that Esther moved out of her parents' house and started to live in a student flat together with people from different backgrounds, whereas Khadija, like most of my unmarried Muslim interlocutors, still lived with her parents. Given these divergent personal biographies, Esther was quite abruptly confronted with alternative points of view when she moved to Rotterdam, whereas Khadija had grown up in Rotterdam and was therefore much more accustomed to encountering difference. This contrast held for my Christian and Muslim interlocutors in Rotterdam more generally: most of the Christians had grown up in villages or towns outside of Rotterdam and moved to Rotterdam for their studies, while most of the Muslims had grown up (and were often born) in Rotterdam. It can indeed be argued that, on the level of the city, the label of "immigrant" might be more applicable to the Christians than to the Muslims I met during my fieldwork.[14] Accordingly, living in a pluralist urban setting required more adaptation from these Christians than from the Muslims, engendering a more far-reaching relativist doubt among the former.

The challenge that this encounter with difference entailed was vividly illustrated by Esther. When we talked about the difficulties she experienced in living out her faith publicly, she noted:

> I think that the most difficult thing is the aspect of tolerance. We live with so many cultures next to one another here and everyone believes in something. And on top of that we are postmodern, so what is truth? ... I think that I do find that the most difficult, that I very easily go along with it myself, as in: okay, you believe this, you believe that and I... Yes, I am Christian. Then I do need to keep a sharp focus for myself, as in: okay, [being] Christian is a *faith* and if I consider this truth, then it is of crucial importance that others know that too, that I tell others about it.

Thus, Esther felt that she too easily slipped into regarding her Christian faith as just another option in a world where everyone has his or her own truth. She experienced this during her work with a home care organization, when she was visiting families who were observing the Islamic feast of Ramadan. While she was interested in learning more about their religion, it would cross her mind that she might take an overly "tolerant" view and that she could be more vocal about her Christian convictions. Esther said she respected Islamic practices such as fasting, adding contemplatively: "Yes, I don't yet always perceive as sharply that they are actually beside the truth to put it that way. Somehow I have a sense that this doesn't get through to me as much as it should. And that uhm… if it did, I would speak out against it more."

It has been suggested that the difficulties Western Christians experience in speaking about their faith publicly result from a conflict between ideals of Christian proselytization on the one hand and the impersonal norms of interaction and indifference characterizing everyday urban practice on the other (Strhan 2015, 101–3). While this certainly seems the case, Esther's struggle went even further in the sense that it did not sufficiently "get through" to her that Christian convictions represented the only valid truth. She struggled with an internalized "postmodern" relativism, as she herself described it.

Nonetheless, when I asked her whether she entertained the idea that Muslims might worship the same God, Esther's answer was clear:

> No, the big difference [with] Muslims, or Buddhists, or whatever is, uhm, Jesus. What you see is that the other faiths are often focused on what they have to do, they have to fast, they have to … follow Buddha's rules and all will be good. … And Christianity is of course: it is *done* [*het is gedáán*]. Jesus has given His life, has thereby, uhm… yes, paid the price.

These words can be understood as a move toward epistemological closure, induced by the very indeterminacy of Esther's relativist thoughts. In this light, questions and doubts like Esther's appear to invite disambiguating moves, directed at keeping one's faith strong. In the last section of this chapter, I will turn to this productive potential of doubt and look more closely into the intertwinement of doubt, community, and conviction.

In Conclusion: The Interactions between Doubt, Community, and Conviction

In the introduction to his edited volume on the ethnographic study of doubt, Mathijs Pelkmans (2013) points out that doubt can be both an obstacle to and a trigger for belief. Rather than the philosophical technique of employing "systematic" doubt as a method to reach certainty, as found in Descartes, he focuses on "lived doubt" as it is experienced by people in particular social situations. Such doubt can be profoundly unsettling, reflecting uncertainty in both ontological terms ("what is?") and pragmatic terms ("what to do?"). At the same time, Pelkmans argues, lived doubt underlies and energizes thought and action by fueling the need for resolution and certainty (cf. Engelke 2005, 783-4). Often this entails "domesticating" rather than overcoming doubt (Pelkmans 2013, 22).

A compelling example of this is provided in the volume by Giulia Liberatore's (2013) chapter on young Muslim women of Somali descent in London. As these women become practicing Muslims, they occasionally experience doubts, anxieties, and worries, for example about the reward of paradise or the efficacy of their religious practices. While these experiences of ambivalence may threaten their faith, they can also be seen to invigorate it. As Liberatore explains, within their communities of peers these newly practicing Muslims learn to interpret these uncertainties as instances of "low *iman*," which result from a lack of religious discipline, from evil thoughts and feelings deriving from *Shaitan* (Satan), or from one's impure self. Signified and rationalized as "low *iman*," doubts encourage these Muslims to improve their acts of worship and that commitment to God. Thus, doubts are encapsulated within their "system of faith" (Liberatore 2013, 245). Luhrmann has similarly described a form of domesticating doubt among American evangelicals: she argues that they co-opt secular doubt into their religious experience by deliberately triggering their as-if imagination, resulting in an image of God as "realer than real" (2012a, 383).

The lived doubts of the young Christians and Muslims with whom I worked similarly motivated them to seek resolution and certainty, particularly by involving themselves in spaces of religious pedagogy. They maintained social networks of support and accountability and participated in services, communal prayers, talks, and classes on a regular and habitual basis. In these contexts, they learned to interpret the alternative views and behaviors that instigated their doubts as aberrations from the true faith, signs of an overly permissive take on their religion, or—parallel to what Liberatore describes—indices of personal failure. In this way, living in a pluralist society vitalized my interlocutors' religious pursuits, as it encouraged them to actively seek affirmation of their convictions within pedagogical religious environments. It moreover stimulated a highly reflexive religiosity, as my interlocutors did not—and could not—take their faith for granted, but had to work actively on their convictions, effectively persuading themselves of their religious truth claims on a daily basis.

It is telling in this regard that my Christian interlocutors often turned out to *embrace* this challenge of pluralism. They used to stress the value of being confronted by alternative views and beliefs, because these stimulated them to ponder upon, and ultimately strengthen, their own convictions. Thus, Esther described her encounters with other viewpoints as "provocative" [*prikkelend*], conveying the sense that these encounters constituted both a challenge and an opportunity. Many of my Christian interlocutors, especially those living in Ede, talked about the drawbacks of staying within a "little Christian world" [*christelijk wereldje*]. Elise, a student in Pastoral Theology, told me that she had always moved within Christian environments, first at home and later at the Christian vocational university in Ede and her Christian student association. "At some point," she said, "I would like to see beyond the end of my nose, [I would like] that the little Christian culture [*christelijke cultuurtje*] also becomes somewhat less self-evident, that I also become somewhat more challenged to explain what I believe and why." It is telling that this lack is experienced by people like Elise, living in the Christian student world of Ede, and far less by people like Esther, who already met ample challenges in the pluralist city of Rotterdam.

My Muslim interlocutors talked less about the need to be "provoked" by people outside of their religious community. Even more than the Christians living in Rotterdam, being challenged on the basis of their faith was a very common experience for them in an environment where they often encountered suspicion of, if not hostility to, Islam (cf. Jouili 2015). Still, many of the Muslims I talked with did, surprisingly, see a positive aspect in the recurrent criticism of Islam by public figures like Geert Wilders, because it had stimulated them to gain a better knowledge of their religion and they thought it might have the same effect on others. Ironically, then, these young Muslims experienced a degree of pressure that some Christians, in a way, seemed to desire. In the small group in Ede, Alwin once referred to the American missionary Paul Washer who had said that he knew he was on the right track after someone had thrown a stone at him while he was praying. The others in the small group concurred: you know you are on the right path when you experience oppression as a Christian (of course, living in a post-Christian society, they were in a comfortable position to make this remark).

My observations in this chapter resonate with what various authors have written about the ways in which secular dynamics may induce religious community participation. Peter Berger already argued that conditions of pluralism make some form of community necessary for the preservation of religious worlds. He held that religious plausibility relies on the social structures within which one lives and on the significant others with whom one is in conversation. "If such conversation is disrupted," he wrote, "the world begins to totter, to lose its subjective plausibility" (1967, 17). The more this happens, the stronger the need for the creation of "sub-worlds" that provide renewed plausibility structures (47, 132–3). Along the same lines, Danièle Hervieu-Léger (2000; 2006) has proposed that the conditions of uncertainty in "high-modern" societies re-invigorate a desire for community. She argues:

> Deprived of the security of stable communities which supplied evidence of a code of meaning that was fixed once and for all, deprived too of the great universalist visions imparted by modernist ideologies, individuals are adrift in a universe without fixed bearings. ... Given such a context, the deliberate choice of invoking the authority of a tradition, by becoming incorporated into a continuing lineage, constitutes one possible, post-traditional way of constructing self-identity among others, all of which call upon an individual's affectivity and are fed on his or her search for community, and his or her memories and longings.
> (Hervieu-Léger 2000, 165)

In "post-traditional" religion, Hervieu-Léger argues, tradition and community no longer generate individual obligation but are now *generated by* individual commitment. Today, "being religious is not so much knowing oneself begotten as willing oneself to be" (2000, 167).

My analysis of the significance of communities of conviction for my Muslim and Christian interlocutors, however, differs from the approaches of these authors on two counts. First, I do not take these communities to signal a full-blown retreat from modern secular culture. Berger described religious "sub-worlds" as "specific enclaves of social life that may be effectively segregated from the secularized sectors of modern society" (1967, 133) and, in a more recent work, as anti-secular "resistance" movements "with beliefs and practices dripping with reactionary supernaturalism" (1999, 4, 11). Hervieu-Léger refers to "closed spaces" (2006, 66) and another prominent sociologist, Manuel Castells, points to religious and other "cultural communes" that reject the hegemonic structures of global network society, while "retrenching themselves in a communal heaven" (2010, 68–70). By contrast to these depictions of some sort of fortified islands of—traditional or reactionary—religiosity, I have shown that the communities of conviction in which my interlocutors participated were dynamic spaces in which personal convictions were inculcated and strengthened in interaction with a wider pluralist society in which these young believers also participated. Indeed, key to the social force of these communities is the ongoing interrelation between young people's encounters with difference in their everyday lives and the work of affirmation established in these communities. If these communities offer a retreat from pluralist or secular culture, then this can only be a partial and temporary one. Moreover, rather than being isolated from the global world, these religious communities are strongly located in global networks of ideas and people, as Kevin McDonald (2006, chap. 8)—in a critique of Castells—points out with respect to new Islamic movements.

Second, the community participation of my interlocutors cannot be sufficiently understood as the result of primarily individual quests of meaning. In Hervieu-Léger's reading, communities make it possible to "declare one's personal search," ground meanings that are "individually produced" and confirm one's "spiritual experience" (2006, 67). Thus, community participation is understood to ensue from personal beliefs. This assumption is also reflected in Berger's comparison of religious activity in pluralist societies to a market situation, where individuals can choose what religious traditions they want to adhere to, based on their personal preferences (1967, 137).[15] Berger further argued that the condition of modern religion is characterized by a "heretical imperative," the requirement to pick and choose, bringing about "the deliberate construction of a community of consent" (1979, 28). Likewise, while Taylor acknowledges that "our relation to the sacred" is "mediated by collective connections" (2007, 516), he too appears to give more weight to the individuality of spiritual quests than to the potentially constitutive work of community. He argues:

> The new [religious] framework has a strongly individualist component, but this will not necessarily mean that the content will be individuating. Many people will find themselves joining extremely powerful religious communities. Because that's where many people's sense of the spiritual will lead them.
>
> (Taylor 2007, 516)

This interpretation of communal religious life as the result of subjectively construed beliefs and quests for meaning does not adequately reflect the situation of my interlocutors. They tended to be thoroughly socialized in Christian or Muslim families and environments, and could therefore not be seen to be completely "adrift in a universe without fixed bearings" (Hervieu-Léger 2000, 165). As I demonstrated in Chapter 2, the religious pedagogy with which they engaged did not represent an entirely new tradition for them, but by and large fitted in with the beliefs, orientations, and dispositions they had acquired in their upbringing. To invoke Bourdieu's terms once more, their general habitus pre-conditioned them to "gravitate" toward the specific habitus associated with these spaces (Desmond 2006, 391). What is more, the religious pedagogical settings in which these young Muslims and Christians participated continued to shape and generate their personal convictions.

For my Christian and Muslim interlocutors, personal convictions *relied* for an important part on their routinized participation in communities. Recall, here, the observation of Smith and Snell (2009, 251-4) that "internal" and "external" religion tend to come together for American young adults. My material suggests that these "internal" and "external" dimensions can be seen to be inextricably linked. Just as my interlocutors' community participation was stimulated by their personal convictions (and their desire to find affirmation of these), so too were their personal convictions structured by their community participation. These convictions were not constructed and maintained autonomously, but through repeated affirmation and re-affirmation in conversation with others. "Outward" religious practice was not subsidiary but essential to my interlocutors' religiosity. It was through their engagement with social-pedagogical settings that they were able to circumscribe, develop, and strengthen their personal convictions.

Thus, it is important, as Birgit Meyer has argued, "to acknowledge *the indispensability of form,* understood not as a vehicle but as a generator of meaning and experience, in all religious practice" (2012, 11–12, italics in original). Building on the work of, among others, Asad (1993) and Keane (2007), Meyer (2012, 8) criticizes the resilience of a "mentalistic approach" to religion, connected with a Protestant bias in scholarly approaches, which privileges the "inside" (concepts, ideas, beliefs) over the "outside" (rituals, objects, pictures). In contrast, she suggests that subjective religious experiences—and, I would add, convictions—depend on "authorized structures of repetition" that are conveyed to, and appropriated by, religious practitioners through material, sensorial, and ritual forms (Meyer 2010; cf. Van der Stoep 2007). Saba Mahmood (2005) has similarly argued that religious interiority and exteriority are closely interrelated. She shows that it was through ritual performances that the pious Muslim women with whom she worked in Cairo were able to cultivate particular sentiments, dispositions, and even spontaneous expressions such as weeping. For them, "outward behavioral forms were not only expressions of their interiorized religiosity but also a necessary means of acquiring it" (Mahmood 2005, 147).

The social-pedagogical spaces that my interlocutors engaged with provided precisely such routinized and ritualized settings that enabled them to shape and strengthen their personal convictions. This chapter has demonstrated that this role of religious communities has become especially important for young Dutch

Christians and Muslims who struggle with doubts about their faith, resulting from their encounters with alternative worldviews and lifestyles in the pluralist context in which they live. Next to such doubts, however, my Muslim and Christian interlocutors also faced more practical challenges to their faith. In the next two chapters, I examine how their engagements with faith were strongly conditioned by the practices and routines of a fast-paced and mass-mediatized society.

5

Fitting God In

"I'm not an exemplary Christian, unfortunately," Rachel said when we spoke about the place of worship in her daily life. Rachel was a 24-year-old psychology student who had grown up within a strictly orthodox Protestant family and later joined an evangelical student association and a Reformed church. I got to know her as someone who was not only passionate about prioritizing Christian faith in her everyday life but also particularly vocal about the struggles this entailed for her. She told me she had recently discussed the issue of making time for worship practices in her peer Bible study "small group" within her student association:

> Everyone is simply struggling with this, as in: How do I give it space in my life from day to day? That's just really *so* difficult. Because you get up, you straight away start doing your everyday stuff and, uhm, at night you drop into your bed tiredly. Yes, that's the reality of each day. And what we came up with in the small group was that it can be very helpful to already pray in the morning, before you start your day, and that you sort of put the day in the hands of God. And I did try that and it is indeed very nice to start your day like that. But, when I say that now, I realize: ah, that also sort of slips away again.

Rachel's reference to her small group indicates how social spaces of religious pedagogy not only, as the previous chapter showed, worked to confirm one's religious convictions in the face of intellectual doubt, but also provided encouragement in coping with one's felt inadequacies of religious practice. What I want to focus on here, however, is Rachel's enduring experience of falling short in the light of what she called the "reality" of her everyday life. At all times and places, Christians—and adherents of other religions—have grappled with feelings of imperfection. Indeed, Rachel's self-diagnosis as "not an exemplary Christian" signals a familiar trope among Christians and other believers. What is striking in her account, however, is the particular problem she addressed of integrating religion into her day-to-day life. Her remark about her morning prayer routine "slipping away again" denotes the way her religious practice seemed to be inadvertently pushed to the margins of her everyday life. This struggle to devote as much time and energy on her religion as she wanted to was widely shared among the young Christians I came to know. It denotes the particular challenge they faced of making and finding time for practices of worship against the backdrop of the rhythms and routines that shaped their everyday lives.

The young Muslims I met during my fieldwork shared this quandary. Consider Ismael, also aged twenty-four, a student in econometrics in Rotterdam who frequently attended Islamic classes and talks organized by mosques or Muslim student associations. When I met him for an interview, he had recently performed the *umra*, the non-compulsory pilgrimage to Mecca and Medina. Reflecting on his experience of coming back to the Netherlands afterward, he told me:

> Over there things go nicely, quite peacefully, you're only occupied with worship.... And then you come here, you have to go to school again, everything goes fast again, and again you have no time, everything goes fast, you are tired.... Yes, you are actually almost kept busy to put it that way. In that way [my faith] does ebb. At first when you come back you are still pretty much at it [practicing worship], but at a certain point, yeah, then, yeah, you actually sort of re-adapt.

What Ismael felt he "re-adapted" to were the rhythms of everyday life that Rachel also described, rhythms that were less shaped by religious routines than by the demands of school, university, and work, as well as by the general quick pace of social life. Ismael's remark about his faith "ebbing" reflects a sense of an unintentional decrease of focus on one's religion that is similar to what Rachel expressed.

In this chapter, I examine these common struggles among my Christian and Muslim interlocutors with regard to integrating religion, and prayer particularly, in their everyday lives. While the previous two chapters focused on their more intellectual and reflexive troubles with faith, in this as well as the next chapter I turn to the ways in which the social practices and routines of everyday life shaped and constrained their religious pursuits (in turn causing more reflexive troubles—these intellectual and practical processes should not be seen as entirely separated). I argue that the struggles with pursuing religious commitment in "busy" everyday lives have to be understood against the backdrop of social processes of acceleration in today's "fast capitalist" society (Agger 1989; 2004; Holmes 2000). My Muslim and Christian interlocutors experienced these processes of acceleration through, among other things, their academic studies, incipient careers, professional aspirations, and—as I discuss in the next chapter—their engagement with modern media.

By looking at the impact of fast capitalism on my interlocutors' religious lives, this chapter builds on longstanding theoretical debates on religion and capitalism. An important field of inquiry in this regard is the relation between religious ethics and capitalist economic activities. Max Weber's (2003) classic account of the impact of an ascetic Protestant ethic on the emergence of capitalism in early modern Europe has often been revived and reworked. Examples include Peter Berger's (2010) description of an "affinity" (Weber used the term *Wahlverwandschaft* or "elective affinity") between Pentecostalism and economic development in the Global South, and Daromir Rudnyckyj's (2011) analysis of a "spiritual economy" in Indonesia where Islamic practices are taken to be conducive to business success. Other authors have pointed to religion's historical relationship with not only production but also consumption—that other key dimension of capitalism (Bauman 2005): in an influential study, Colin Campbell (1987) analyzed the affinity between what he called "the other Protestant ethic" (a Sentimentalist rather than a Calvinist one) and modern consumerism. Particular attention has been given to the ways in which Pentecostal churches, especially those featuring the "Prosperity Gospel," encourage their members to participate in the neoliberal cultures of wealth, consumerism, and success (see e.g. Coleman 2000; Martin 2001; Van de Kamp 2016). The emphasis on both worldly and spiritual prosperity has also been observed in other contemporary religious movements (Woodhead and Heelas 2000, chap. 6). Studies of Islam have for example pointed to the emergent "halal market," characterized by the production and promotion of products advertized as religiously permissible (see e.g. Fischer 2008). More generally, the focus in the literature on religion and consumer-capitalism tends to be on the commodification and marketing of religion, the emergence of spiritual marketplaces, the success of "prosperity religions," and the provision of welfare by religious movements (Gauthier, Martikainen, and Woodhead 2011; 2013).

Unlike these main areas of inquiry in the literature, this chapter focuses neither on the affinity between religious and capitalist practices, nor on the commodification or marketing of religion itself. Rather, it examines the tensions between religious aspirations and the demands of fast capitalist society. I show that the quickening of the pace of life and the fast capitalist work ethic put pressures on my interlocutors' aspirations to give religion a primary place in their everyday lives. Indeed, the very capitalist ethic characterized by the norms of hard work and efficient time use, which Weber understood to be historically inspired by Calvinist religious culture, now seemed to constrain the religious pursuits of these young Christians and Muslims. At the same time, the social conditions of fast capitalism not only thwarted but also induced these young people's religious pursuits. Religious practices, and prayer in particular, were typically experienced by both the young Muslims and Christians to provide "peace" or "tranquility" (*rust*): precisely those qualities of mind of which they felt deprived in the context of their "busy" lives. The chapter, then, also demonstrates how today's accelerated culture gives practices of worship a renewed impulse and significance. Here, religion and (fast) capitalism emerge neither as congruous nor as merely conflicting, but rather as dialectically related.

Prayer and Closeness to God

Prayer played a central role in my Christian and Muslim interlocutors' aspirations to a strong personal faith. The young Christians commonly set aside specific moments during the day for prayer, often in combination with Bible reading. While their prayers varied in terms of content, they generally followed common styles, utterances, and bodily postures. In their prayers, the young Christians sought to petition, listen to, and express their gratitude to God. The young Muslims practiced the *salat*, the prescribed ritual prayer, which ought to be performed five times a day within set time intervals and in a state of ritual purity. The *salat* is a structured prayer with a fixed sequence of bodily postures and utterances, but it also leaves room for personal supplication or petitioning (*duʿa*). Both my Muslim and Christian interlocutors regarded prayer as a personal moment of connecting to, or communicating with, God. They performed their prayers either individually or in a group—with friends, partners, student groups, families, or, for the young Christians who live in student flats, housemates. For my Muslim interlocutors, Friday prayers in the mosque (considered to be obligatory for men) were important communal events, as were the prayers in the Sunday church services for my Christian interlocutors. These communal settings were also significant as recurrent moments in which the young Muslims and Christians were encouraged to give prayer a central place in their lives and were offered formats and techniques to do so.

My interlocutors felt that prayer affected the ways in which they navigated their everyday lives. If practiced systematically, prayers were understood to be constitutive of particular moral dispositions, experiences, and emotions (Asad

1993, 65; Mahmood 2005). For example, some of my Christian interlocutors pointed out that performing prayer in the morning changed the way they experienced the day. They felt that it made them more "aware" and stimulated a Christian ethics that motivated them to stay away from sinful behavior. My Muslim interlocutors said that praying regularly, ideally five times a day or even more, helped them to remain focused on God and to harness themselves against temptations. Some explained that the *salat* offered moments during the day in which they could pause and reflect on their behavior and ask for forgiveness for what they regarded as wrongful deeds. The young Muslims and Christians talked, in quite similar terms, about the ways in which prayer ultimately contributed to an everyday sense of closeness to God. It was, however, understood that this could only be realized by making prayers an integral and habitual part of their daily lives.

For both my Muslim and Christian interlocutors, performing prayer was also an expression of—and a means of cultivating—a sense of being fundamentally dependent on God. Through their regular prayers, experienced as moments of return to—and reconciliation with—God, they could put their worries into perspective and foster the feeling that their lives were guided by a supreme Being. The notion of dependence on God was also informed by their view of themselves as necessarily imperfect beings: the young Christians treated prayers as pedagogical practices by which they learned to build up a personal relationship with Jesus, which was understood as the only path to redemption from their sinful nature. For the young Muslims, prayer was a crucial part of an ongoing process of obeying and submitting themselves to God, which enabled them to correct and discipline the (carnal) self (*nafs*), so as to move closer to God and to salvation. For both groups, then, prayers were part and parcel of continuous moral and spiritual work on the self, aimed at becoming closer to God.

While anthropologists have carefully examined how Muslims and Christians cultivate prayer as a technique of moral and spiritual self-fashioning (see e.g. Henkel 2005; Mahmood 2005; Luhrmann 2012b; Reinhardt 2017), less attention has been paid to those moments and contexts in which people fail to practice prayer in ways they deem to be consistent or adequate (but see Simon 2009; Jouili 2015; Kloos 2018b). The next sections discuss precisely how my Muslim and Christian interlocutors, despite ascribing such important qualities to their prayers, struggled to make these an integral and habitual part of their everyday lives.

Struggles with Finding Time for *Salat*

The young Muslims with whom I worked regarded it as each individual's own responsibility to meet the requirements of prayer, or *salat*. As Farida, a pedagogical consultant in Rotterdam, said:

> At all of these times He is waiting for you. And it is up to you to keep that appointment. ... Look, we say: in the Quran God is talking to you, these are His words. And in prayer you come into contact with God, you talk with Allah. And, yes, for me prayer is really... yes, I mean, what is more beautiful than having five appointments with your own Creator? We attach a lot of value to appointments at work, with friends, with other people, but there isn't anything better than keeping to these five appointments and also really taking time for them. ... Prayers are the pillars of faith actually.

Farida's words put the emphasis squarely on the temporal component of the Islamic prayer. Yet, it was exactly this, taking time for prayers, that my Muslim interlocutors found difficult to accomplish in their everyday lives. This was expressed especially clearly by Naima, a student in law I met in the context of a Muslim student association in Rotterdam.

At around sixteen, Naima had "started to practice," particularly by trying to consistently observe the daily prayers. Yet, at the time of our interview, when she was twenty-four, she had come to find it difficult to fit the prayers into her busy schedule. Next to pursuing a master's degree in law, Naima had a job with the city council in Rotterdam for twenty-four hours a week. At her job she lacked both an adequate place and the time to perform the ablutions and prayer, given that she needed at least half an hour to "do the whole process correctly." This would give her a "bit of a hurried feeling," whereas she preferred to "pray comfortably [*op m'n gemakje bidden*]." She had only once conducted her prayer at work, at a time when both of her direct colleagues were out of their shared office room.

Even more than these practical concerns, Naima related this difficulty to pray to the work pace at her job: "you are really doing so many things, and also meetings, and people coming in asking things, phone calls and that kind of stuff.... Sometimes I'm really very busy and then I also have my sandwich behind my ... PC at work." She noted that it would be convenient if there was a mosque next door to her work, in which everything would be already "set up" in such a way that she could quickly go and pray in her thirty-minute break. At the Erasmus University in Rotterdam, where she studied, there was a prayer room for Muslims. Yet, Naima pointed out, it was only a small room with just one single space to perform one's ablutions, while there were often many people who wanted to pray. So this meant waiting and subsequently having to rush through one's ablutions and prayer.

On her workdays, Naima would "catch up" all the prayers she had missed after she got home—a practice that some of my interlocutors mockingly called the "marathon prayer." This made her feel dissatisfied with herself, as she was not "really doing it as it ought to be done." Apart from not following the Islamic prescription to pray on time, she disliked having to catch up her prayers in the evening, because "after a whole day at work" she would feel tired and her concentration would have dropped, diminishing the emotional engagement she would feel during her prayers. Naima pointed out that her feelings during prayer depended on the state in which she performed them. She tried to strengthen her emotional experience of prayer by cultivating, in her words, "awareness" and "conviction," trying to realize "what I'm actually saying" (when reciting a *sura*, or chapter, from the Quran during prayer), "to whom I'm actually praying," and "why I'm actually praying."

The emotional experience to which she aspired during prayer was *ihsan*, which, she said, meant "perfection," the "finest" form of worship and being "really very close to God." A *hadith* in the collection of Al-Bukhari gives this definition of *ihsan*: "to worship Allah as if you see Him, and if you cannot achieve this state of devotion then you must consider that He is looking at you" (Khan 1997, 81–2). To reach that stage of faith, Naima pointed out, one needs to "constantly improve oneself." What was at stake was precisely that cultivating *ihsan* was a long-term, cumulative process of committing oneself to prayer. The result of not consistently performing one's prayers on time was that "you also come to have that feeling [of being close to God] less and less. Thus, you miss that feeling, and to get that going again [*weer op te krikken*], yes, that doesn't come easily. You really have to strengthen yourself in that." Sometimes she was afraid of losing this feeling altogether, "because of all the other things, activities here in the world, that *that* will finally dominate and push the practice of your religion, like, to the background."

It is notable that Naima presented the impediments to prayer due to her work almost as an inescapable reality. She did not seem to seriously consider the option of privileging the religiously prescribed prayers over her obligations at work. "You have to of course live here in this, this world," she said. "So you simply have to work, you have to participate in society." And that, she said, meant one cannot always observe one's prayers. This statement contrasted with the repeated encouragement by Islamic preachers and teachers—within the revivalist, often Salafi, circles I attended during my fieldwork—to give high priority to the *salat* and, if needed, to request one's employer for space and time to perform one's prayers. Naima's position in this regard reflected her professional ambitions. She aspired to a position in a government institution and wrote to me in an e-mail correspondence that her main motivation to do her current job was to "acquire experience in a municipal work environment." Thus, her work was a relevant asset to her CV that could help her forward in her career.

Many of my other Muslim interlocutors, often as highly educated and ambitious as Naima, similarly seemed to accept as a fact the restrictions on religious practice resulting from their jobs and studies, even if they were—like Naima—dissatisfied with having to miss prayers. Most of them, indeed, struggled with performing their prayers on time, because of their obligations of study and work, the absence of adequate facilities at their workplaces, and a general sense of hurriedness and lack of time. At home, many of my interlocutors were especially struggling to observe *fajr*, the early morning prayer that takes place before sunrise. They often did not manage to get up in time, particularly when they had stayed up late; for example because they had been studying for exams. In the evenings, they often felt tired after a whole day of work, studies, or other activities. This, they felt, decreased their concentration during prayers.[1]

Khadija, the nineteen-year-old student introduced in the previous chapter, mentioned to me that the problem in balancing work and faith was that one perceived the duties and consequences of the former more directly than those of the latter. For her, this meant that she often found it hard to give priority to her prayers during her work in a supermarket. When she did pray at work, it was difficult for her to ignore (as she thought she should) cashiers' calls for assistance, out of fear to lose her job. Even if she would choose to continue her prayer on those moments, she said, she would be very distracted by her anxieties and far from focused on the prayer itself. By contrast, some of my other interlocutors noted that when they explicitly voiced their religious needs, their employers were often prepared to accommodate these. For example, Idris, a student in Islamic spiritual care in Amsterdam, said: "You can hide your religion, but you can also simply be candid about it. ... My experience is always, if you're candid about it, they also respect you and actively search for a solution together with you."

The constraints my interlocutors experienced on regularly performing prayer were related to a more general structuring of everyday life. Several of my Muslim interlocutors pointed out that the rhythms and routines of everyday life in the Netherlands were unfavorable to consistently practicing their prayers. Some drew a contrast with Muslim societies in this regard, occasionally with

Mecca and Medina, but more often with Morocco or Turkey, the countries in which their parents were born and which they occasionally visited. They pointed out that the rhythms of Islamic prayer were part of social life in these countries, especially because of the publicly audible *adhan*, the call to prayer, which many respond to (cf. Tamimi Arab 2017, 7). For example, Hasan, who studied political science in Leiden and volunteered for a Gülen-inspired association in Rotterdam, pointed out that at university he would often be the only one who needed to pray, while his fellow students continued to work. He said that in Turkey, where his family hailed from, there would at least be a substantial minority of students who would also pray. This made it more difficult for him to practice his religion in the Dutch context. Haniya, a 28-year-old graduate in law, similarly explained why she had come to pray less and less since she turned eighteen:

> I simply forgot it, I simply forgot my faith, because of, uhm, other things, other social things, work things. And, uhm, when I went to Morocco again I realized: Oh, yes, there's Islam too (*islam is er ook nog*). … There you're also being reminded of it, because of the call to prayer.

Indeed, one reason these young Muslims found it important to pray regularly was that, as Aisha, a twenty-year-old student in Rotterdam, put it, prayers were moments of the day on which you "remember that you believe." Since the *salat* is not part of generally shared social rhythms in the Netherlands, Dutch Muslims who want to pray regularly rely on their self-discipline to do so. As Idris put it:

> When you hear [the *adhan*], then you get an *urge* to go and pray, because you hear the call, you hear a call as in "Come to prayer!" Then, even though you're sometimes lazy, when you hear it, you're stimulated to go. But if you don't hear a call to prayer then … you have to depend on yourself far too much [*veelsteveel beroepen op jezelf*], you have to keep track of the time yourself, you see, *you* have to activate yourself to go.

Surely, many people in Morocco do not consistently respond to the *adhan* in the way Idris described and regularly neglect prayers (Ababou 2005, 34). Still, different from those living in Morocco or other Muslim-majority societies, my Muslim interlocutors had to create a prayer routine in a social context in which such a routine could not be taken for granted. They did have resources at their disposal to do so, including lists with prayer times published on websites and distributed at mosques, as well as *adhan* apps. Furthermore, they were often motivated to pray by—and often prayed together with—their family members, friends, and fellow Muslim students.

The struggles of these young Muslims with performing their prayers on time, then, were strongly related to the routines and the structuring of time in their everyday lives. Some also noted that they ran up against restrictions and hostile attitudes when it came to performing their prayers within the public domain (cf. Fadil 2013, 740–1; Jouili 2015, 155–61). Others might experience embarrassment, especially, perhaps, when it came to performing the ablutions (cf. Jouili 2015, 159–60). Yet, the major constraint my interlocutors referred to in this regard was a "daily rhythm" of life that "had nothing to do with Islam," as Hasan put it. This conflict between religious and secular rhythms was clearly pronounced for my Muslim interlocutors due to the daily temporal program of the *salat*. Yet we should not be too quick in framing conflicts like these as unique to Muslims in—and as opposed to—a secular Europe, as some academic work tends to do (on this point, see also Schielke 2010, 5–9). To the contrary, in the next section, I show that my Christian interlocutors struggled in very similar ways with the secular rhythms of their everyday lives.

Struggles with Finding Time for Prayer and Bible Reading

At Pilgrim Students in Rotterdam, busyness and time constraints were recurrent themes. Many of the association's members found it hard to find a balance between devoting time to their studies and jobs on the one hand, and to their faith on the other. To illustrate, in the men's club in which I participated, the members had set themselves the ambitious task of reading the entire Bible in one year. This required setting aside at least fifteen minutes a day for Bible study. The four young men with whom I met in a small group found it hard to keep up with the reading schedule (as did I) and often did not manage to read the entire text assigned between our fortnightly meetings. In the course of the months in which we met, the men's commitment to keeping up with the schedule waned increasingly, until the project was abandoned altogether. They turned out to prioritize other activities and obligations in their everyday lives. Johan, who participated in another small group within the club, similarly told me that he did not manage to keep up with the schedule. "You simply don't make it [*Je redt het gewoon niet*]," he said. By using the impersonal "you," rather than "I," he seemed to imply that his failure to keep up did not reflect his personal character but rather the impossibility of the whole business in the first place. Johan often only read the Bible late at night, when he was already tired and eager to go to bed. He noted that he should open his Bible earlier in the evening but that at such times he often "simply forgot it." "It's sort of not part of your rhythm," he mused.

More generally, the young Christians I worked with often expressed their dissatisfaction with the extent to which they managed to set aside moments for practices of worship during the day. This was commonly discussed as a problem of "being busy." Echoing Rachel's words about her worship practices "slipping away" in her day-to-day life, Robert, a student in economy and member of Pilgrim Students, told me that he often "forgot about" his faith as a result of the routines of his everyday life. On an average day when he had to work and hurry up in the morning, it would happen that he would take a moment for prayer before having lunch, or even only before having dinner, and realize that he had not yet "thought about God at all" that day. He felt that the practice of his religion often moved to the background of his everyday life, due to the "busyness of the world, in the sense that everything simply keeps on moving."

Some spoke more specifically about their struggles to "fit" God into their day-to-day schedules. Paul, a Christian student in medicine who played an active role in Pilgrim Students, said: "[Serving God] does not come by itself, you really have to choose for it, otherwise you indeed have no time left in your agenda, or you rather go and watch a movie, or there are all kinds of other things that come first." A parallel point was made by Isabel, a business consultant in Rotterdam who had converted to (Pentecostal) Christianity a couple of years before I met her, when she talked to me about "things that keep one away from God":

> I think that for me the most important now is, uhm, time. That sounds a bit, well, stupid, but because I make such a full planning, God simply slides off constantly—to put it that way [laughs]—in my schedule. ... Also with colleagues, spending one Friday night going out, or doing something else. Your week is full before you know it and, as I said, when you are away twelve hours [a day, because of work] and you sleep seven hours, well, see how much there's left. And you have to do your housekeeping and you have to eat.

When I prompted her to elaborate on these experiences, Isabel said:

> I make a resolution: I will read the Bible tonight, you know. And I'm *so* tired after I get home, uhm that I switch on the television and it simply doesn't happen anymore. Or that I say at half past ten: I go to bed. And that that happens once in a while, look, I don't think that God minds. I think that he ['ie] says: just go and sleep, tomorrow there is another day, as long as you think of me and uhm... You know. But I just notice that it is too much. ... I just have to make choices.

When she did find "time for God," as she put it, Isabel felt that such time was often "lousy" (she used the English term), as she would already be tired because of everything she had done that day. The consequence of having too little (quality) time with God, Isabel said, was that God felt "further away." She explained:

> And it's not so much that I think that God retreats or something like that … , but it is more for myself that I notice like, when I'm more occupied with God … , for example when I'm taking a shower that I'm not thinking like "hmm, what shall I wear today?", you know, but that I think about the texts that I've read or… you know. So you feel that you're closer to God. … I also believe that the Holy Spirit can do more in you, if you're focused more on Him.

Isabel's example about where her thoughts wandered to while she was taking a shower—her clothes or religious texts—nicely illustrates her point that the less time she devoted to God, the less prominent her religion became in her everyday life. Like her, many of my interlocutors felt that the busyness of their everyday lives decreased their religious engagement and drew them away from God. They effectively talked about the challenge of "fitting" God in their already packed schedules. Isabel formulated it almost literally in these terms when she noted that God constantly "slides off" her schedule.

Like my Muslim interlocutors, these young Christians regularly pointed to the role of self-discipline in this regard. Thus, Rachel said that it was important to constantly "activate" the feelings of peace and trust that she drew from her Christian faith, by reading the Bible, praying and speaking to people about faith. When Charlotte, who had just finished her studies in social work at the Christian college in Ede, told me that she prayed and read in the Bible every day, she noted:

> And that's also really something, uhm, you have to do an effort for. It requires a degree of discipline and personal will to do that. Because, of course, time is something you're always lacking, and [worship] is something you also really have to make time for … . Because, yes, the worldly things can consume your time so fast, so that you're occupied with yourself, your studies, with all kinds of things, except with [worship].

These experiences are strikingly similar to the ways in which my Muslim interlocutors felt challenged by the busyness of their everyday lives. Indeed, to some extent both groups used the same terms to describe these difficulties, including "being busy," "simply forgetting about one faith," and "having to activate" religious practices or experiences. Both also felt that negligence of worship moved them away from God.

A notable difference between them, however, was that the young Muslims had to relate themselves to the prescription to pray on set times during the day while the Christians did not. Hence, the former faced the particular problem of integrating the prayers in their daily occupations, more specifically at their workplaces or universities, and they were confronted with feelings of inadequacy when they missed prayers. Young Christians enjoyed more flexibility with regard to setting their own moments for prayer and religious contemplation. Yet this also meant that they could support less than the young Muslims on a prescribed temporal structure for daily worship practices. While they were familiar with conventional moments and formats for prayer such as morning prayer, prayer before and/or after meals and evening prayer, these did not constitute clear guidelines. Possibly even more than the Muslims, they had to rely on self-discipline when it came to "making time for God." Arguably, the risk of settling into the prevalent secular rhythms of everyday life was even greater for them.

This difference was occasionally remarked upon. For example, Rachel, who had some experience in "interreligious dialogues" with Muslims, mentioned to me that an ordinary day for her was just like that for a non-Christian. She noted that she saw a difference with Muslims in this respect, given their prescription of the five-daily prayers. "I find that somewhat compulsive, but on the other hand I also see it's positive side, because indeed for Christians it always kind of slips away again."

Nonetheless, my Muslim and Christian interlocutors shared the sense that their lives were so "packed" with activities and events rapidly succeeding one another, that there was often little time left to practice their faith. They often felt that worship practices were unwittingly pushed to the margins of their everyday lives—or, as Isabel put it, that God constantly "slid off" their schedule. While they aspired to consistently practice prayers as a means of getting "closer to God," they found it hard to realize this in their busy everyday lives.

The Acceleration of Everyday Life

Feelings of falling short, sinfulness, or imperfection are part and parcel of most religious lives, especially for those who are actively cultivating a pious or committed self. These feelings are prompted by individual concerns over one's salvation or virtuosity, often invoked by religious authorities, and deliberately cultivated within religious contexts (Strhan 2015; Beekers and Kloos 2018; Kloos 2018a; Laidlaw and Mair 2019; Fahy 2020). Such senses of failure are also, as the material presented here indicates, substantially shaped by particular social conditions. The struggles of my Muslim and Christian interlocutors with making time for prayer resulted not just from their strong religious ambitions, but also from a social context in which religious practices tended to be constantly pushed to the background of everyday life. In their hurried and packed lives, falling short of their religious aspirations was a basic condition of their religious lives. For these young believers, experiences of failure were continuously recurring, rather than sporadic and singular moments of "moral breakdown" (Zigon 2007).

Two issues stand out in the accounts of felt busyness of both my Muslim and Christian interlocutors: the time and energy taken up by their studies and jobs, and the more general sense of hurried everyday lives. Most of the people I worked with were studying full time and working part time on the side—a common practice among Dutch students today, who face substantial study as well as living costs and only a modest state benefit (which was still a gift at the time of my fieldwork, but has since been turned into a loan). Their dissatisfaction with the ways in which these activities constrained their religious engagement generally did not move them to reconsider these pursuits of study and work, but rather to negotiate moments of prayer and religious contemplation around them. My interlocutors' experience of hurriedness resulted not only from these daily occupations, but also from social contacts and obligations, as well as the continuous influences of modern media and entertainment. They often mentioned that television, internet, e-mail, and smartphones kept them "busy" (the next chapter will look at the influence of such media use in more detail). All this thwarted the consistent, everyday practice of faith. The result of neglecting worship practices, or of performing them without much concentration, was a felt distancing from God. This is another manifestation of the ways in which these young believers' religious submission, as I argued in Chapter 3, relied strongly on the activity and commitment of the self, and was therefore always contingent on that self.

The experiences of busyness and hurriedness among my interlocutors correspond to wider social patterns. Statistical research in the Netherlands has pointed to increasingly widespread feelings of hurriedness among the population (Cloïn 2013, 161). These experiences can be related to changes in time use: since 1975, Dutch people have come to spend more time on—what in this research is termed—"obligatory" activities, including education, housekeeping, childcare, and especially paid labor (34–6). The Dutch are also increasingly combining work and household tasks (Breedveld and Van den Broek 2002, 20). Moreover, propelled by processes of economic rationalization in the 1980s and 1990s, the pace of work has quickened in recent decades (17). The introduction of flexible work in these years has resulted in a decrease of fixed contracts, linear careers, predictable sources of income, and steady everyday routines (28–9). At the same time, Dutch people increasingly have to "multitask," both at work and at home (Haegens 2012, 67, 114–16).

These patterns of societal acceleration and the increased encroachment of work on everyday life have also been extensively described in the international sociological literature on high capitalist societies. This scholarship points to a restructuring of time related to two key socio-economic developments: first, the onset of a new phase in capitalism that has been described as post-Fordism,[2] characterized by the acceleration and increased flexibility of modes of production, consumption, and accumulation (Harvey 1989; Sennett 1998; Bauman 2000; Muehlebach and Shoshan 2012); and, second, the rise of "information society" since the 1990s (Castells 2000; cf. Eriksen 2001; Agger 2004). These developments represent recent phases of what David Harvey has described as "the overwhelming sense of *compression* of our spatial and temporal words" (1989, 240, italics in original).

Flexible accumulation, the 24/7 economy, and the "digital revolution" have instigated a quickening of the pace of everyday life in recent decades. As Thomas Hylland Eriksen has pointed out, "more and more information, consumption, movement and activity is being pushed into the available time" (2001, 101), resulting in a reduction of "slow, continuous time" (139). Acceleration under conditions of "fast capitalism" (Agger 1989; 2004; Holmes 2000) is not restricted to the economic domain, but spills over into other domains of life. Thus, David Harvey (1989, 291) argues that "everything, from novel writing and philosophizing to the experience of laboring or making a home, has to face the challenge of accelerating turnover time …." This accelerated culture is characterized by instantaneity, simultaneity or "multitasking," volatility and short-term planning (Harvey 1989, 286–7; Bauman 2000, chap. 3; Agger 2004, 5–6). It has been strongly reinforced by the emergence of the internet in the 1990s and the continuous introduction of new digital media and technologies since then (Coleman 2010). Eriksen argues that this new information technology "removes distance, shortens time and fills the gaps with cascades of information" (2001, 76).

The "spillover" of fast capitalism is particularly expressed by the relation between work and other domains of life. While the increasing flexibility of production processes has liberated workers, at least high skilled ones (Bauman 2005, 35–6), from the "time clock" and made them more autonomous, it has also increasingly erased the boundary between work on the one hand and home, family, and leisure on the other. Ben Agger (2004, 65) writes that work "sets the agenda" around which family and personal life get organized. He argues that work has become "omnipresent," due to "its anywhere/anytime-ness (using e-mail and cell phones)" and "its encroachment into other domains no longer temporally separable from it" (2004, 80). Together with the quick turnover of information and images in the context of intensified consumerism, new media, and digitalization, this encroachment of work into other domains contributes to an increased fragmentation of everyday life (cf. Sennett 1998).

The impact of this accelerated culture on everyday religious lives has not yet received much scholarly attention. An exception is Anna Strhan's work on the members of an evangelical Anglican church in London, for whom, she observes, the "pressures and rhythms of everyday middle-class metropolitan life make it easy to forget about God …" (2015, 192). Likewise, in their study of religion among young adults in the United States, which focuses on people from white Christian milieus, Christian Smith and Patricia Snell point out that their respondents "talk repeatedly about how busy they are" (2009b, 77). They suggest that for young adults in particular the demands and activities of everyday life can "feel all-consuming" in the light of their studies, emergent careers, often strong engagement with consumer and popular cultures, and experienced use of new communication technology. These young people "would have a hard time imagining—if they thought about it—squeezing the demands of a committed religious life into their hectic and unpredictable schedules" (Smith and Snell 2009, 77).[3]

As young people living in an urban environment, studying, working, consuming, and extensively using (new) media, my Muslim and Christian interlocutors, too, participated actively in today's accelerated culture. They were receptive to the continuous influences of modern media, entertainment, and consumer culture. Even though many of them criticized the excessive materialism and undue focus on "making a career" that they regarded as characteristic of contemporary Western society, most also pursued the modern ideals of a good life measured by material prosperity and professional success (Hage 2003, 13). They worked hard to obtain good university degrees and to set off on promising careers. Indeed, the social conditions of contemporary fast capitalist society posed such strong challenges to my interlocutors' religious pursuits because they constituted a realm of practice and aspiration in which these young people were themselves strongly embedded.[4] These social conditions marked their daily routines and rhythms, their feelings of hurriedness, and their concomitant struggles to "fit God in."

The Tranquility of *Salat*

Yet, the young Muslims and Christians with whom I worked were not merely positioned ambivalently between the conflicting aspirations of religion and those of capitalism. Rather, the impact of processes of acceleration was two-sided: it not only constrained their practices of worship, but also endowed these with a renewed significance. When my Muslim interlocutors talked about prayer, they typically put a strong emphasis on the Dutch term *rust*, which carries such connotations as tranquility, quietness, rest, peace, or peace of mind. They generally noted (often without any direct prompts from my part) that the *salat* allowed them to temporarily let go of their worries, forget about the concerns of—what they described as—"this life" or "this world," and to connect with God. Many were also quick to point out that this was the ideal state to be reached through prayer: whether they succeeded in achieving it depended on their "intention" and the level of concentration with which they entered the prayer.

Asked why they desired such peace of mind, they pointed to the stress, demands, or "chaos" of their everyday lives, to work and to personal problems. Fouad, a 21-year-old student in Islamic theology from Rotterdam, told me that his prayers gave him repose from the "hectic" character of his daily life and from his "busy agenda." During prayer, he said, "it's God's turn," you "close yourself off." In the same vein, Idris said:

> Five times a day you make a phone call with God as it were, you talk with Him, if something is bothering you, if… anything. So that also gives peace [*rust*]. You know that, that in any circumstance, however bad things are going, whatever stress you're experiencing, whatever deadline you need to meet, Allah sees you, Allah knows that you're in that situation. … So you know that you, that Allah is continuously with you. And prayer confirms that all the time. And that's a, yes, comforting thought.

Fatima, a psychology student in Rotterdam, told me that she would sometimes actually "spend more time" on her prayers when she was very busy with school, as this would give her a feeling of peace (*rust*), and she hoped she would also be rewarded for these prayers in her studies.

The embodied practice of the ablutions preceding prayer and the physical movements during prayer may be seen as both expressing and stimulating the acts of letting go of "worldly" concerns and finding tranquility through worshipping God. As Ahmet, an active member of the Gülen-inspired association mentioned before, remarked:

Because when you do this, right [raises his hands up to his ears], you say "Allah is great" and you start the prayer. This has a symbolic expression as in: I leave *everything* behind that happens here in the world. And then I enter into communication with God, [recites:] *Allahu Akbar*. Then everything is gone. ... Just like a soccer player who says, like, that he forgets everything when he is on the field, well, it's something like that that you should feel.

In relation to this, some of my Muslim interlocutors described prayer as an extraordinary moment, temporarily taking them beyond the here and now. Farida, who had referred to the prayers as five appointments with God, described her experience of prayer as "really a feeling of peace [*rust*].... You even hear your own breath, you even start to concentrate on the way you are breathing." She enthusiastically told me about a particularly strong emotional experience she had had during prayer:

> The other day, it really felt as if my heart trembled, it was a *very* unusual [*apart*] moment. On that moment I was kneeling, I was on the ground, and I continued to kneel, I thought: I'm not going to get up as long as I have that feeling. ... I breathed very little, but I felt *very* calm ... and I had let go of everything. And I wasn't at all focused on the worldly life or that I was at home, I wasn't even aware of that. But that contact I had at that moment, I thought like, wow, you know, you don't experience such a beautiful feeling every day, so hold on to it.

Farida's account resonates with more widely shared Islamic repertoires of what Charles Hirschkind (2006, 75) calls "the affective-kinesthetic experience of a body permeated by faith (*iman*)." And as he points out, the Quran describes believers as "only they whose hearts tremble whenever God is mentioned."[5]

While Farida's description of this deeply affective experience of prayer was quite exceptional, many of my Muslim interlocutors did to some extent share the experience—or at least ideal—of completely letting go of the here and now during prayer. A striking formulation of this was given by Mustafa, a student in law who had come to the Netherlands as a refugee from Azerbaijan at the age of twelve (he was raised as a Shi'i Muslim but now identified himself as a Sunni Muslim) and whom I frequently met at Islamic talks organized at the Erasmus University in Rotterdam. He said he sometimes found it difficult to concentrate during his prayers, especially when he had just been studying or watching soccer. "Something you can't see, you can't always concentrate on," he pointed out. Yet, he continued to say: "I do try it and it really is a good feeling.

It's a feeling that you can only describe when you, uhm, experience it yourself." And after a moment's thought Mustafa added: "We are now in a time and space, but prayer takes you above these, above time and above space. Really a, yes, travelling toward God."

The experience of peace that prayer provided was also described by my Muslim interlocutors as a sense of relief. Some compared it to the feeling they had when they had done their exams and no longer had to worry about them. Fatima described it as the feeling of having fulfilled one's duty. Mustafa said that when he spent hours on any one activity, his soul (*ruh*) would start to become sour, it would become hungry, and this hunger could only be satisfied by prayer. Khadija's account made clear that such understandings of prayer were also encouraged within Islamic pedagogical settings. She said: "During a talk I heard like: You know when you get home tired and you just come from work and you think 'oh, I still need to pray, I still need to pray everything'? This prayer should rather make you more lively, less tired, as if a weight is lifted from your shoulders." Khadija still found it hard to experience prayer in this way. She thought she could achieve it by strengthening her *iman* to such an extent that, during her prayer, "all worldly affairs no longer matter, that those exams no longer matter."

While the "other-worldliness" of prayer was often emphasized, some of the young Muslims I met also talked about the ways in which prayer helped them to structure their everyday, "worldly" activities. Thus, Ahmet said that prayer contributed "a certain discipline" to his daily life, as the combination of "worldly" activities and prayers forced him to plan his days well. When Idris and I were talking about prayer at their family home, his 24-year-old brother chipped in to make a similar remark:

> When you do your prayers on time, you can also reflect on what you have done between two prayers. Have you made good use of your time or not? ... So you're constantly focused, consciously focused, on using your time efficiently. ... When you don't pray, at least for me, it feels as if I'm wasting my time, throwing it away. Because then I don't, like uhm... Then I don't keep to my agenda to put it that way.

In contrast to the sense of struggling to fit one's prayers into one's schedule, it is suggested here that prayers themselves help to organize one's use of time efficiently. This shows how, for some of these young Muslims at least, prayer is perceived not only as opposed to the normativities of (fast) capitalist culture but also as conducive to them (cf. Rudnyckyj 2011).

The Quietness of Christian Worship

The young Christians I met also regularly talked about prayer and other worship practices as activities that brought them peace, tranquility, or quietness. They, too, often used the Dutch term "rust" in this respect. Many of my Christian interlocutors described prayer and reading the Bible as providing moments of tranquility (*rustmomenten*) in their otherwise busy and chaotic everyday lives. An important concept for these young Christians in this regard was "quiet time" (*stille tijd*), a term they—like many other Christians (see e.g. McGrath 1996)—generally used to describe the moments of prayer, Bible reading, and contemplation that they set aside during the day, typically in the mornings and/or evenings, and that were directed at cultivating personal intimacy with God (cf. Luhrmann 2012b). Starting to read in one's Bible was often the practical act that marked such quiet times and set them apart from other activities in one's everyday life. They held that what communion with God should entail was not only them talking to God, but also God talking to them (through the Bible or other media), allowing them to be "edified" (*opgebouwd*) by His word.

Quiet time entailed moments in which one became literally quiet, by sitting still and retreating from the buzz of everyday life. For my Christian interlocutors, this often meant retreating to a private space, like one's bedroom, and "closing oneself off" from external, distractive influences as much as possible. Thus, Adam, the pastoral theology student I referred to earlier, told me that he deliberately created such moments a couple of times a week, switching off his computer and television and making everything "quiet" (*rustig*):

> Sometimes I also simply switch off the light in my room, then I only see the light entering from outside. Simply uhm praying in a delightfully peaceful [*rustige*] way and reflecting [*stilstaan*, lit. "standing still"] on what is important in life, instead of going along with all that busyness and being confronted with your limits one day [*jezelf op een dag tegenkomen*].

In this atmosphere without, as he put it, "noise" and things that "distract you," Adam could "come to God." This "closing off" of oneself from the outside world bears a resemblance to the (ideal) practice of *salat* among my Muslim interlocutors.

My Christian interlocutors commonly pointed out that, as Robert put it, such moments of "focusing [one's] thoughts on God" brought them peace during the day and made them "more relaxed." Similarly to Fatima, some of them noted that such practices of worship were particularly important in busy times. Thus, Charlotte told me: "I notice that especially when I'm very busy, I should actually take time for [prayer and Bible reading], because it makes me more peaceful [*rustiger*] and you can get the bigger picture again, so that you can continue again." In relation to this, prayer and reading the Bible were understood to help one to put things into perspective. Thus, Rachel noted that these practices allowed her to "activate" feelings of peace and trust, which put all of her "daily worries," about her exams or her internship, for example, into "a bigger picture"—the "perspective of eternity"—that made such worries seem irrelevant. Likewise, when Jantine had graduated from the Christian college in Ede and started her first full-time job, she struggled with feelings of stress. When I met her some months after she had started the job, she pointed out: "I have really been learning lately that when I indeed read my Bible in the morning, and pray, and bring [things] to God, this gives me so much more peace [*rust*] in my whole life."

Prayers, for my Christian interlocutors, were opportunities for contemplation and reflection, helping them to put their concerns into perspective, make decisions, and seek guidance. Frank, the employee of a small company I introduced in Chapter 3, said that when he was struggling with issues, like having a bad day at work, it was prayer that gave him peace (*rust*):

> Perhaps in normal terms you could say: every second you can walk into the room of the psychologist. Uhm… So each moment you need it, you can simply come to your Father again and sit still for a moment and order your thoughts with Him, for Him. … And just that already recharges you as it were.

What is striking in this statement is not only that Frank articulates a form of secular normativity by contrasting Christian prayer with the "normal" activity of seeing a psychologist, but also that he emphasizes the ways in which prayers provide support for his everyday activities at the office. Many of the young Christians told me, as did the young Muslims, that they often prayed to God about issues at work or about their exams at university. Some also said that taking time for prayer and Bible reading in the morning helped them to be positive and energetic during the day at their jobs or studies. To some extent, then, practices of worship were not separated from other concerns in everyday life, but entangled with them.

These young Christians set the Sunday apart as a "day of rest" that they observed in varying ways and to varying degrees. They commonly sought to spend their Sundays differently from other days, by going to church, reading the Bible or other "edifying" literature, and refraining as much as possible from work, study, and shopping. Some, like Charlotte, also kept their televisions and computers switched off on Sundays, because these, she said, "can also very much hurry [*opjagen*] you." She told me that she experienced the Sunday differently from other days, particularly because of its "slower pace." Ruth, a student in commercial economy at a vocational university in Rotterdam, told me that on Sundays she usually went to her parents, who lived in a small, predominantly Christian village in the province of Zeeland. For her, this was "a day to spend a lot of time on God." She would go to church twice, did not work on her studies, read "good books" and the Bible, prayed a few times, sometimes slept the whole afternoon, and looked back on the previous week and forward to the coming one. Because of the rest she took and the experience of "coming very close to God" on Sundays, she said she found renewed energy to start the following week.

Apart from these notions of quietness and rest, my Christian interlocutors also employed a notion of "stillness," particularly with respect to the ways in which particular experiences, thoughts, or images could give them pause for reflection. The Dutch phrase they recurrently used in this regard was *stilgezet worden*, which literally translates as "being brought to a standstill." I have rarely—if ever—heard people use the phrase in this way outside of the Christian settings in which I worked. It seems to be part of a particular Dutch Christian vocabulary. Generally used in the sense of bringing to a halt something that would otherwise continue running (like a clock or a machine), for my Christian interlocutors *stilgezet worden* denoted a momentary suspension of the ordinary, incessant course of events that, in their experience, filled up their days. To give just one example, Johan used this phrase to indicate those moments during his work in a supermarket when something made him pause to reflect on the things that mattered to him, such as his relationship with his girlfriend, his identity, or his faith. Such experiences, he said, really changed the way he experienced his afternoon or behaved toward his team members. *Stilgezet worden* was commonly used in the passive sense: being brought to a standstill was not so much something one did oneself, as something that happened to you—directed, perhaps, by God.

In Conclusion: Practicing Worship as Slowing Down Time

The young Muslims and Christians with whom I worked aspired to a strong personal faith, which for them meant giving religion a central place in their everyday lives and committing themselves to prayer and other practices of worship. Yet, today's fast-paced culture, combined with the lack of generally shared religious rhythms in contemporary Dutch society, made it practically difficult to "fit God" into their daily schedules. For them, leading busy, hurried, and accelerated lives seemed to be an inevitable condition of the contemporary world. At the same time, their busyness also resulted from their professional ambitions. Indeed, alongside their aspirations to religious commitment, they pursued aspirations to professional success, well-being, and the fulfillment of one's potential through one's career. That is, they gave shape to both an ethics of religious piety and an ethics of hard work and personal achievement within the framework of neoliberal capitalism. In this sense, my interlocutors' lives were characterized by a moral ambivalence (cf. Schielke 2015) that manifested itself in their everyday lives through conflicting rhythms, routines, and structures of time.

Yet my findings also show that the relation between these—religious and capitalist—aspirations and rhythms was not merely one of ambivalent coexistence. Both my Muslim and Christian interlocutors emphasized the ways in which prayer and other worship practices provided them with experiences of tranquility, rest, or peace. Worship, then, offered them precisely those qualities they missed in today's accelerated, fast-paced culture. In line with authors who have suggested that religion can provide an alternative to, or means to cope with, the speeded-up culture of contemporary capitalism (Van Harskamp 2008, 16–17; Gauthier, Martikainen, and Woodhead 2011, 295), I argue that for the young Muslims and Christians with whom I worked, worship gained a renewed significance in the context of conditions of fast capitalism. Apart from constituting an expression of their devotion to God and of their adherence to religious prescriptions or conventions, worship was felt to provide repose from—and indeed a slowing down of—the quick pace of life. Practicing worship not only required making time, but also allowed for a particular quality of time, characterized by deceleration and contemplation, inner peace, and, in Mustafa's words, a "traveling toward God." It was experienced as a time-out from the continuous flow of events, influences, and incentives in everyday life.

The social conditions of fast capitalism, then, not only constrained but also gave a new impetus to these young people's religious engagement. Religious and capitalist aspirations and rhythms were not merely opposed, but rather dialectically related and productive of a particular kind of religious engagement in which the tranquility offered by worship was emphasized. This dynamic played out in similar ways for the young Muslims and Christians, who faced the common challenge of putting their ambitions of religious commitment to practice in a fast capitalist context.

What does this emphasis on tranquility say about my interlocutors' understanding of worship? The value they put on deceleration could, to some extent, be interpreted as a kind of secularization of religious practice. These young believers' search for tranquility through prayer resonates with desires for "slowing down life" (*onthaasten* in Dutch) that are more widely shared in society, particularly among the (upper) middle classes—captured by such concepts as "slow food" (Petrini 2003) and "slow tourism" (Fullagar, Markwell, and Wilson 2012). In this regard, the role that prayer played for my interlocutors seems to resemble the role that mindfulness, wellness retreats, or going on a hike plays for others. It is notable in this regard that my interlocutors occasionally compared their prayer practices to non-religious activities such as playing soccer (Ahmet) or seeing a psychologist (Frank). Moreover, if interpreted skeptically, their worship practices could be seen to provide only snippets of release from the quick pace of life, while these practices are subsumed in the fast capitalist economy as yet another activity that needs to be "squeezed in." In such a reading, religion too becomes incorporated in a temporality of "accelerating turnover time" (Harvey 1989, 291).

At the same time, however, these young believers' practices of worship did also entail an ethics and a realm of experience that potentially allowed them to move beyond the conditions of fast capitalism. For both the Muslims and the Christians, prayer provided not merely a snippet of release from their hurried lives, but also the cultivation of a sense of closeness to—and dependence on—God. This importantly entailed alternative modes of experiencing and structuring time. As Mustafa's notion of "traveling toward God" suggests, prayer involved attempts at moving beyond the very organization of space and time dominating their everyday lives in today's capitalist society. Besides, deceleration itself can be a significant and even political act. Ben Agger, building on Marcuse's analysis of the decline of critical thought in advanced industrial societies, argues that in today's fast capitalist society "people's lives are so accelerated that they cannot slow down sufficiently to take stock let alone begin to change things" (2004, 132). In this regard, engaging in day-to-day religious practices that decelerate the pace of life could be one way of enabling alternative visions on how to lead one's life and how to organize society. Daily "quiet times" and a weekly day of rest for the young Christians and, even more perhaps, the five-daily *salat* for the young Muslims can be seen as activities that puncture prevalent secular rhythms and counter the structures of time under conditions of contemporary capitalism.[6]

Yet the young people I worked with felt that the desired ethical and spiritual effects of worship could only be realized if its practice became an integral and habitual part of their everyday lives—and one on which they invested sufficient time and concentration. It was here that they often felt to be falling short. Time and again, the practice of worship appeared to be "slipping away" in their day-to-day lives. For these young believers, religious commitment was a perpetually incomplete project that required ongoing work and investment. Their practices of worship were part and parcel of such ongoing moral and spiritual labor, aimed at becoming closer to God. In that way, prayers and other worship practices not only gained a renewed significance under conditions of fast capitalism, but also constituted attempts at coming to terms with self-perceived imperfections and inadequacies, without ever fully solving them.

6

Distraction, Habituation, and Closeness to God

In one of the meetings of the men's club of Pilgrim Students in which I participated, Paul, who was given the task of leading the twenty-five or so young men of the club in spiritual matters, showed a fragment of the television program *Op zoek naar God* ("In search of God"). This show, broadcasted by the Dutch evangelical broadcasting company (*Evangelische Omroep*), invited and followed Dutch celebrities or media personalities on a quest for God. The fragment featured the DJ and judo champion Dennis van der Geest, who turned out to be frustrated in his quest. He felt he had already given it everything he got, but so far God hadn't given any "feedback." And without any "response" from God, he found it very difficult to "make it real." After showing this fragment, Paul commented that Dennis's despair was recognizable, even for Christians. Following God entailed "a degree of spiritual discipline" (*een stukje geestelijke discipline*). God's grace is there for everybody, "but it doesn't come by itself" (*komt niet aanwaaien*). It involves making "conscious choices." Paul doubted whether Dennis was making these choices. One cannot simply wait for faith to come by itself.

The following morning, Paul and I met for an interview in his flat, located in a diverse neighborhood of Rotterdam, which he shared with two other members of Pilgrim Students. As often happened, Paul had only gotten home from the student association during the early hours of the morning, and it took him a few cups of coffee to properly wake up. But this did not seem to make him any less articulate. When I invited him to elaborate on what he had called the need for spiritual discipline the night before, he readily pointed out that this aspect of discipline, which came down to "maintaining one's relationship with God," turned out to be a "very difficult" task and a "weak spot" among the club members. To explain this, Paul pointed to the continuous distractions from faith that Christians like themselves encountered in their everyday lives:

> So around us there are all kinds of means like that: music, television, internet, which continuously distract you and which also engage you at a very low level [*op*

een heel laag niveau insteken]. ... So when you have to choose between reading a book and switching on the television, uhm, then we choose for the most fleeting [*vluchtig*], so then it's television. ... Also your phone that rings ten times a day, or twenty times... Yes, e-mail... all things that distract. ... So if you have to choose, like, well, I'm going to find God or watch TV, then watching TV is very easy and finding God, reading the Bible, something much more demanding. ... The 'entry level' is high to put it that way.

It was precisely because one received "so many stimuli throughout the day," Paul said, that living a life of faith required a "very conscious choice" and did not "come by itself," especially, he pointed out, in a prosperous and media-saturated society like the Netherlands.

This sense of being continuously distracted from faith was widely shared among both my Christian and Muslim interlocutors. The distractions were seen to derive especially from mass media, popular culture, and digital media technologies. Both the young Christians and Muslims actively engaged with these realms of modern media in their everyday lives. Like other young people in the Netherlands, they were assiduous consumers of music, films, television series, social media, and media technologies. In this chapter, I continue my inquiry into the practical and routine challenges my interlocutors faced in their pursuits of faith by analyzing the ways in which they experienced such mass media and mass-mediated popular culture as both appealing and distractive. I demonstrate that they shared the feelings of distraction that are widespread in today's digitalized and accelerated society, but re-signified these in a markedly religious register. Distraction, for them, meant being drawn away from God.

The theme of religion and media has received much attention in the literature.[1] Many scholars in this area have focused on the appropriation of modern mass media by contemporary religious movements. They argue that these manifestations of modern culture are not incompatible with religion, but rather productively adopted by religious movements as tools of religious communication, instruction, proselytization, and cultivation (e.g., Hirschkind 2006; De Witte 2009; Schulz 2012; Stolow 2012; Meyer 2015). The young Muslims and Christians with whom I worked also made extensive use of modern mass media in their religious pursuits. Yet I was struck by their close engagement with the wider fields of mass media and popular culture that can be described as secular in the sense that they are not produced and disseminated by religious groups and usually do not convey religiously inspired messages, images, or sounds. This aspect of religious subjects' media use has received less attention in the literature. An important exception is Stewart Hoover's (2006) examination of the pervasiveness of secular media in American Christian evangelical households. He notes that self-identified "born-again" Christians tend to accept the presence of these media as a "fact of life" (2006, 266) and "live more on the 'secular' media map than they live separately from it" (165). In Hoover's interviews, "religious television never rose to the surface as the kind of interesting, attractive, or meaningful programming that even the Evangelicals found in 'secular' media" (274).

In this chapter, I aim to further develop the analysis of the often central place of this broader media landscape in religious people's everyday lives (cf. Oosterbaan 2017, chap. 6). Looking at the ubiquity and appeal of mainstream media and popular culture among my interlocutors in the Netherlands, I show that their stances on these were characterized by a marked ambivalence. They were strongly attracted to popular television programs, movies, and music, while also apprehensive of the felt threats these posed to their faith. At the same time, I demonstrate that these threats stimulated them to invest actively in their faith. Since, for my interlocutors, faith entailed a strong relation with God in everyday life, it required constant work in the context of the ongoing stream of stimuli experienced as distractions from God. Such work entailed committing oneself to religious practices such as prayer, Bible reading, listening to Quran recitations, and attending sermons (notably, these often also implicated the use of modern media technologies). As anthropologists like Talal Asad (1993, 72–9) and Saba Mahmood (2001) have shown, these kinds of religious practices should be seen not merely as expressive but also as constitutive of faith. They are what Ruth Marshall, noting that "faith is an experience realized in action," calls "acts of faith" (2009, 146–7). What this chapter highlights is that such active work on faith does not take place in "empty space," but in particular socio-cultural contexts, such as the media-saturated worlds in which my Muslim and Christian interlocutors moved.

Muslims, Movies, and Music

A particularly evocative account of felt distraction was shared with me by Ismael, when he told me about his return to the Netherlands after he had performed the *umrah*, the non-compulsory pilgrimage to Mecca and Medina. As mentioned in the previous chapter, once back in the Netherlands, Ismael noticed that his *iman*, or faith, tended to "ebb." With regard to his arrival at Schiphol Airport in Amsterdam he said:

> I clearly remember that I, uhm, returned from Mecca and, yeah, on that moment your picture is... there you actually only see women with *niqab*, very many with *niqab*, with *burqa* that is,² and that becomes a normal picture. ... And then you come here. And I clearly remember that at Schiphol, you suddenly see a billboard with women in lingerie... That is quite a shock [*dan schrik je wel weer*]. ... So that really required adjusting.

For Ismael, the encounter with the billboard meant an involuntary confrontation with the world of advertisement and its sexually explicit images, which, he made clear to me, he experienced as a negative influence on his *iman*. He referred to this encounter not as an unusual incident but rather as an exemplary one for his ordinary life. It made him realize that he was back in the Netherlands, where "things are simply different." My Muslim interlocutors more often talked about distractions caused by their encounter with immediate temptations in public life, such as the sexually explicit images emanating from the worlds of consumerism and advertisement. Particularly the men I spoke with indicated sexual attraction as one of the major "tests" to their *iman*.

Even more commonly, these young Muslims referred to distractions resulting from everyday practices they regarded with less suspicion, such as internet use. To illustrate, the twenty-year-old Zainab, whom I met through the student association An-Nur in Rotterdam, told me that she did not recite from the Quran as much as she used to do some years ago. She blamed this on her own "slackness." She explained that it was much easier for her to take her laptop and open Facebook or YouTube. Hasan, who studied political science in Leiden, likewise recounted: "I'm at university, I have a one-hour break, I'm a bit tired, I'm on the internet, I have to look up a few things. But I can also go to [the prayer room at] the medical center, take a couple of moments to pray [*effe bidden*]." Hasan described such choices in terms of a fight with his *nafs*, which he defined as "the devil within yourself, the bad will within yourself."³ An important point here, which also came out of Paul's statement quoted above, is that using the internet, for example to visit Facebook, was felt by my interlocutors to be less demanding than practicing their religion. Moreover, the alternatives to worship practices were felt to be all-pervasive in their everyday lives. Thus, Fatima, who studied psychology in Rotterdam, told me that it is very difficult to maintain "a strong *iman*": "Because there are simply so many other things that you can do, there are so many other things that also occupy you, that it is simply *very* difficult to bring along that *one* feeling in everything you do."

At the same time, my Muslim interlocutors' internet use also reveals the extent to which they appropriated new media technologies within their religious endeavors. Internet took an integral place in the acquisition of religious knowledge, communication about religious events, and the sharing of ideas and religious inspiration between peers. My interlocutors used the internet extensively to update themselves about Islamic events, to download Islamic talks, sermons, and Quran recitations, and to look up religious information. In addition, many shared thoughts, observations, Quran verses, *hadith*, and so forth on Facebook. They also occasionally participated in Islamic web forums.[4]

Yet, both online and offline, these young Muslims encountered and participated in a wider field of popular culture, media, consumption, and entertainment in their everyday lives, which was not religiously coded and which frequently ran counter to their aspirations to piety. Indeed, they generally did not shy away from, but rather embraced, the wide and constantly renewed offer of goods, movies, television, and music. When I asked Aisha, a law student I had met at An-Nur, about her hobbies, she replied: going to town, going shopping (laughingly: "what girls do"), hanging out with her friends, going out for dinner, and going to the movies. She told me that Quintin Tarantino's *Kill Bill* (2003/2004) was one of her favorite movies. When we met she had recently gone to see *True Grit* (2010), by Ethan and Joel Coen, "a bit of a tedious movie [*slome film*], but it does briefly take you out of the world, into that world for a moment." At home she likes to relax by watching TV, "not having to think." She watched comedy series (even though "you don't get anything out of these in the end") and, like many of my Muslim interlocutors did, Dutch talk shows that were popular at the time, such as *Pauw & Witteman* and *De wereld draait door*. While not all of my Muslim interlocutors pronounced their enthusiasm for television and movies as strongly as Aisha did, most shared her close familiarity and engagement with this kind of popular culture.

Their stances toward such forms of popular culture were however characterized by ambivalence. While these young Muslims enjoyed watching television and going to the movies, they were also apprehensive of the perceived moral dangers of these activities. As Aisha put it, while going to the movies is "fun," it does make you "forget why you're actually here." She felt that it could distract her from a consciously lived faith and from staying tuned to her goal in life. That "higher goal," which she "easily lost sight of," was making it to Paradise in the afterlife. Like the Brazilian Pentecostals who watch "sinful" popular television shows in Martijn Oosterbaan's ethnography (2017, chap. 6), the stance of my

Muslim interlocutors on music and movies can be characterized by "a dynamic of attraction and rejection" (2017, 178): attraction to the enjoyment and relaxation offered, combined with rejection of the sinful, impure or inappropriate content often involved. The way Aisha talked about going to the movies is instructive in this regard: she both liked the fact that it took her out of her ordinary world *and* she worried that it made her forget her true goal in life. Differently put, the distraction emanating from this kind of popular culture was both embraced and mistrusted by young Muslims like her.

This ambivalence was expressed most clearly among my Muslim interlocutors with respect to music. While many of them frequently listened to music, most agreed that listening to music including instrumental sound (in contrast to unaccompanied vocal music, or *anasheed*) is prohibited in Islam. This view was informed by their strict interpretation of Islamic doctrine, representing one of a large variety of approaches to music among Muslims.[5] The young Muslims I worked with linked this prohibition to the perceived corrosive effects of music on one's faith. This issue came up among my female interlocutors especially. Asked how she felt about listening to music, Fatima told me:

> So difficult. I listen to music. I really listen to all kinds. … Sometimes I'm listening and then I think: oh, this is actually really not good for me. Because recent songs especially are so much sex related… . The latest artist that I had that feeling with was, [in a matter-of-fact tone:] yes actually Justin Timberlake, and uhm… Enrique Iglesias. I really like both of them, I think they have good music. But lately their songs are also so much… wrong actually, that you, yeah, should actually make a choice in that respect. But the temptations are great and I do it [laughs].

Fatima added that she found this kind of music inappropriate because it wasn't "pure" (*rein*) and because it had a "bad influence" on her *iman*. Nonetheless, because she "simply liked" it, she couldn't get herself to stop listening to it.

Strikingly, the dangers of listening to music were often described in terms of habituation and sense perception. Zainab, for example, noted:

> The more you listen to music, the more difficult the Quran uhm… comes into your ears. You notice that. I notice it in the case of my younger sister, because you could mistake her for a DJ. She has all sorts of music and dancing and… But when she hears the Quran she goes: "no, Ahmed [their younger brother, whom Zainab described as very committed to Islam], turn it down, I don't want it!" It is as if she feels guilty. The more music you listen, the further away you move from faith.

Here, Zainab described the danger of music not so much in terms of the content of the lyrics, but rather in terms of embodied habituation: one's sense of hearing becomes attuned to a different register (I will elaborate on this issue in the next section). For many of my Muslim interlocutors, listening to popular music had become a habit that was difficult to abandon. As Khadija, a nineteen-year-old student in Rotterdam, put it: "I don't know how many times I've really removed all my music from my iPod and thought like: 'well, today it's the last day'. And then, well, tomorrow [I listen to it] again [laughs]."

While music was a recurrent concern when it came to temptations, some of the young women quoted above remarked that listening to music was not a major wrongdoing. The laughter that frequently accompanied their statements about music illustrates this. It did not feel like committing "a very bad sin," Zainab told me. "You're only human." As Fatima noted: "I find it more important that you're for example good and perform your prayers. ... I also think like, I don't know, I've grown up with it." Khadija, by contrast, was stricter with herself. She said she wanted to get rid of her sins, like listening to music, rather than merely thinking, as she put it, "bad [*foei*], Khadija." But this was difficult for her precisely because listening to music, like shaking hands with a man, was something she had gotten used to.

Incidentally, the issues of shaking hands and sitting in a closed room with a man often came up in my interviews with young Muslim women, as most of these took place in rooms at university.[6] While they generally regarded both issues as prohibited or at least inadvisable from an Islamic point of view, they told me that they often treated these norms in flexible and pragmatic ways. Reflecting on this, Khadija noted:

> These are small examples that, like, I actually take for granted now, that creep in so much that you no longer know that it is a sin, or at least no longer even see that it is a sin, because it's so self-evident in the Western world.

Thus, Khadija suggested that habituation to what she regarded as non-Islamic practices as a result of living in a predominantly non-Islamic society could make young believers like herself overlook the fact that these were, in the end, sinful practices.

Those who continued to listen to music developed a couple of ways to respond to, or deal with, their indulgence in this "small sin." First, abandoning music was approached as part of a personal process of religious development. Those who still listened to music often told me that they were "not yet" strong enough to stop doing so. Similarly to what David Kloos has shown for villagers in Aceh,

Indonesia, religious imperfection is approached here less as an obstruction to faith than as part of an "ongoing, personalized and future-oriented process of ethical formation" (2018b, 102). Likewise, Zainab remarked to me that her sins, like watching MTV, show that her *iman* is "weak." She could nonetheless try to make her *iman* stronger by setting the intention to abstain from these perceived sinful practices for longer periods of time and by, when she did give in to them, "feeling bad about it and directly changing channels." In such ways, she said, she could "build it up."

Second, some of my interlocutors sought to practically regulate their exposure to the perceived malevolent influences of popular cultural forms such as music. Aisha, for instance, had made the resolution to stop listening to music altogether, but she still sometimes watched new video clips of artists she liked. "But then I try to put the music down," she said laughingly. When it came to watching movies, Aisha recounted that during scenes containing explicit sexuality she usually changed channels or, in cinemas, closed her eyes or turned to look at her friend. Through such "pious micro-practices" (Jouili 2009), these young adults sought to mitigate the negative impact of particular sounds or images. This suggests that religious self-fashioning may include not only particular "ways of looking," which are cultivated within specific aesthetic religious traditions (Meyer 2006, 303; cf. Morgan 1998, 3), but also acts of *not* looking, of closing one's eyes, or looking away at the right moments (Meyer 2015, 146–9; Oosterbaan 2017, 193–7). The temptations produced by movies, music, and other mediated forms of popular culture, then, not only brought about distraction from faith, but also offered opportunities to affirm one's faith by giving shape to a pious response. As occasionally noted in the Islamic talks I attended during my fieldwork, the dangers posed by temptations are also chances to, as one Salafi preacher at a youth conference in The Hague put it, "adorn oneself with Islamic behavior."

Christians, Mediated Popular Culture, and the "Antennas to God"

My Christian interlocutors expressed similar anxieties about everyday distractions. Within the student associations, and in their conversations with me, they often discussed the risks of being drawn away from God as a result of their engagements with the affairs of "the world," as they often put it. Like the Muslims, they strongly related such distraction to the pervasiveness of mass media and (new) media technologies in their everyday lives. Many of the young Christians told me that they found it difficult to keep focused on their faith in the context of the profusion of things that asked their attention: not only friends, social contacts, study, and work, but also television, movies, music, and the internet. With the widespread use of new digital devices, the internet had become a pervasive influence in their everyday lives. Johan, a member of Pilgrim Students in Rotterdam, characterized the internet as "deadly" because of the amount of time it consumed, especially when it came to social media like Facebook and Twitter. The internet, he said, "really occupies your whole life."

Like my Muslim interlocutors, however, these young Christians also adopted (new) media technologies and popular culture in their religious endeavors. Among other things, they listened to evangelical worship songs on CDs or YouTube, occasionally watched sermons online, and searched information on the internet to prepare for small group meetings.[7] Such involvement with media and popular culture has often been highlighted in studies of contemporary Christianity, and the evangelical movement in particular (e.g., Shibley 1996; Miller 1997; Roeland 2009; Luhrmann 2012b). Mark Shibley has in this regard argued that contemporary evangelicalism in the United States should be seen as "a world-affirming faith" (1998, 69), a phrase that runs counter to the (Weberian) association of Protestant Christianity with worldly avoidance. Shibley points out that contemporary evangelicalism "fits comfortably with many aspects of popular culture" (1998, 72).

Yet my Christian interlocutors' stance on popular culture and media was marked not only by affirmation, but also by ambivalence and caution. The Christians I met were often wary of what they regarded as the tempting or evil aspects of TV programs, movies, music, and advertisement, which included explicit sexual content, the promotion of materialism, and references to the occult. Many of them had grown up in Christian communities in which mass media and popular culture were, and still are, looked upon with a fair amount of suspicion (cf. Roeland 2009, 189–90). And many had grown up in families without televisions—or with televisions that only received the non-commercial, public service broadcasting channels—and with a lock on the internet to prevent children's exposure to perceived malevolent material. This upbringing, which was in many instances reinforced within the social religious spaces in which these young Christians moved as young adults, contributed to something of an "in-built" watchfulness regarding secular popular culture. This was expressed particularly strongly with regard to pornography and other sexually explicit material.

Accordingly, while consumption, mass media, and popular culture were part and parcel of these young Christians' everyday lives, their engagement with these fields was characterized by constant moral negotiations. To illustrate, Rachel, who spoke about her faith "slipping away" in the previous chapter, told me that she often watched the TV series *Desperate Housewives*. While she enjoyed watching such—as she put it—"nonsense," she also noted that the "emptiness" of this series could have a negative influence on her, making her feel "less holy." At the same time, she distinguished *Desperate Housewives* from such series as *The Bold and the Beautiful* and *As the World Turns*, which, she noted, were replete with "treason and blackmailing" and which she simply found "re-pul-sive." She also regularly watched movies with her boyfriend and his flatmates (all Christians). When a film didn't "feel right," for example because it featured ghosts, she would "take a stance" and tell the others she didn't feel comfortable about it. She told me that she would not want to watch a horror movie like *House of Wax* (2005), because it was "clearly not of God." She would however watch *The Sixth Sense* (1999) because, although it is a movie about ghosts, she thought it was "very good." While watching pornographic movies was "out of the question" at the student-flat, Rachel noted that sex features in most movies and is therefore hard to avoid. They had recently watched *Shame* (2011), a movie about sexual addiction, which she liked. It featured "lots of sex, bordering porn," but this "served a purpose." During one scene, which was "pretty intense," she and her boyfriend "partly looked away" or, rather, "watched half-heartedly [*halfslachtig*]." Like some of my other Christian interlocutors, Rachel expressed an intricate "ethics of watching television" (Bakker 2007). Birgit Meyer defines such an ethics of watching among Pentecostals in Ghana as a "moral exercise" by which spectators negotiate "the modality of their own receptivity and moral personhood" (Meyer 2015, 148). For Rachel, this ethical practice was based on criteria of not only religious appropriateness but also artistic quality.

Many of the Christians with whom I worked also felt ambivalent about listening to music. While they neither rejected music altogether nor considered it to be prohibited in Christianity, they were generally cautious about the kind of music they listened to and how frequently they did so. Isabel, the recent convert to Christianity to whom I referred earlier, described herself as a big fan of music, particularly of hip-hop, R&B and dancehall. After her conversion, she was relieved to find out that there was very good Christian music in these genres. She removed all of her, as she put it, "secular music" from her phone and only kept music "about God." She contrasted this Christian music with the "plain devil worship" and "glorification" of sex, power, and money that she heard when she went clubbing. She did nevertheless—though less frequently than before—continue to go clubbing and watch MTV at times, because, she pointed out, she did not want to completely isolate herself from people who did not believe.

My Christian interlocutors, then, were wary of exposing themselves to music, movies, and television programs they regarded as harmful or irreconcilable to their religious convictions. This often involved personal struggles when it came to abstaining from downloading songs and music videos, listening to the radio, or watching a movie. Even if not necessarily sinful, the melodies of a song, images from a movie, or narratives of a TV series risked pushing their thoughts away from God and weakening the focus on their faith. Thus, similar to my Muslim interlocutors, their stance on consuming such forms of popular culture was characterized by both rejection and attraction. They themselves often connected this to the classic Protestant maxim of being "in the world" but not "of the world" (cf. Stoffels 1995, 106). Rachel, having noted that it is not always good to watch movies about ghosts, added that she also did not want to be "out of touch with the world" (*wereldvreemd zijn*).

Yet some of my interlocutors with a strictly orthodox Protestant background put the emphasis on the second part of the maxim: "not being of the world." For example, Ruth, the student in commercial economy introduced in the previous chapter, said:

> God also asks Christians to be, in a way, strangers on earth [*God vraagt ook een bepaald vreemdelingschap van christenen op aarde*]. And I think that it is good to simply, uhm, let go of certain things that can very much occupy you, that give a highest place to music rather than to God.

Vreemdelingschap, or being a stranger, is a familiar, Bible-based concept in the vocabulary of Dutch Protestants, particularly within strictly orthodox church communities.[8] For these Calvinist Protestants, similarly to what Susan Harding has shown for evangelical Christians in the United States, the aspiration to being "a stranger on earth" inspires "little rites" of "interlacing virtually every step they [make] into the world with ways of staying out of the world" (2000, 151). In different ways and to different extents, the young Christians I met engaged in similar practices of separation, while also continuing to participate in "the world."

Similarly to my Muslim interlocutors, the felt risks of popular culture and mass media were not only understood to be determined by their particular content. Rather, the young Christians regarded the time and attention demanded by various media and forms of popular culture as a problem in and by themselves, because these tended to displace the salience of faith in their everyday lives. Thus Paul, whom I quoted at the beginning of the chapter, described television, music, and the internet as "things that grab your attention [*aandachtstrekkers*]." Rachel similarly said: "You are al-ways *more* inclined to check your mail, or to go on your Facebook—and I'm not even a Facebook freak—or to watch a series. That's short-term effect, nice. To go and read [the Bible] is different, difficult." Rachel's use of the term "inclined" (*geneigd*) is important here. It points to the embodied dispositions she had developed in the context of today's media-saturated society (Hepp 2013), which made it "natural" for her to open her laptop to check her e-mail or to turn on the television. The young Christians commonly shared a *habitus* (Bourdieu 1977, 82–3) that is attuned to the worlds of entertainment, consumption, and new media. While praying and reading the Bible were also significant parts of their everyday lives, many felt that these tended to come less naturally and required more self-conscious effort.

Importantly, Rachel pointed out that her engagement with (new) media and other, as she put it, "profane" (*aardse*) stimuli, risked not only supplanting her engagement with faith, but also making it more difficult for her to relate to God. Parallel to Zainab's remarks about listening to the Quran, she pointed to the dangers of media in terms of habituation and sense perception. Referring to a book she had read by the preacher and former evangelical TV presenter Henk Binnendijk, she said:

> No wonder that you don't experience God, that your spiritual [*geestelijk*] life is dead. That's just because your antennas are not at all directed at God, but at all the profane stimuli and things that are fun here. ... Yes, I simply always compare it to a relationship between two people. If I'm continuously on my phone, do you think the other will be happy about that? If I'm in a restaurant with [my boyfriend] and if he's constantly busy with his [phone]. That would also completely piss you off wouldn't it? Then I also wouldn't be able to reach him anymore right? That's exactly the same thing.

The metaphor of one's antennas to God implies that one's faculties of perception should be, as it were, attuned to the particular frequency on which the divine can be received (Oosterbaan 2017, chap. 5). As Binnendijk (2008, 78) puts it: "The intoxication [*roes*] in our heads is so great, that it becomes hard to find peace [*tot rust komen*]. We squander our antenna to heaven and can no longer make out God's voice [*God verstaan*]."

"Making out God's voice" required a particular embodied receptivity, which can be realized by a training and honing of one's senses (cf. Hirschkind 2006). For Binnendijk and for young Christians like Rachel, the stimuli of modern media were understood to have the *adverse effect* of attuning the senses away from "heaven's frequency," making one disposed to perceiving the sounds and sights of these media (most of which were seen by my interlocutors as "non-Christian"), rather than perceiving the voice of God. Zainab's observation that listening to music made it more difficult for the Quran to "come into your ears" points to a very similar dynamic.

The Christians with whom I worked often described the way God manifested Himself in terms of a voice that one needed to be able to discern and listen to (cf. Luhrmann 2012b, 39–71). Hearing this voice required some effort. My interlocutors typically characterized it as "soft and subtle," as opposed to the loud noise of modern media and advertisement—domains in which they understood the devil to be at work. Their reflections on the overpowering loudness of modern media and consumption reflect the strongly felt presence of these realms in my Christian interlocutors' everyday lives. The internet, television, consumption, and advertisement were inescapably part of the social world they inhabited. They felt that the presence of God in their everyday lives was, effectively, less inescapable. If they were not alert and did not invest in their faith, but got carried away by "worldly" affairs, the subtle voice of God could easily be outcried by the many stimuli in contemporary Dutch society. In this way, Rachel told me, one could even "remove" God from one's life.

Yet if one allowed God to play a role in one's life, my interlocutors believed, this could be a fulfilling experience. The low "volume" of God's voice should not be taken to signify a lack of divine power. Instead, it might indicate the way in which God was understood to transcend this world and its cacophony of sounds and sights, connecting believers with a source of fullness (Taylor 2007) beyond the scattered experiences of everyday life. As the twentieth-century theologian Paul Tillich put it: "Religion opens up the depth of man's spiritual life which is usually covered by the dust of our daily life and the noise of our secular work" (1959, 9).

Distraction as Being Drawn away from God

More often than not, my Muslim and Christian interlocutors experienced using the internet, watching television, going to the movies, or listening to music, as well as being confronted by—especially sexually explicit—advertisements as *distractions* from the concentration on faith to which they aspired. Such distractions were omnipresent in their everyday lives in contemporary Dutch society, where they were enveloped—and attracted—by the recurrent impulses and stimuli of popular culture, entertainment, and consumption.

Arguably, the intensity of such everyday distractions has strongly increased in today's high capitalist society. Important reasons for this are the dynamics of acceleration and the onset of the digital revolution described in the previous chapter. Consumption, including that of mass-mediated popular culture, has become increasingly ubiquitous (Agger 2004; Bauman 2005; Lury 2011). At the same time, the break-through of the internet and the continuous introduction of new digital technologies and devices have made information and entertainment increasingly accessible, while also allowing people to obtain these in the privacy not only of their homes but also of their personal electronic devices. In her review of the ethnographic literature on digital media, E. Gabriella Coleman notes that "in some instances, digital media have extended their reach into the mundane heart of everyday life" (2010, 488). This was true for most of my interlocutors, for whom e-mailing, visiting websites, texting, chatting, and using Facebook were integral and self-evident parts of their day-to-day lives. They generally did not consider these media as immoral in and by themselves—and, indeed, they often also integrated them in their religious endeavors. Yet their accounts are replete with a sense of anxiety about the ways in which their extensive use of modern media, and their consumption of popular culture, tended to constrain the time and energy devoted to their faith in their everyday lives, and to pull them away from God.

Distraction, in the sense of a disintegration of attention, has today become a widespread concern (North 2012; Lovink 2013). This perceived crisis of attention has a striking precursor in the early twentieth century. As Carolin Duttlinger (2007, 33) notes: "Today's digital culture has its equivalent in the early twentieth-century media revolution triggered by innovations in photography, radio, and film." Thus, writing in 1903, Georg Simmel (1950, 410) already identified the "intensification of nervous stimulation" as a distinguishing mark of modern urban life, as opposed to small town and rural life. Around the 1930s, theorists associated with the Frankfurt school—most notably Siegfried Kracauer, Walter Benjamin, and Theodor W. Adorno—identified distraction (*Zerstreuung*) as a characteristic experience and mode of perception of the modern subject. They pointed out that in modern culture, and particularly in the growing world of mass entertainment, "the subject was exposed to a heterogeneous succession of heterogeneous stimuli and impressions that defied mental synthesis" (Duttlinger 2007, 33). Siegfried Kracauer described the Berliner picture houses as "palaces of distraction" (*Paläste der Zerstreuung*) that "[assault] every one of the senses using every possible means" (1995, 323–4). Walter Benjamin similarly viewed distraction as "mentally numbing," but he also argued that the "constant, sudden change" of cinematic images elicited a particular mode of apperception among spectators: "reception in a state of distraction" (Benjamin 2007, 238–40), which trained the senses "to take in the stimuli of modern life in a casual, detached state of distraction" (Duttlinger 2007, 42).

The German *Zerstreuung* translates into English not only as "distraction," but also as "dispersal," "dissemination," or "scattering." This points to the spatial and dynamic connotations of the term (Weber 1996, 92; Rutsky 2002, 284). In fact, the English verb "distract," which derives from the Latin *distrahere* (to draw in different directions, to pull asunder), carries similar connotations. It includes such meanings as to draw away from actual purpose, to divert, and to divide attention (*Oxford English Dictionary*).

In today's fast-paced and digitalized culture, these dynamics of distraction have intensified. As media theorist Petra Löffler notes: "Distraction has become normalised now that network society has taken command" (in Lovink 2013, 548). R. L. Rutsky points to the "pop-up effect" created by the dispersive tendency of contemporary media and information culture: "As ever more texts and media forms become linked or popped, as meta-information proliferates, we often feel ourselves overwhelmed by the information that continually pops up around us, caught up in its unpredictable movements" (2002, 288). This pop-up effect is all the more strengthened by a pervasive consumer culture characterized by an emphasis on instant gratification and by a rapid turnover of consumer goods, including forms of popular culture and entertainment (see Chapter 5).

Notably, my Muslim and Christian interlocutors re-signified these familiar experiences of distraction within the framework of their reflection on personal faith. In their view, the everyday stimuli of popular culture, entertainment, and (digital) media distracted them—indeed, drew them away—from the concentration on faith to which they aspired, and thus from a strong engagement with God in their everyday lives. Distraction (*afleiding* in Dutch), a term the young Muslims and especially the young Christians regularly used themselves, denoted not only absentmindedness or lack of concentration for them, but also a diversion, a movement away from God. Indeed, their distracted engagement with television, music, films, e-mail, Facebook, and so on was seen to generate a distance between themselves and God. These stimuli were experienced as an almost physical pull, drawing them away from a strong engagement with God. The young Christians, particularly, talked explicitly about the ways in which music or films "kept" or "drew" them away from God.

Different from the challenges to faith discussed in Chapter 4, this movement away from God resulted not so much from intellectual doubt as from my Muslim and Christian interlocutors' day-to-day, routinized use of media and consumption of popular culture. Because of the constant lure and the modalities of instant gratification and "fast time" of mass media and secular popular culture, these tended to take an important place in my interlocutors' everyday lives, thereby compromising—they felt—their commitment to God. Although they sought to regulate their exposure to particular images and sounds, my interlocutors shared a habitual mode of perception that was adapted to the dispersed sensory stimuli they encountered in their everyday lives. They believed, however, that their religious pursuits required a focused attentiveness and receptiveness to God. Differently put, the lure of a *general* surrender to the multiple, scattered stimuli of "the world" jeopardized their aim of a *specific* surrender to God. I will now turn to their attempts at strengthening their faith in the light of their everyday experience of distraction.

Nourishing Faith, Drawing Close to God

The young Christians with whom I worked emphasized the need to constantly "invest" in, and thereby "nourish," their faith. To illustrate, Jantine, who had studied in Ede and now lived with her husband in the rural village in which she had grown up, tried to keep her faith "strong" by reading the Bible and praying each morning. When she "forgot [to do so] for some time," she got "far less nourishment [*voeding*]." Rachel noted that "to have faith" (*geloven*) is no "child's play." While you do "get it for free," you need to "keep on nourishing [*voeden*] it." Such nourishment includes reading the Bible, praying, listening to the sermon on Sunday, and talking to people about faith. Isabel told me that on some Sundays she got so much "spiritual nourishment" (*geestelijke voeding*) from her church that she didn't get hungry until the evening, even if she hadn't eaten anything the whole day. Going to church, she said, gave "a boost to your life of faith." The much-used term *opbouwen* ("edify" or "build up") among my Christian interlocutors, which referred to the experience of being formed in one's faith, reflects the emphasis on spiritual nourishment. Conversely, I was often told that not practicing one's religion brought about a feeling of "emptiness" (*leegte*), which was also talked about in terms of restlessness or a lack of energy or motivation. As Adam, a student in pastoral theology in Ede, put it: "It simply starts to itch, ... it feels strange, it feels, you're missing something." Rachel likewise noted that before she began to consistently pray in the morning she felt that her life "wasn't quite complete, something was simply missing."

These young Christians typically envisioned faith as a *relationship* with God. Just as one needs to actively maintain one's relationship with a friend or a partner by investing in it and making time for it, so one needs to devote oneself to one's relationship with God. The words of Sarah, who attended an evangelical congregation in Rotterdam, offer a good illustration of this:

> Of course, when you become less involved [*minder d'rmee bezig gaat*], or when you think on Sunday "oh well, I will sleep in" ..., or never pray anymore or never read the Bible anymore, yes, than how can God still speak? Because you don't have that whole relationship with Him. That's also gone. Just like a friend you haven't spoken to for two years, [laughingly:] you also don't know how he's doing, what has happened in the meantime. It's the same with God. You do actually have to talk with Him or listen to Him and become conscious that He's there. Only then that relationship can grow.

As Sarah suggested here, Christians needed to cultivate an awareness of God's presence in their everyday lives. Recall also Rachel's comparison between not being attuned to God because one is occupied with the "things of the world" and not being able to reach one's boyfriend because he is constantly checking his phone. It is striking that Rachel noted that these two things are "exactly the same." Apart from this, the personal character of one's relationship with God was deemed to be important. Jantine, for example, told me that in the evenings she and her husband read the Bible and prayed together, but in the mornings they both did so by themselves. "Because," she said, "we do find it important that we both keep our own personal relationship with God and continue to grow in it."

What a strong faith and relationship with God were understood to accomplish was the experience of *being close to God*. Time and again, my interlocutors emphasized this goal, which they phrased as "living with God," "walking with God," or "remaining close to God." It was understood to be enabled by nourishing the self with prayers, Bible texts, and sermons, and it was seen to shape the ways in which one acted in the world. This points to what Asad analyzed as the constitutive work of ritual practice, that is, the ways in which "systematic practices" can be seen to create and maintain "particular moral dispositions and capacities" (1993, 65). As Isabel, who converted to evangelical Christianity, put it:

> The way I would like to see it is that I'm really working toward growing closer to God everyday day, and that by doing that, uhm …, that I, from within [*uit mezelf*], or in any case that it becomes more normal that I, uhm, don't kind of do bad things. So through my relationship with God, and also the Spirit that dwells in me, that that is so strong, that I don't even think of going and gossiping, … or lying or whatever.

While not all of my Christian interlocutors would share Isabel's phrasing—particularly her reference to the Spirit dwelling in her, which was informed by her charismatic orientation—they did generally share the idea that having a strong relationship with God shaped their behavior, anchoring within them a Christian ethics that may eventually result in "naturally" staying away from sin.

Such an interiorization of a Christian ethics was an ideal that these Christians were working toward, without necessarily ever fully realizing it. Yet, in their day-to-day lives, they did experience how religious practices shaped their behavior in small but significant ways. During one of our small group meetings in Ede, for example, the group members shared their experience that when they made resolutions for the day during prayer, such as not "bad-mouthing" people, they would go through the day with more "awareness" as a result. Similarly, Esther, the young nurse from Rotterdam introduced earlier, noted that reading the Bible in the morning "sharpened" her, kept her "critical" of how she lived, and made that she did "not easily fall back into habits."

Sebastian, a student in medicine and member of Pilgrim Students, had visualized his aspiration to "be as close as possible to God" by painting a big blue spot on the wall of his student room. He had painted it during one of the weekly meetings he had with two friends to talk about faith. The point of Christianity, he explained, was not to stay "close enough" to God—represented by the blue spot—by following the rules and keeping to the law, while always remaining outside of Him. Rather, the point was that Jesus, through His redemption, brought people *in* that spot, "in God." The spot also reminded Sebastian that, as he put it, "whatever you do, you may come directly to God." He explained that he sometimes felt that when he had committed a sin, he couldn't "come to God":

> Because the sin was between me and God and I actually first wanted it to wear off before I came to God again, you know. As if you are too impure to come before God. Well, that's not possible. And it is also very dangerous, because

when you do that, you do not come to God for a while and, later, the desire to come to God will also decrease.

Here, Sebastian pointed out that the experience of closeness to God was fostered by continuously returning to God in prayer and repenting one's sins, while not doing so for a longer period of time had the exponential effect of further reducing the desire to pray and repent, thereby increasing one's distance from God.

For my Christian interlocutors, it was by committing oneself to religious practices that one could nourish one's faith, increasing one's receptivity to God and decreasing one's inclination to sin. Faith needed to be constantly "fed" in order to stay strong. While distractions were signified as impulses that eroded their faith and *drew them away* from God, religious practices were understood to strengthen their faith and *draw them closer* to God again. The strong concerns of these young Christians with "investing" in their religious practices, then, were closely related to their everyday experiences of being drawn away from God due to the distractions of mass-mediated popular culture.

Strengthening *Iman*, Cultivating Closeness to God

A similar dynamic was at play among my Muslim interlocutors. Like the Christians, they strongly emphasized the need to continuously work on one's faith. The "level" of one's personal faith, or *iman*, was an object of recurrent concern and discussion among them: faith was seen to be constantly fluctuating, or going through "ups and downs," as it was sometimes put.[9] They held that they could strengthen their *iman* by committing themselves to such religious practices as prayer, listening to Quran recitations, and attending Islamic talks or classes (cf. De Koning 2013, 79; Roex 2013, 238). Like my Christian interlocutors, the young Muslims sometimes noted that these religious practices gave a "boost" to their faith (*iman*). Their ideas about "keeping their *iman* strong" through this kind of active religious commitment carried a similar connotation to the Christian notion of "nourishment."

For the young Muslims I worked with, prayer constituted a crucial means of strengthening one's *iman*. As I noted in the previous chapter, praying several—and ideally at least five—times a day was seen to increase one's focus on God, protect the self against the temptations encountered in everyday life, and provide moments for self-reflection and for asking forgiveness. In a strikingly similar way to the young Christians, they described missing prayer in terms of feeling "empty" (*leeg*), either in the sense of missing out on a routine that had become part of their everyday lives and that was experienced to nourish one's self, or in the sense of missing an essential source of meaning in life.

Performing prayer was also understood to give shape to particular ethical dispositions that made one averse to sin. Idris, the student in Islamic Spiritual Care referred to earlier, explained: "The moment you want to commit, like, something that's wrong, it's already time for prayer again, so you have to come clean again with God [*in het reine komen met God*]." For my Muslim interlocutors, such a dispositional, "inbuilt" aversion to sin—the sign of a strong *iman*—could be cultivated by committing oneself actively to one's faith through prayer and religious study. At the same time, a strong *iman* required cultivating a sense of incongruence when committing sins. Zainab, a bachelor student in psychology, used the notion of cognitive dissonance to explain this: "It is, yes, theory of dissonance, so the moment you do something that goes against your faith, it leaves you with a bad feeling." And then "you want to compensate it by doing something good."

Idris related this longing for prayer directly to the tempting distractions he encountered in the "outside world":

> Look, on the streets, nowadays also in Morocco in fact, you simply see a lot of non-Islamic things. For example, uhm, you see a lot of nudity on the streets, on billboards too you know, lingerie advertisements, those kinds of things. … Well, looking at these, well, gets you sins, you're not allowed to look at them. And at some point, when you are outside for a long time, you've done so many of those things that you feel very heavy and dirty. Then you long for prayer to become clean again, to take it off of you again. You see. And then you really feel very good again.

This statement illustrates the way in which distractions do not only instigate a drawing away from God, but also encourage a renewed movement toward God through prayer.

Notably, the association Idris made between distraction from God and impurity on the one hand and closeness to God and purity on the other was recurrent among both my Muslim and Christian interlocutors. Among both groups, this sense of impurity pertained especially to sexual temptations. To return to my Christian interlocutors for a moment, Sebastian said he was "susceptible" to an "addictive" engagement with "sexuality," for example by "looking up videos on the internet." He noted that these videos "keep me away from God, make me dirty or something." Likewise, Judith, a pastoral theology student in Ede, told me that she often looked away from certain TV images she came across in public spaces, because she didn't want these to "soil" her "retina." Mustafa, a law student of Azerbaijani background, drew a contrast between the purity of Islam and the impurity of sin. He told me that he had had a girlfriend for more than one year and remarked that while they "of course abstained from [sexual] intercourse," he could still commit sins with her. "Islam is *so* pure," he said, "it's just like water, when you throw something in it, throw mud in it or something, you feel that straight away, it clouds [*vertroebelt*]. And your faith is like that too, it clouds easily." Mustafa said that he was particularly relieved from his sinful tendencies during the month of Ramadan. That month, he said, felt like "taking a shower": "Your dirtiness goes away, you become pure, spiritually pure."

Apart from prayer, my Muslim interlocutors also regarded frequenting Islamic classes and listening to recitations of the Quran as important means toward strengthening their *iman*, reducing their susceptibility to sin, and bringing them closer to God. Attending classes, by contrast to studying the religion at home, was valued because of the stimulus offered by collective study and the lack of distractions in a mosque or classroom setting. During one of his classes on the biography of the Prophet Muhammad, the youth imam Omar Khalil recounted to his audience that some people told him they were too busy to make time for his classes. He would say to them that "*one* lesson a week can make all the difference." Khalil pointed out that "when you go on the streets your *iman* weakens instantly, but if you come to lessons regularly you become steadfast." Classes were seen to provide a protection against everyday temptations and distractions, almost as a layer of faith between the believer and the distractive world "out there."

Yet activities geared toward strengthening one's *iman* could also take place while being out "on the streets," as the common practice of listening to Quran recitations makes clear. Musa, a student at a vocational university in Rotterdam and a professional kickboxer, told me that he regularly listened to Quran recitations on his MP3 player, in the car, or at home on his laptop, commenting: "If you start to constantly listen to these, then, uhm, you keep yourself under control.... How can I put it, it keeps you closer to God, you see?" Idris also told me that he had a sound file with the recitation of the entire Quran on his iPhone, so he could listen to it "everywhere." These examples confirm the point that modern media technologies not only brought about distractions from faith, but also provided means of (re-)adjusting a religious focus.

Religious practices such as listening to Quran recitations enabled these young Muslims to try and stay focused on God and to stay clear of—or indeed clean from—sin. Thus, Idris told me about his experience of listening to recitations while traveling to his university in the metro:

> It also gives me a feeling like: God is always with you, regardless of where you are, regardless of uhm anything. ... And it's just as if God is talking to me, like: Idris, you have to do so and so and if you do good you will end up here, and know the rights of men and the rights of such and such. So I am alert all the time, regarding everything I do. And when I listen to the Quran, I also have the feeling that my heart becomes softer, with respect to my fellow human beings also. ... When someone is rude to you, you will much less quickly react in a, uhm, harsh way, as you would perhaps normally do.

Listening to Quran recitations stimulated a disposition in Idris toward "being good" and "doing good," and toward being vigilant with regard to tempting distractions. His use of the term "alertness" is telling given its connotation of non-distractedness.

My Muslim interlocutors attached particular value to hearing Quranic verses on death and the Day of Judgment and to listening to preachers or teachers explain these verses. They occasionally pointed out to me that this helped them to "stay alert" or "stay awake," particularly when it came to the realization that one could die at any moment and that one should therefore not postpone breaking off one's sinful behavior (cf. Hirschkind 2006, 176). Listening to such verses was felt to stimulate a God-fearing disposition (*taqwa*) that raised one's awareness about the urgency of living a pious life (cf. Mahmood 2005, 140–5).

Similarly to my Christian interlocutors, for these young Muslims having a strong *iman*, or faith, entailed a feeling of proximity to God. They discussed this sense of proximity in terms of "having contact with God," "talking with God," or "being close to God." What they sought to accomplish through religious practices was the sense that God was nearby throughout their everyday lives. The aversion to sin and the disposition to do good that my Muslim interlocutors talked about were understood to be part and parcel of the condition of being close to God. They sought to bring this closeness to God, which they tended to experience most strongly on their prayer mats, into their everyday lives. As Yessin, a committee member of the student association An-Nur, once put it to me, he strove as much as possible to "remember Allah" in everything he did (a practice known as *dhikr* in Islamic theology).

Conclusion

The young Muslims and Christians I became acquainted with felt that the fields of mass media and secular popular culture posed a threat to their faith because of the ways these tended to become part and parcel of their everyday routines. Turning on the television, listening to music, and checking one's e-mail tended to be sheer habits, activities that by and large came natural to them. By contrast, religious activities were typically understood to be less inescapable, and to require more effort, as a result of which these continuously risked moving to the background of their everyday lives. Moreover, the engagement with media and popular culture was also seen to shape one's embodied dispositions, making one less receptive to God's word or voice. These young people strongly felt that, for a large part, the internet, social media, movies, music, and television distracted them, drew them away, from the concentration on faith to which they aspired, thereby creating a felt distance between themselves and God.

My interlocutors also appropriated (digital) media technologies within their religious endeavors. Indeed, they were not so much critical of these media technologies in and by themselves, as of particular ways of using them. Their religious adoption of media technologies, however, did not constitute the kind of mediatized religious environments that have been described in other contexts. Thus, in his study of cassette sermon audition in Egypt, Charles Hirschkind (2006) traces the contours of an "ethical soundscape" in the public sphere of Cairo. There, he notes, "the cassette sermon has become an omnipresent background of daily urban life" (2006, 2), constituting "a line of defense, infusing the car, the shop, the street, and the home with acoustic conditions" that encourage Islamic piety (185). Birgit Meyer has described a visual—and Pentecostal—counterpart to this, characterizing the public sphere in Ghana as replete with a Pentecostal "image economy," whereby Christian visual (as well as auditory) signs have come to pervade "the surface of social life" (2006, 294, 299).

The young Muslims and Christians with whom I worked did not lead their day-to-day lives within such public spheres suffused with religious aesthetics. The public worlds in which they moved—the streets, city centers, schools, work spaces, buses, and marketplaces—generally had little to offer by way of religious imagery or acoustics (Muslim sartorial practices form an exception here). Furthermore, the popular culture they encountered was commonly shaped less by religious than by secular forms, including popular television shows, top of the charts pop music, fashionable consumer goods, and box office movies. This is not to say that the Dutch public sphere is altogether devoid of perceivable Islamic and Christian markers, but rather that such markers—such as mosques and churches—take up a rather marginal place in the public worlds in which my interlocutors moved.[10] In these worlds, neither did Islamic sermons "infuse" the ordinary shop (cf. Hirschkind 2006, 185), nor did Christian bumper stickers decorate the average car (cf. Meyer 2006, 299). Rather, as the example of listening to Quran recitations on one's MP3 player illustrates, my interlocutors had to set themselves the task of actively integrating auditory and other religious forms in their personal lives and within their religious communities—often making use of (digital) media technologies.

Such self-conscious efforts at integrating religious forms and practices in everyday life point to the ways in which experiences of distraction play a crucial role in my interlocutors' pursuits of faith, despite—or perhaps rather because of— their felt effects of fragmentation and dispersal. These young people's antagonism toward listening to the radio, going to the movies, or watching music videos effectively enabled them to explicate—and pursue—their religious aspirations vis-à-vis these forms of popular culture. In other words, their very struggle with these distractive stimuli was part and parcel of their endeavors of crafting a faithful self. Moreover, they responded to the distractions they encountered by actively investing in religious practices, trying to make these practices an integral part of their everyday lives so as to reinforce their faith. This was understood to counter precisely the felt disruptive effects of everyday distractions in terms of (sensory) habituation and a concomitant distancing from God.

The aspiration to making religious practices part of everyday routines was of central importance here. Both the Muslims and Christians held that the strength of their faith depended on the time and energy they invested in it. Their notion that practices such as prayer constituted—or ought to constitute—a believer's "second nature" (Bourdieu 1990, 56) was expressed in terms of the feelings of "emptiness" that abstaining from prayer brought about. Furthermore, my Muslim and Christian interlocutors believed that by giving religious worship and contemplation an important place in their everyday lives they cultivated ethical dispositions that made them inclined to stay away from what they perceived as wrongful or sinful behavior, and thus remain "pure." An active religious life, they felt, made them less disposed to surrender to the distractions and indulgences of mass media and popular culture and, whenever they *had* succumbed to "tempting" distractions, it made them more disposed to "return" to God, to pray and ask for forgiveness—that is, to strive for a reconciliation and rapprochement with God. Indeed, both groups held that the practical acts of strengthening one's faith accomplished an enhanced closeness to God, thus mitigating the continuous drawing away from God that they experienced in their media-saturated life-worlds. In these ways, their continuous struggles with everyday distractions were central to their attempts at living faithful lives.

7

Conclusion

In the Euro-American world, Muslims have frequently come to be perceived as potentially disruptive if not dangerous "others." In the Netherlands, they are often seen as an exception in a self-professed liberal and secular nation, requiring special attention when it comes to their "integration" in society. In the light of dominant secularization narratives, the decreased, but still substantial, Christian population in the Netherlands tends to receive fewer attention. When it is being discussed, Christianity is often treated as a remnant of a more religious past or—from a perspective that is more favorable but still relegates the religion to history—as valuable cultural heritage. These stereotypes were vividly portrayed in the focus group discussion this book started with, in which the participants drew a sharp contrast between Christians having to demonstrate they are not "dull" and Muslims having to prove that they do not "kill people." Although these widespread representations are also widely contested, they do to a large extent set the terms of the debate, in which the relation between Christians and Muslims is framed by such dichotomies as self and other, majority and minority, native and migrant, and past and present.

This book has reached beyond such conventional oppositions by approaching the religiously observant Muslims and Christians I worked with as young adults who have grown up in a shared pluralist European context. To be sure, these groups differed from one another in many ways—as most of my interlocutors would themselves readily point out and as the orthodox and revivalist teachings they were exposed to often emphasized. Nonetheless, they importantly shared the experience of pursuing paths of religious commitment within a wider social environment that offered little support of such endeavors. I have examined these everyday religious pursuits in relation to prevalent social dynamics in today's Dutch and European society. This has exposed both shared pathways and situated differences in how these young Christians and Muslims shaped their religious lives under these circumstances.

In this regard, I have sought not only to move beyond dominant representations but also to cut across longstanding boundaries between the academic study of Muslims and Christians in Europe—and between the kinds of analytical questions asked with respect to these religious groups. Thus, this book has aimed to destabilize established modes of knowledge production in the social scientific study of religion in Europe by developing an explicitly comparative approach that has so far suffered from neglect. In this conclusion, I reflect on my findings by looking more closely at, on the one hand, a predicament of precarious piety that is largely shared by my Christian and Muslim interlocutors and, on the other hand, the ways in which this common predicament relates to the different social positionalities of these groups and to the widespread politics of difference.

Precarious Piety

The young Sunni Muslims and Protestant Christians with whom I worked strongly emphasized the importance of a self-conscious, sincere, and pro-active religious commitment. They did not want to approach faith as secondary, as something one does on the side, but rather as integral to, and constitutive of, their everyday lives. They aimed to lead their lives in a state of surrender and closeness to God. In this respect, my Muslim interlocutors put a strong emphasis on acquiring religious knowledge so as to learn about what they regarded as the correct Islamic doctrines and worship practices. My Christian interlocutors focused more on their emotional relationship with God and their subjective experience of the significance of Christ's redemption in their lives. But these emphases were not mutually exclusive: while the young Christians gave much weight to Bible study, the young Muslims longed for spiritual experiences of contact with God. As I suggested in Chapter 2, these latter orientations seemed to reinforce my interlocutors' bonds with the mainstream orthodox religious traditions in which they had been brought up. More than the revivalist tendencies they engaged with later in life, these mainstream traditions encouraged religious learning in the case of Christianity and spiritual experiences in the case of Islam.

The emphasis on a personal and self-conscious religious commitment among these young Muslims and Christians signified a demanding approach to religion. This was all the more so because both demarcated faith in rather strict ways, setting it apart from major domains of social life including work, study, and consumption. Faith was understood to entail religious acts and qualities such as cultivating a state of devotion, being close to God, and giving religious practices and thoughts a central place in everyday life. Accordingly, my interlocutors felt that their involvement with domains such as work should be determined by their faith. Yet these domains themselves were commonly seen to center on what these young people described as "worldly" concerns. Indeed, while contemporary religious believers often treat faith and work (or study) as complementary (see e.g. Ammerman 2014a, 294ff.), and while my interlocutors occasionally did so too, they more generally approached the latter as an area of social life that risked moving them away from God. This illustrates their perception of everyday public life: they experienced their universities, jobs, and the urban spaces through which they moved as overwhelmingly secular. They felt that religion could only play a marginal role in these normatively non-religious places. Although they wanted faith to pervade all aspects of daily life, they tended to situate it mostly in their private lives and in the socio-religious settings they attended. Arguably, it was precisely because the secular world was never far away in their everyday lives that they experienced the need to distinguish it sharply from their religious endeavors.

At the same time, my interlocutors' approach to faith exposes the influence of particular religious teachings, particularly those of evangelical and Salafi revivalist movements. These centered on the aims of achieving a "true" or "pure" religion, a high level of personal commitment, and a prioritization of faith in everyday life, which were all seen to demand a degree of detachment from the "world." These teachings did not seem to leave much room for regarding "worldly" engagement as an expression of faith or spirituality, or for treating the boundaries between religious and non-religious domains as porous. Rather, they emphasized the temptation and appeal emanating not only from the worlds of consumption, entertainment, and popular culture, but also from personal ambition and the prospect of professional careers—even if the latter were also encouraged.

In line with these revivalist approaches, my Christian and Muslim interlocutors strove to prioritize a self-conscious religious commitment in their everyday lives. This ideal was however hard to realize. This book has shown that their embrace of a socially proliferating ethics of authenticity contributed not only to their understanding of submission to God as a privileged path to self-realization, but also to their emphasis on a sincere and deliberately chosen personal faith as a prerequisite of true submission to God. While this was perceived to make faith more genuine and durable, it also made it dependent on the volition, sincerity, and moral scrutiny of the self, thereby bringing in a degree of contingency. When it came to such moral scrutiny, my Muslim interlocutors emphasized the sincerity of their religious worship practices whereas the young Christians worried more about mistakenly taking their subjective feelings as indices of God's will.

Moreover, these young people's recurrent encounters with alternative convictions and commitments in today's pluralist Dutch society provoked a measure of relativist doubt. Again, this occurred in somewhat different ways: while doubts among the young Christians tended to center on religious truth claims, those among the young Muslims pertained more to the salience that religious prescriptions should be given in their everyday lives. As I argued in Chapter 4, this divergence signifies less a distinctive emphasis on orthodoxy in Christianity and orthopraxy in Islam, than a difference in the degree to which my interlocutors were prone to relativize their beliefs: the young Christians tended to question these somewhat more extensively than the young Muslims. What both groups nonetheless had in common was that they constantly faced the risk of regarding the rigorous surrender to their religion as optional rather than inescapable. Consequently, their religious commitment could remain neither self-evident nor unquestioned, but necessarily became deliberate, reflexive, and reliant on the routinized "input" from social settings of religious pedagogy.

Next to these challenges centering on reflexive thought, these young Christians and Muslims also faced constraints at the level of routine practices. Thus, because of their participation in a fast capitalist culture, which quickened the pace of life and fostered processes of acceleration in a variety of social domains, they often struggled to "fit God in." Their practices of worship tended to unwittingly move to the background of their everyday lives. As a result, integrating prayers and other religious practices into daily life required deliberate action and self-discipline. My Muslim interlocutors, in contrast to the Christians, could in this regard resort to the prescribed daily prayer times as a temporal structure. Furthermore, these young people's active engagement with "secular" mass-mediated popular culture, which has become increasingly pervasive and intrusive in today's accelerated and digitalized consumer culture, confronted them with what they experienced as a relentless stream of distractions. Because of its ready availability and appeal, this mass-mediated popular culture constituted a virtually inescapable presence in my interlocutors' everyday lives. While they were attracted to it, they also felt that this popular culture drew them away from God.

These findings show that the constraints on my interlocutors' religious pursuits resulted not only from the particular kinds of revivalist-oriented, committed faith to which they aspired, but also from the ways in which these religious endeavors articulated with prevalent social dynamics in today's pluralist, predominantly secular and fast capitalist society. While they were confident about the religious paths they wanted to follow, their efforts at leading their lives in a condition of religious surrender and closeness to God were inherently vulnerable. Rather than finding themselves in a closed-off religious world, they lead highly heterogeneous lives in which their pursuits of faith co-existed, competed, and became enmeshed with other, in their eyes, more "worldly" activities. They were constantly enticed, both intellectually and practically, to imagine and organize their lives in alternative ways. And they were apprehensive of the appeal that such alternative lifestyles, which always seemed to be in close reach, had on them. The personal piety to which they aspired continuously risked slipping away.

The instability of my interlocutors' pursuits of faith further becomes apparent in the ways in which their religious commitment depended on ongoing personal investment, dedication, and critical introspection, and on frequent engagement with fellow believers in social-pedagogical settings. In a social context characterized by the sharply abated influence of organized religion on social and public life, and by secular and capitalist constraints on religious convictions and practices, faith could not be taken for granted but had to be self-consciously cultivated by these young people. My Christian and Muslim interlocutors, then, shared a predicament of what I call precarious piety: a condition in which the pursuit of a religiously committed life is inherently fragile and, precisely for that reason, continuously requires deliberate care and nourishment.

This condition of precarious piety may well characterize the pursuit of religious commitment in secular capitalist societies more generally. At least for religious practitioners who adhere to exclusive truth claims and seek to prioritize worship practices in their everyday lives, such pious endeavors inevitably run up against the pull to understand and shape their lives differently. This argument resonates with, and is indebted to, Charles Taylor's (2007) analysis of how, in our secular age, religious faith has become one option among others—and one that is often hard to embrace. Yet I have shown that the precarious condition of my interlocutors' religious pursuits does not only result from skepticism or doubt about the plausibility of faith—as emphasized in Taylor's and other analyses of secularity (e.g., Berger 1967; 2014; Luhrmann 2012a). It is also, and substantially so, the effect of everyday routines and embodied habits that have more to do with the taken-for-granted organization of everyday life than with skeptical thought, and that pose more of a practical than an intellectual challenge to religious commitment. These routines and habits are largely grounded in the social forces of advanced consumer capitalism. My findings, then, suggest that to grasp the present conditions of religious engagement, we should not just look at those factors that are commonly associated with secular society, including value pluralism, moral individualism, skepticism, and—from a more Asadian perspective—the political modes of regulating religious expression. We should also pay close attention to the structuring of everyday life in today's accelerated, digitalized, and high capitalist world.

In this respect, an important finding of this study is that the Muslims and Christians with whom I conducted fieldwork themselves actively engaged with, participated in, and often embraced these secular and capitalist dynamics. These young, committed believers did not fully retreat in religious "enclaves" that protected them from a hostile, secular world—to echo a depiction of modern religion regularly invoked in the sociological literature (see Chapter 4). By contrast, that secular world was part and parcel of their everyday lives as much as it was reflected by their ambitions, ideals, interests, and desires. They adhered to the demanding work ethic that prevails in today's fast capitalist society, embraced the relaxation and entertainment offered by mass-mediated popular culture, assented to the proliferating ideals of authenticity, and accepted the social reality of living in a pluralist society (my Christian interlocutors sometimes even mentioned that they welcomed the condition of pluralism as a stimulus for cultivating a self-reflexive faith). This closeness to "the world" did however cause worries among these young believers about the ways in which it contributed to a backgrounding—or de-prioritizing—of faith in their everyday lives.

My interlocutors' participation in the secular and capitalist world did not, however, mean that their religious aspirations were simply eclipsed by that world. Rather, this book has demonstrated that it stimulated a reinvigoration of their pursuits of religious commitment. Thus, the young Muslims and Christians often explicitly contrasted their religious ideals with their "worldly" engagements: they talked about following "God's will" rather than one's own desires, adhering to an exclusive religious truth as opposed to assenting to cultural relativism, making time for God despite one's busy schedule, and "connecting" to God in a world of distraction. Indeed, it was partly through their very opposition to, and negotiation of, these challenges to their faith that these young Muslims and Christians gave shape to their religious aspirations and pursuits. Their practice of drawing sharp distinctions between "faith" and "the world" was part of this dynamic, enabling them to clearly formulate and pursue their aspirations to religious commitment.

The tensions that my Christian and Muslim interlocutors experienced in contemporary Dutch society, further, stimulated them to regularly participate in social spaces of religious pedagogy as a means of attaining reaffirmation and encouragement of their religious lifestyles. These tensions also motivated them to invest in religious practices as a way of finding tranquility and moving closer to God, thereby countering the adverse effects of acceleration and distraction. In a social world in which they felt they were continuously drawn away from their religious focus, my interlocutors deliberately strove to, in the terms of the young Christians, "nourish" or "build up" their faith, or, in the phrasing of the young Muslims, "strengthen" their *iman*.

Without doubt, there will be many believers for whom the combination of a demanding religious ethics and the everyday pressures on realizing these will result in disillusionment and perhaps a waning or abandonment of religious ideals. This has been documented for evangelical or "fundamentalist" Christians in particular (see e.g. Babinski 1995), and it has also been observed among Salafi Muslims (Schielke 2015, 128–48; cf. De Koning 2013, 79). Because I have followed my Christian and Muslim interlocutors for a relatively short period of time (my fieldwork was spread over three years), I cannot say whether, and to what extent, their religious paths may have changed afterward. Yet focusing on Muslims and Christians who—at least for the time being—continued to pursue demanding religious ideals, this book has shown that the challenges posed to a committed religious life do not necessarily result in a deterioration of faith, but can be appropriated within, and be made productive for, religious pursuits. But this requires work: my interlocutors had to deliberately invest in giving faith a central place in their everyday lives. Furthermore, the self-reflection on which they put so much emphasis was more than just an ideal; it was a necessity. Their ideals of living their lives in a condition of surrender to God required an acute awareness of the challenges to their faith and a self-conscious effort at responding to these.

Muslim Exceptionalism and the Politics of Difference

My exploration, so far, of the shared dynamics of everyday religiosity leaves open the question how the disparate public discourses on Muslims and Christians may affect their religious pursuits in different ways. There is reason to expect that the "othering" of Muslims in particular adds to the precariousness of their religious endeavors, especially when it comes to issues of belonging. Given today's negative climate toward Islam in Western Europe, Muslims face particular pressures on their religion that Christians in this region do not share—or to a much lesser extent. The young adults I worked with grew up in the late 1990s and 2000s, a period in which the signifiers "Muslim" and "Islam" became increasingly essentialized and associated with problems of social integration, gender inequality, lack of freedom, and extremism. My Muslim interlocutors routinely encountered questions and criticisms, as they were being taken to task to account for the problems associated with their religion. *Being Muslim*, then, was—and still is—a strongly ascribed social identity that is surrounded by public anxieties. In this context, it has become almost inevitable for people with a Muslim background to speak out and take a stance with regard to ongoing debates on Islam.

My Muslim interlocutors told me that the public debates on Islam had an impact on how they talked about, and represented, their religion. And several of them also mentioned that these debates triggered their desire to learn more about their religion. However, their narratives about their personal religious processes show that, different from what is frequently assumed, public criticisms of Islam seldom seemed to be the most important factor in their turn to religious commitment. These narratives centered more on their changing life-phase, the influence of peers, personal questions about meaning, experiences of misfortune, and encounters with revivalist-oriented religious pedagogy (preachers, books, websites, and so forth). In this sense, their pathways toward becoming committed were not so different from those of my Christian interlocutors.

In widespread public perceptions, nonetheless, expressions of Islamic piety do, more often than manifestations of Christian religiosity, come with negative connotations. Islamically inspired acts such as demanding a prayer space at work (Jouili 2015, 156), not shaking hands with a person of the opposite sex (Fadil 2009, 440), or articulating conservative sexual values (Mepschen, Duyvendak, and Tonkens 2010, 967–70) is potentially read as a lack of integration or good citizenship. Writing on revivalist Muslim women in France and Germany, Jeanette Jouili (2015, 14ff.) shows how their pursuit of a pious lifestyle runs up against, and becomes intertwined with, "moral struggles over representation" aimed at countering negative perceptions of Islam in the "inhospitable context" of today's secular Europe. The young Muslims I worked with expressed a similar sense of responsibility with regard to improving the image of Islam, even if they were sometimes weary of having to do so.

My Christian interlocutors, notably, shared this felt responsibility to present a good image of their religion in public. Both the Christians and Muslims occasionally described themselves as "ambassadors" of their faith (cf. Van Es 2019), with both using this very term. For the latter, this—sometimes reluctantly accepted—role was mostly motivated by a desire to counter stereotypes of Muslims as unintegrated, uncivil, threatening, or backward. While my Christian interlocutors also felt the need to counter stereotypes (such as being old-fashioned, boring, or odd), their self-prescribed task of ambassadorship also seemed to be informed, more strongly than I observed among their Muslim counterparts, by a missionary aim of exposing the appeal of their religion.

Of particular consequence to my Muslim interlocutors was the often made association between Islam and radicalization or violent extremism (Fadil, Ragazzi, and De Koning 2019). In Dutch public discourses, like those in many other places in Europe and beyond, discussions about orthodox Islam frequently slide into concerns about extremism and terrorism. As Sara Ahmed (2004, 132) has argued, in global normative discourses following 9/11, the figures of the Muslim and the terrorist tend to "stick together." This discursive framing is based on the occurrence of violent and terrorist acts committed in the name of Islam, which are at times generalized as characteristic for the Muslim population as a whole. Although many refrain from making these essentialist linkages in Dutch debates, others tend to assume that it is a "slippery slope" from strict religious observance to extremism.

In recent years, these worries have exacerbated due to the rise of ISIS and its appeal on sections of the Muslim population in Europe, including the Netherlands. From this country, an estimated three hundred people traveled to Syria or Iraq to engage in militant *jihad* (AIVD 2019). As a jihadi-Salafi organization, ISIS has induced global attention to Salafism. As a result, anxieties about a "slippery slope" are directed most strongly at Muslims inspired by Salafism. Although research has pointed out that most Salafis do not support the use of violence as propagated by ISIS and other *jihadi* organizations (see Chapter 2), Salafism has increasingly come to be equated with violent extremism in Dutch public debates. Moreover, occasional reports about the propagation of segregation and intolerant views in a number of Salafi mosques and Quran schools have raised concerns, also within Dutch Muslim communities. Although my fieldwork took place before the establishment of ISIS in 2014, public worries about Salafism had already begun to emerge. Consequently, participating in Salafi-oriented settings, as many of my Muslim interlocutors did, could potentially raise suspicion and concern. As I have shown in Chapter 2, it is however highly problematic to assume that all of those who engage with Salafi renditions of Islam inevitably move toward radicalism or extremism.

These politicized debates around, and negative connotations of, Islam meant that the socio-political position of my Muslim interlocutors differed in important ways from that of the Christians I worked with. The young Muslims faced recurrent public anxieties about their integration, belonging, and potential radicalization. To some extent, these issues were echoed by Salafi pedagogies, which emphasize the moral boundaries between Islam and secular Dutch society as well as between different branches of Islam (De Koning 2013). For a small number of Dutch Muslims, these negative representations, combined with Salafi teachings, have kindled a desire to undertake *hijra*: to migrate to a country identified as Islamic, such as Morocco, Egypt, or Saudi Arabia (Ter Laan forthcoming). My Muslim interlocutors did not seem to share this desire. Like Christians oriented toward evangelicalism—which also emphasizes the moral perils posed by secular culture—they rather sought to carve out a religiously committed path within Dutch society, of which they considered themselves to be part. At the same time, they faced widespread public discourses that, based on their pursuits of religious commitment, questioned their very moral membership of the Dutch nation. Centering on questions of identity and belonging, these pressures particularly affected their experiences of feeling accepted, their senses of attachment, and the ways they represented themselves in wider society.

Even though struggles over representation can have a notable influence on the quest for a religious life (Jouili 2015; Van Es 2016; Liberatore 2017), it has struck me that my Muslim interlocutors put a greater emphasis on the ways in which their religious pursuits were challenged by everyday habits, routines, and social encounters in today's pluralist, high capitalist Dutch society. This was not merely an external, "hostile" secular context (Jouili 2015, 3), but one they were in many ways attracted to, and participated in, themselves. Thus, they were engaged in moral negotiations not only between Islamic ethics and dominant representations of Islam, but also, and importantly so, between their pursuit of religious aspirations and their active participation in secular and capitalist culture. In contrast to the specific representational troubles they faced, these young Muslims shared these negotiations with respect to their enmeshment in a secular, capitalist world with my Christian interlocutors. This finding suggests that we need to shift our perspective more than we have so far done from an analysis of Muslims *as opposed to* secular Europe to one of Muslims *as part of* secular Europe.

With regard to this proximity to—and indeed participation in—mainstream, predominantly secular society, my Christian interlocutors in particular expressed concerns about the extent to which they were distinct from that wider society. In their conversations both with me and among themselves, they sometimes wondered out loud what difference it actually made that they were Christians. This question also formed a more tacit background to some of their reflections about their everyday lives as Christians, for example when it came to leading busy lives, watching box office movies, going out for drinks, or dating. Did being a Christian, they wondered, have any effect on how they confronted such "worldly" activities? How could they "give witness to their faith," as they often put it, while being engaged in such mundane pursuits? And how did they differentiate themselves from their secular peers in this context?

Strikingly, these questions seemed less urgent for the young Muslims with whom I worked. As pointed out above, they tended to be readily identified *as* Muslims and their "otherness" was already assumed by many of the people they encountered. By contrast, my Christian interlocutors were not necessarily identified as religious people in public, except on those moments they practiced or talked about their faith. Moreover, in a context of rising Islamophobia, an increasing shift in the target of secular critique from Christianity to Islam, and an emerging emphasis on the relevance of the "Judeo-Christian roots" of Dutch culture, Christians are generally not stigmatized and set apart to the same extent as Muslims. In other words, their moral and cultural particularity as Christians did not necessarily speak for itself. At the same time, the Calvinist and evangelical traditions my Christian interlocutors drew from taught them to be "in the world but not of the world," as the popular Christian adage goes, and thus to be morally distinct from wider secular society.

In response to this quandary, these young Christians often welcomed external "input" that stimulated them to explicate their convictions and identities as Christians (my interlocutors in Ede told me that they were happy about my presence as an outsider for precisely this reason). Furthermore, they emphasized the Christian character of particular behaviors and views, while drawing an explicit contrast with those of their non-Christian peers. Thus, they for example rejected—or were at least reserved about—premarital sex, they sought to restrict their alcohol consumption, and aimed to abstain from watching "occult" or sexually explicit movies. They linked these choices, more than my Muslim interlocutors tended to do, to an explicit moral critique of wider society—not in the least in terms of what they perceived as its excessive "sexualization" (Beekers and Schrijvers 2020, 149). This resonates with what Anna Strhan (2015) has observed for conservative evangelicals in London. Since these Christians understand themselves to be "shaped by the same moral currents as those they seek to be different from" and since "the lines marking them out as different are fragile," Strhan writes, they seek to "clearly stake out symbolic moral boundaries of distinctiveness" (2015, 169).

My comparative analysis has demonstrated that while both the young Muslims and Christians with whom I worked were deeply affected by the moral and cultural norms that prevail in wider Dutch society, the Christians were more worried about their moral distinctiveness. This is related, I suggest, to their divergent socio-political positions: while Dutch Muslims tend to be always already framed as "other," Christians are perceived to be more closely positioned to the dominant population. Ironically, as I described in Chapter 4, my Christian interlocutors longed for a degree of pressure that was all too familiar for the young Muslims I worked with.

Despite the distinct positionalities and public discourses surrounding them, these young Christians and Muslims shared substantial common ground. The comparative approach taken in this book has revealed that the predicament of precarious piety was not unique to either my Muslim or Christian interlocutors, but shared by both. A separate study on either of these religious groups may have been more likely to follow the prevalent approaches of research on European Muslims and Christians respectively, entailing a focus on minority politics and religious-secular tensions in the case of Muslims and on the effects of the decline of institutionalized Christianity and the closeness to majority secular culture in the case of Christians. My aim has not been to argue that these approaches are misguided, but rather that they are part and parcel of a wider disciplinary split between research on Muslims and Christians—in Europe and beyond—that has resulted in an oversight of parallel processes and dynamics as well as situated differences. Directly comparative work on lived religious experiences among Muslims and Christians enables a move beyond well-trodden approaches and categories, and offers fresh perspectives that may otherwise remain concealed.

Like my Muslim interlocutors, the young Christians with whom I worked effectively constituted a religious minority in Dutch society. They strove toward strict religious commitment in an environment where religious piety has become a fairly marginal phenomenon that can count on limited support and understanding. Meanwhile, the young Muslims I encountered were, similarly to my Christian interlocutors, not simply positioned in opposition to an "outside" secular world but rather embedded in prevalent secular and capitalist dynamics in today's Dutch society. Placing these groups alongside one another within one ethnographic framework, then, has enabled me to look at Christians through an analytical lens that is more commonly focused on Muslims, and vice versa. Such cross-fertilization through comparative work opens new windows with respect to each of these groups. Thus, an important insight of this study is that the struggles inherent to leading a religiously committed life in today's secular Europe are not exclusive to Muslims, despite the particular pressures on religion they experience. My focus has not so much been on the issues of stigmatization, representation, and societal integration that so often take central place in contemporary political and scholarly discussions on religious minorities, as on the complex everyday dynamics of pursuing a life of religious commitment within a pluralist, high capitalist, and predominantly secular context.

The Dutch Christians and Muslims whom I have come to know in the course of my research were, in many ways, leading very ordinary lives as young adults in the Netherlands. They devoted themselves to their studies, prepared for their future careers, forged friendships and—in many cases—romantic relationships, redefined the bonds with their parents, yielded to the pleasures of modern media and popular culture, and moved along with the stimuli, thrills, and fast movements of contemporary urban life. It is precisely because they were leading such largely unexceptional lives in the context of today's Dutch society that they often struggled to give their religious faith the priority they felt it ought to have. This book has revealed that such shared experiences of inadequacy, imperfection, and struggle did not paralyze these young people's pursuits of religious commitment, but rather energized and revitalized them.

Notes

Chapter 1

1. On the whole, 12.8 percent of the Dutch population self-identify as Protestant and 4.9 percent as Muslim. Other religious groups include Roman Catholics (11.7 percent), members of other Christian churches (0.8 percent), and adherents of other non-Christian religions (2 percent) (Bernts and Berghuijs 2016, 21).
2. The SCP argues that the trend among young Protestants cannot be sufficiently explained by a "hard core" effect, whereby the more committed church members remain in church while the less committed leave (De Hart 2014, 63–5, 89–90).
3. While I give attention to issues of age, generation, and youth culture, my goal is not to theoretically explore the relation between "youth" and "religion" as such. Rather, I focus on young people because this enables me to study, in an especially productive way, how the religious pursuits of Muslims and Christians play out in a shared Dutch context. For the extensive literature on religion and youth see, for example, Collins-Mayo and Dandelion (2010); Giordan (2010); and Arweck and Shipley (2019).
4. The number of Christians with a migration background in the Netherlands is estimated between 500,000 and 1.3 million (De Hart 2014, 110).
5. It is often overlooked in current discussions, which tend to frame Islam as a recent phenomenon in the Netherlands, that the Dutch colonial presence in Indonesia involved extensive encounters with, and the development of elaborate government policies on, Muslim populations (Kennedy and Valenta 2006, 342; Kloos 2018a, 33–8).
6. Smaller Muslim groups include Shi'is, Alevis, and Ahmadis (De Koning 2019, 483). It has been estimated that Shi'is make up around 10 percent of the Dutch Muslim population (Schlatmann 2016, 37).
7. CBS StatLine, 2019, "Bevolking met migratieachtergrond; geslacht, leeftijd, 1 januari." https://statline.cbs.nl/StatWeb/publication/?PA=70787ned. Accessed September 23, 2019.
8. I occasionally use composite terms such as Moroccan Dutch as shorthand expressions to specify the migration background of those designated. Like most identity labels, such hyphenated identities (i.e., dual identity markers that can be connected by a hyphen) are far from flawless. I should therefore stress that by using these terms I do not want to make any assumptions about questions of belonging. Rather, I employ them sparingly and particularly for the purpose of distinguishing between different post-migrant groups, such as people of Moroccan and Turkish descent. My interlocutors did not

tend to use hyphenated identities themselves. Rather they identified as, for example, both Moroccan and Dutch, depending on the context.

9 "In de koranschool leren kinderen dat Nederland niet hun land is," NRC, September 10, 2019. https://www.nrc.nl/nieuws/2019/09/10/in-de-koranschool-leren-kinderen-dat-nederland-niet-hun-land-is-a3972824. Accessed September 18, 2019.

10 For more explicitly comparative approaches to religion and gender, see Bartkowski and Read (2003), and to religion and sexuality, see Beekers and Schrijvers (2020).

11 Scholars have even referred to the "return of the religious" in a post-secular era (see e.g. De Vries and Sullivan 2006, passim). The term "post-secular" is employed in different ways and it is not always clear whether it is used descriptively or prescriptively (cf. Calhoun, Juergensmeyer, and VanAntwerpen 2011, 18). Yet most scholars use the term in order to criticize longstanding secularist assumptions and to address the significance of religious arguments and emotions in public debates and political subjectivities (see e.g. Braidotti et al. 2014). While in my view such post-secularist critique is valid and important, describing our time in terms of a "post-secular age" seems unwarranted—at least in Western European contexts like the Netherlands—given the limited power and influence of religious organizations in society and the prevalence of secular reasoning in public and political discourse. Nonetheless, it is striking that religious categories and identifications have gained a renewed significance in—especially right-wing and populist—public and political discourses across Europe (Van den Hemel 2014; Marzouki, McDonnell, and Roy 2016; Brubaker 2017).

12 This is not to say that all religious believers, at all times, worry a great deal about moral shortcomings, even if many do. As Maya Mayblin and Diego Malara (2018) point out, a pro-active ethical engagement with self-perceived inadequacy may be particularly salient in revivalist or reformist versions of Abrahamic religions, like those I focus on in this book. As a counterpoint to this realm of pious reflexivity and discipline, Mayblin and Malara suggest that lenience, deviation, and deferral with respect to ethical norms are central to many "religious systems" and crucial to their maintenance and reproduction (cf. Bandak and Boylston 2014).

13 I have replaced all real names of Christian and Muslim organizations with pseudonyms.

14 See Centraal Bureau voor de Statistiek, "Helft Nederlanders is kerkelijk of religieus." December 22, 2016. https://www.cbs.nl/nl-nl/nieuws/2016/51/helft-nederlanders-is-kerkelijk-of-religieus. Accessed September 23, 2019.

15 For a more detailed account of the social and institutional characteristics of An-Nur, see Beekers (2015).

16 The Gülen movement, or *Hizmet*, is a transnational Islamic movement founded in Turkey by Fethullah Gülen. The movement emphasizes education, religious and ethical discipline, and civic responsibility. It is particularly popular among highly educated young Muslims, both in Turkey and in the diaspora (Landman and Sunier 2014, chap. 6).

17 All names of the Muslim and Christian preachers, teachers, and mentors I encountered during my fieldwork are replaced by pseudonyms.
18 All interviews were audio-recorded and transcribed.

Chapter 2

1   Larkin and Meyer's argument has recently been revisited in a collection edited by Janson and Meyer (2016b).
2   Throughout this dissertation, I have transcribed Arabic terms using a minimum of diacritical marks. I have done this not only for reasons of convenience, but also because this "minimalist" style of transcription is common among my Muslim interlocutors themselves.
3   The root of the word *iman*, *'mn*, denotes "being secure, trusting in, turning to" (Gardet 2012c).
4   In this regard, Asad (2011, 38) has criticized Smith for treating faith as an essentially individual, unmediated, experience.
5   Martijn de Koning (2008, 311–12) draws a similar picture of the young Moroccan-Dutch he studied in the 2000s.
6   This turn to a self-conscious religious commitment has also been described for young Muslims elsewhere in Europe, see, for example, Jouili (2015, chap. 2) on Muslim women in France and Germany.
7   In Muslim discourses in the Netherlands and elsewhere (e.g., Norway, see Jacobsen 2011, 297–301), the turn to personal religious commitment is at times represented as a *return*. This notion conveys that one goes back to one's "natural disposition" to submit oneself to Allah—based on the notion of Islam as *din-al-fitrah*, the "natural religion" (Jacobsen 2011, 298). The term "return" was used more often by Muslim preachers than by my young Muslim interlocutors themselves.
8   Studies of the generation of these parents have shown that their engagement with Islam is directed, more than that of their children, at fulfilling ritual duties, social cohesion, and unity (De Koning, Wagemakers, and Becker 2014, 161). Yet some research on first-generation Muslim migrants to Europe has also pointed to a shift from social norms to self-determination in their approach to religion (see e.g. Schiffauer 1988).
9   Quran 51:56, Sahih International version.
10 My Muslim interlocutors generally used the term "God" (which is spelled identically in Dutch and English), rather than "Allah" when they spoke with me. Yet "Allah" was generally used in sermons and other Islamic settings.
11 As mentioned earlier I have replaced the real names of preachers, religious leaders, and institutions by pseudonyms.

12 See, for example, Douwes (2001, 12–14), Cesari (2003a, 261), Buitelaar (2008, 241–2), De Koning (2008, 72–82, 104), and Nagra (2011). The notion of "reactive identification" (Nagra 2011) builds on the concept of "reactive ethnicity" (Portes and Rumbaut 2001, 148) and on the broader "societal reaction" and "labeling" theories—developed, among others, by Howard Becker (1963)—that look at the consequences of public perceptions or "labeling" on the behavior of those addressed.

13 See, for instance, Joep de Hart (2012). For an example from the Dutch media, see Maarten Keulemans, "Thanks, mister Wilders, for your contribution to the Islamization of the Netherlands" (translation mine), *De Volkskrant*, November 8, 2012.

14 I should note here that my fieldwork took place a couple of years before the rise of ISIS in 2014 and the violent acts its members perpetrated in Europe and worldwide, which has reignited debates about Islam and particularly about violence conducted in its name.

15 Scholars commonly distinguish between three factions among Salafis: purists or quietists (who stay away from politics), politicos (who engage in politics and activism), and jihadis (who advocate holy war, not only against non-Muslim invaders of the world of Islam—the classical interpretation of *jihad*—but also against leaders in the Muslim world who in their view have strayed from Islam) (Wiktorowicz 2006; Meijer 2009; Wagemakers 2016, 51–9).

16 Many Muslims who are designated as "Salafis" by researchers would not use that term to identify themselves, possibly because they find it presumptuous to do so, they want to distance themselves from the label's negative connotations (Roex 2013, 91–2), or because they claim to represent the only "true" Islam (De Koning 2009, 380). Instead, some describe themselves as people of the *hadith* or *Sunna* (e.g., "ahl al-hadith") (Roex 2013, 92).

17 The PKN (Protestantse Kerk in Nederland) was established in 2004 as a result of a fusion between the two largest Protestant denominations (both Calvinist) and the Lutheran Church in the Netherlands. The PKN is now the largest Protestant church in this country, with around 2 million members in 2015 (De Hart and Van Houwelingen 2018, 37). Many of my Christian interlocutors had a background in member churches of the PKN, while others hailed from orthodox Reformed churches outside the PKN, such as the *Gereformeerde Kerken vrijgemaakt*. A smaller number had grown up going to strictly orthodox churches within the Dutch tradition of pietist Calvinism (known in Dutch as *reformatorisch*). The orthodox and strictly orthodox groups of churches, both outside the PKN, each counted a little over 200,000 members in 2006 (De Hart 2011, 44). Another small segment of my interlocutors had grown up in evangelical and Pentecostal churches. While the membership of these churches is relatively small—142,000 people in 2006 (De Hart 2011, 44)—the evangelical movement transgresses the walls of these churches and effectively influences hundreds of thousands of Christians in the Netherlands—through evangelical and Pentecostal organizations, conferences, festivals, media, literature, and worship music (Roeland 2009, 26–36).

18 In evangelical circles, the term "worship" refers to the act of singing Christian praise songs, usually in a group and typically accompanied by contemporary music (with someone playing the guitar or a whole band). It is characterized by accessible lyrics and, often, by bodily involvement (standing, dancing, and raising or clapping one's hands). My Christian interlocutors generally preferred the English term "worship" over the Dutch "lofprijzing."
19 Opwekking 581, "Til mij op," Stichting Opwekking.
20 "Build up" or "edify" (*opbouwen*) is a Bible-based term (see e.g. Romans 15:2, 1 Corinthians 14:4, Ephesians 4:29, New International Version, 1984) that was frequently used by my Christian interlocutors to describe the experience of being formed in one's faith.
21 Members of the *Gereformeerde Kerken vrijgemaakt*, established in 1944 after a schism within the "Reformed Churches in the Netherlands" (now part of PKN).
22 Sarah is referring to disagreements among different Protestant currents as to whether Christians should be baptized as infants or as adults, and as to the nature of the liturgical blessing. My interlocutors identified baptism in particular as a main bone of contention between different churches (cf. Klaver 2011, 362–6).
23 Covenant (*Verbond*) refers to the relationship between God and mankind. In Calvinist Reformed theology, the concept is employed to demonstrate the coherence of the Old and New Testaments and to frame baptism as a "sign and seal of God's covenant of promise" (Kamphuis 2005). In the New Testament, Christ's redemption is described as the fulfillment of a "new covenant" (e.g., Hebrews 8:6-12, World English Bible).
24 This characterization of evangelicalism draws from Stoffels (1990), Van Harskamp (2000), Roeland (2009), and Klaver (2011).
25 Given their strong historical and theological links, charismatic and Pentecostal Christianity are often regarded as part of the evangelical movement, but there is some scholarly debate on this point (Klaver 2011, 44–5).
26 See Bebbington (1989, chap. 1), Shibley (1998, 69), Van Harskamp (2000, 139), Roeland (2009, 27), and Klaver (2011, 45).

Chapter 3

1 The anthropology of ethics has emerged as a self-conscious sub-field in anthropology in the last fifteen to twenty years. For an overview of the relevant works and debates, which are too many and too heterogeneous to discuss here, see Mattingly and Throop (2018).
2 See, on evangelicals in the United States, Miller (1997), Shibley (1998), and Luhrmann (2012b) and, on evangelicals and Pentecostals in the Netherlands, Van Harskamp (2000), Roeland (2009), Versteeg (2010), and Klaver (2011).

3   See especially Schiffauer (1988), Cesari (2003b), Roy (2004), Peter (2006), and Jacobsen (2011). On Muslims in the Netherlands, see Bartels (2005), Demant (2005), and De Koning (2008). Roy (2004, 26) made the point that the "individual reformulation of personal religiosity" may have such various outcomes as "a liberal reformist view of Islam, a charismatic and spiritual approach ..., or a neofundamentalist stress on *sharia* (laws) and *ibadat* (rituals)."

4   Except where indicated otherwise, quotations from the Bible are taken from the American Standard Version.

5   Psalms 16:2, rendered by Mark as "Ik heb geen goed boven U." The wording in the 1901 American Standard Version is: "Thou art my Lord: I have no good beyond thee."

6   "Door Uw wil te doen/leer ik om vrij te zijn" from *Opwekkingslied* 582, based on "Jesus, all for Jesus" by Robin Mark.

7   These terms can have different meanings according to the context in which they are used. Thus, *nafs* can take on a broader meaning than the self in the carnal sense and it can also be used as a synonym for *ruh* (Esposito 2003).

8   This statement was presented in the exposition "Ik vast" ("I fast"), curated by Vanessa Vroon-Najem at the Amsterdam Museum in 2011.

9   My interlocutors' thoughts on free will raise the complex question of the relation between free will and predestination. This is a thorny issue that has spawned much debate in Islamic theology (Gardet 2012a; 2012b) and that is beyond the scope of my discussion here.

10 For Islamic pedagogies stressing the interaction between outward practices and interior dispositions, see Mahmood (2005, chap. 4). In the next chapter, I return to the relation between interior and exterior.

11 While sincerity usually refers to a quality of speech, Keane points out that non-discursive actions can also become characterized as sincere, but "only insofar as they can be translated into discourse or be treated as some sort of signification" (2007, 209, n8).

12 While Fadil conceptualizes the discourses of autonomy and authenticity in terms of power, more particularly of "liberal secular governance" (2008, 244), Roeland analyzes them as expressions of cultural change, specifically the "massive subjective turn of modern culture" (Taylor 1991, 26). These separate analytical orientations characterize the literature on Muslims and Christians in the West more generally (on Muslims see e.g. Jacobsen 2011; Jouili 2015; on Christians see e.g. Klaver 2011; Luhrmann 2012b). Notwithstanding the interrelations between power and cultural change, these discrete orientations point to different trajectories in the anthropologies of Islam and Christianity, with a stronger influence in the former of Foucauldian theoretical frameworks as developed by Asad (1993; 2003), Rose (1999), and Mahmood (2005). In the anthropology of Islam, this has contributed to a common analytical juxtaposition between religion and (liberal) secularism

(Schielke 2010). In the anthropology of Christianity, by contrast, one common thread has been to indicate the links between Christianity, liberalism, and secularism—particularly between Protestantism and the values of interiority, authenticity, and sincerity (see e.g. Robbins 2004; Keane 2007).
13 Compare Liberatore's (2017, 14–15, 239–41) critique of approaches to Muslim religiosity that focus on moral ambivalence.
14 While doing fieldwork, I participated as much as I could in settings such as the small group. Having to answer this question on my personal faith (I recall placing myself sitting on the side of the pool, with my feet dangling in the water) was one of the recurrent moments in which I found it difficult to balance between detachment and proximity (see Introduction). Asking my interlocutors to open up to me, I felt obliged to share my own feelings and thoughts, to reciprocate (cf. Ewing 1994, 579).
15 For similar discussions on the relation between inner convictions and outward practices among young British Muslims of Somali descent, see Liberatore (2017, chap. 7).

Chapter 4

1 These are *ahadith* 16 and 17 in the authoritative *hadith* collection of the thirteenth-century Imam An-Nawawi, which is taught in the course discussed here.
2 Not all of my female Muslim interlocutors would habitually go to the Friday sermons in mosques, which is seen to be a religious prescription for men only. Most would however regularly visit mosques to attend Islamic classes or talks.
3 On the strong representation of women in settings of Islamic learning in Europe, see for example Jouili and Amir-Moazami 2006, 617; Roex 2013, 47. It is beyond the scope of this study to analyze this phenomenon in detail, but it is likely related to the particular desire among women to learn about their rights in Islam, which I discussed in Chapter 2 (cf. Van Es 2016). Connected to this, Muslim women in Europe may feel a particular need for support to cope with the tensions between religious prescriptions, social expectations, and individual ambitions, for example with respect to issues such as veiling (Roex 2013, 47). Furthermore, gendered socialization processes in the families of these young Muslims may play a role.
4 I borrow the term "communities of conviction" from Gerd Baumann (1996, 70), who has used it in a slightly different way in his study of cultural diversity in Southall, London.
5 See, among other studies, Mandaville (2001, esp. chap. 4), Frank (2006), Jacobsen (2011, esp. chap. 2), and Sunier (2011) on young Muslims, and Roeland (2009, esp. chap. 5), Hopkins et al. (2011), and Vincett et al. (2012) on young Christians. For a comparative discussion of new forms of social engagement among young Muslims, Christians, and New Agers in the Netherlands, see Roeland et al. (2010).

6   Scholars have also used specific concepts such as "third space" (Mandaville 2001, 151; Vincett et al. 2008, 9, building on Homi Bhabha) and—in a different regional context—"free social space" (Martin 1990) to express the potentiality and room for maneuver of particular religious settings.
7   For an elaborate study of religious community formation and learning on the internet, see Carmen Becker's (2013) work on Dutch and German Salafi Muslims.
8   This argument is made in a chapter Smith and Snell co-authored with Kyle Longest.
9   According to Flory and Miller, a crucial factor for the renewed significance of religious community is that post-boomers "don't want to be stimulated so much as loved," because they "grew up with parents who were seldom home" and as a consequence had to "raise themselves" (2008, viii).
10 The same metaphor of religion by autopilot in relation to one's childhood religiosity was used by Irene, one of my Christian interlocutors (see Chapter 2).
11 On the perception of doubts as signs of a "weak *iman*," see also Fadil (2008, 114), Liberatore (2013), and De Koning (2018, 46–8).
12 In his more recent work, Berger (1999; 2014), along with many other sociologists of religion, has revised his argument by stating that pluralism does not necessarily result in the decline of religion.
13 By taking the proliferation of discourses of the expressive self in the 1960s as a central explanatory factor for the decline of organized Christianity in the Netherlands, Van Rooden builds on the work of the British historians Hugh McLeod (1997) and Callum Brown (2009). See also Taylor (2007, chap. 13).
14 Crul et al. (2012, 25–6) make a similar observation based on quantitative data: "young people from the ['immigrant'] second generation are frequently the most established group in the neighbourhoods of Europe's large cities today. … In contrast, many of our respondents of native-born parents had moved from other parts of the country to the major cities in order to study or work. … A student of native-born parents who moves into a cheap and ethnically diverse working-class city neighbourhood will still need some adapting to this new environment—especially if coming from a small town or the countryside, environments usually much less diverse in many ways."
15 The wide adoption of this marketplace metaphor in the sociology of religion has been criticized by several authors (see e.g. Hervieu-Léger 2000, 163–4; Vásquez and Marquardt 2003, 20–4; Aupers and Houtman 2006).

Chapter 5

1   Jeanette Jouili (2015, 58–64) has similarly described the struggles with implementing prayer in everyday life among Muslim women in France and Germany. See also Nadia Fadil's (2013, esp. 737, 740) discussion on performing the *salat* at work among young Muslims of Maghrebi descent in Belgium.

2 David Harvey (1989, 124) has described post-Fordism as "a new regime of accumulation" that emerged after the economic recession of 1973 and that is characterized by "more flexible labour processes and markets, … geographical mobility and rapid shifts in consumption practices." The onset of post-Fordism entailed a move beyond, as Agger (2004, 60) puts it succinctly, "Henry Ford's urban factory with its down-town warehouse, unions, mass production for mass markets, inflexibility of production lines, impermeable national boundaries, Taylorist scientific management, top-down authority, and rigid corporate culture."

3 In his ethnography on social outreach among suburban American evangelicals, Omri Elisha similarly writes: "When I asked ministry directors and volunteer coordinators about the most persistent problems they faced in gathering volunteers, almost all of them complained that no one seemed to have any time" (2011, 147).

4 Samuli Schielke (2015, chap. 5) has similarly pointed out that the aspirations of the Egyptian villagers with whom he worked were simultaneously shaped by both religious and capitalist normative frameworks. Yet his line of argument, highlighting "the shared existential grounds" (106) of capitalist consumption and religious revival, differs from the analysis presented in this chapter.

5 The Holy Quran 8:2, as rendered by Hirschkind (2006, 75–6).

6 The potential temporal politics of contemporary religion has received little attention in both scholarship on religion and that on fast capitalism (for a recent exception, see Haynes 2020). Agger, for one, all too easily reckons today's (American) religion among the "fast" and "superficial" products of an accelerated culture (2004, 22).

Chapter 6

1 See, for different disciplinary approaches and analytical perspectives, De Vries and Weber (2001); Clark (2007); Morgan (2008); Meyer (2009); Lynch and Mitchell (2012); and Knott, Poole, and Taira (2014).

2 Ismael's reference to the *burqa* appears to implicitly take into account Dutch debates on the Islamic face veil, in which the term *burqa* has increasingly, but incorrectly, been used to denote face veils in which the eyes remain visible (Moors 2009, 401). Ismael's observation that most women in Mecca and Medina were wearing such face veils, or *niqab*, seems an exaggeration, which may be indicative of the contrast he experienced between the two places he compared.

3 See Chapter 3 for a more elaborate discussion on *nafs*.

4 The appreciation of Islamic web forums among my Muslim interlocutors was mixed. While they occasionally used these forums to seek answers to questions on Islam, they often expressed their suspicion of such forums as places brimming with unauthorized and unqualified opinions about Islam. On young Dutch Muslims' use of Islamic web forums, see De Koning (2008) and Becker (2013).

5   On the diverse ways in which Muslims engage or disengage with music, including the adoption of music as a method of cultivating religious ethics and sentiments, see Jouili and Moors (2014); Van Nieuwkerk, LeVine, and Stokes (2016); and Ter Laan (2016).
6   The issue of shaking hands with persons of the opposite sex has come to be treated as one of the symbolic markers of the "integration" of Muslims in the Netherlands. It gained currency as a political issue after the highly publicized event of the Syrian-Dutch imam Ahmad Salam who declined to shake hands with Rita Verdonk, then minister of integration (Fadil 2009).
7   It was my impression that the young Christians generally used the internet less intensely for religious purposes than my Muslim interlocutors.
8   See, for example, Psalms 119:19, 1 Peter 2:11. For a detailed study of the process of fashioning the self as a stranger in the world among contemporary conservative evangelicals, see Strhan (2015).
9   See also Chapter 4. This concern with the fluctuations of one's *iman* has also been observed among young Muslims elsewhere in Europe (see esp. Liberatore 2013; cf. Jacobsen 2011, 283ff.; De Koning 2018, 46–8).
10 Dutch cities like Rotterdam contain numerous religious buildings, including thriving churches and mosques. Many churches, however, face decreasing numbers of attendance, while many others have been repurposed, often for secular uses (Beekers 2017). The majority of mosques in the Netherlands are housed in makeshift—rather than purpose-built—sites and most do not broadcast a publicly audible call to prayer, thus reducing their visibility and audibility as Islamic places of worship (Tamimi Arab 2017, 9; Beekers and Tamimi Arab 2016).

References

Ababou, Mohammed. 2005. "The Impact of Age, Generation and Sex Variables on Religious Beliefs and Practices in Morocco." *Social Compass* 52 (1): 31–44.
Adraoui, Mohamed-Ali. 2009. "Salafism in France: Ideology, Practices and Contradictions." In *Global Salafism: Islam's New Religious Movement*, edited by Roel Meijer, 364–83. New York and Chichester: Columbia University Press.
Agger, Ben. 1989. *Fast Capitalism: A Critical Theory of Significance*. Urbana: University of Illinois Press.
Agger, Ben. 2004. *Speeding Up Fast Capitalism: Internet Culture, Work, Families, Food, Bodies*. Boulder, CO: Paradigm Publishers.
Ahmed, Sara. 2004. "Affective Economies." *Social Text* 22 (2): 117–39.
AIVD. 2019. "Uitreizigers en terugkeerders." Algemene Inlichtingen- en Veiligheidsdienst. https://www.aivd.nl/onderwerpen/terrorisme/dreiging/uitreizigers-en-terugkeerders.
Akgündüz, Ahmet. 1993. "Een analytische studie naar de arbeidsmigratie van Turkije naar West-Europa, in het bijzonder naar Duitsland en Nederland (1960-1974)." *Sociologische Gids* 40 (5): 352–85.
Allievi, Stefano. 2003. "Islam in the Public Space: Social Networks, Media and Neo-Communities." In *Muslim Networks and Transnational Communities in and across Europe*, edited by Stefano Allievi and Jørgen S. Nielsen, 1–27. Leiden and Boston, MA: Brill.
Amir-Moazami, Schirin, Christine M. Jacobsen, and Maleiha Malik, eds. 2011. "Special Issue: Islam and Gender in Europe: Subjectivities, Politics and Piety." *Feminist Review* 98 (1): 1–135.
Ammerman, Nancy Tatom. 1997. *Congregation and Community*. New Brunswick, NJ, and London: Rutgers University Press.
Ammerman, Nancy Tatom. 2007. *Everyday Religion: Observing Modern Religious Lives*. Oxford and New York: Oxford University Press.
Ammerman, Nancy Tatom. 2014a. *Sacred Stories, Spiritual Tribes: Finding Religion in Everyday Life*. Oxford: Oxford University Press.
Ammerman, Nancy Tatom. 2014b. "Finding Religion in Everyday Life." *Sociology of Religion* 75 (2): 189–207.
Anderson, Allan. 2004. *An Introduction to Pentecostalism: Global Charismatic Christianity*. Cambridge: Cambridge University Press.
Arweck, Elisabeth, and Heather Shipley, eds. 2019. *Young People and the Diversity of (Non)Religious Identities in International Perspective*. Champaign, IL: Springer.

Asad, Talal. 1986. "The Idea of an Anthropology of Islam." Occasional Papers Series. Washington, DC: Center for Contemporary Arab Studies, Georgetown University.

Asad, Talal. 1993. *Genealogies of Religion: Discipline and Reasons of Power in Christianity and Islam*. Baltimore, MD: Johns Hopkins University Press.

Asad, Talal. 2003. *Formations of the Secular: Christianity, Islam, Modernity*. Stanford, CA: Stanford University Press.

Asad, Talal. 2011. "Thinking about Religion, Belief, and Politics." In *The Cambridge Companion to Religious Studies*, edited by Robert A. Orsi, 36–57. Cambridge: Cambridge University Press.

Aupers, Stef, and Dick Houtman. 2006. "Beyond the Spiritual Supermarket: The Social and Public Significance of New Age Spirituality." *Journal of Contemporary Religion* 21 (2): 201–22.

Baars-Blom, José M. 2006. *De onschuld voorbij... Over reformatorische cultuur en wereldbestormende meisjes*. Kampen: Uitgeverij Kok.

Babinski, Edward T. 1995. *Leaving the Fold: Testimonies of Former Fundamentalists*. Amherst, NY: Prometheus.

Bakker, André. 2007. "God, Devil, and the Work of Television: Modern Mass Media and Pentecostal Christianity in an Evangelical Community in Brazil." Master Thesis, Vrije Universiteit Amsterdam.

Bakker Kellogg, Sarah. 2019. "Perforating Kinship: Syriac Christianity, Ethnicity, and Secular Legibility." *Current Anthropology* 60 (4): 475–98.

Bandak, Andreas, and Tom Boylston. 2014. "The 'Orthodoxy' of Orthodoxy: On Moral Imperfection, Correctness, and Deferral in Religious Worlds." *Religion and Society* 5 (1): 25–46.

Bartels, Edien. 2005. "'Wearing a Headscarf Is My Personal Choice' (Jasmina, 16 Years)." *Islam and Christian–Muslim Relations* 16 (1): 15–28.

Barth, Fredrik. 1999. "Comparative Methodologies in the Analysis of Anthropological Data." In *Critical Comparisons in Politics and Culture*, edited by John R. Bowen and Roger Petersen, 78–89. Cambridge: Cambridge University Press.

Bartkowski, John P., and Jen'nan Ghazal Read. 2003. "Veiled Submission: Gender, Power, and Identity among Evangelical and Muslim Women in the United States." *Qualitative Sociology* 26 (1): 71–92.

Bauman, Zygmunt. 2000. *Liquid Modernity*. Cambridge and Malden, MA: Polity Press.

Bauman, Zygmunt. 2005. *Work, Consumerism and the New Poor*. Second edition. Maidenhead: Open University Press.

Baumann, Gerd. 1996. *Contesting Culture: Discourses of Identity in Multi-Ethnic London*. Cambridge: Cambridge University Press.

Bebbington, D. W. 1989. *Evangelicalism in Modern Britain: A History from the 1730s to the 1980s*. London and New York: Routledge.

Becker, Carmen. 2013. *Learning to Be Authentic: Religious Practices of German and Dutch Muslims Following the Salafiyya in Forums and Chat Rooms*. PhD Dissertation, Radboud University Nijmegen.

Becker, Howard S. 1963. *Outsiders: Studies in the Sociology of Deviance*. New York: The Free Press.

Beekers, Daan. 2015. "A Moment of Persuasion: Travelling Preachers and Islamic Pedagogy in the Netherlands." *Culture and Religion* 16 (2): 193–214.

Beekers, Daan. 2017. "De waarde van verlaten kerken." In *Gods huis in de steigers: religieuze gebouwen in ontwikkeling*, Oskar Verkaaik (with Daan Beekers and Pooyan Tamimi Arab), 161–92. Amsterdam: Amsterdam University Press.

Beekers, Daan. 2020. "Introduction: Toward a Comparative Anthropology of Muslim and Christian Lived Religion." *Social Analysis* 64 (1): 102–10.

Beekers, Daan, and David Kloos, eds. 2018. *Straying from the Straight Path: How Senses of Failure Invigorate Lived Religion*. New York and Oxford: Berghahn.

Beekers, Daan, and Lieke L. Schrijvers. 2020. "Religion, Sexual Ethics and the Politics of Belonging: Young Muslims and Christians in the Netherlands." *Social Compass* 67 (1): 137–56.

Beekers, Daan, and Pooyan Tamimi Arab. 2016. "Dreams of an Iconic Mosque: Spatial and Temporal Entanglements of a Converted Church in Amsterdam." *Material Religion* 12 (2): 137–64.

Bender, Courtney. 2010. *The New Metaphysicals: Spirituality and the American Religious Imagination*. Chicago, IL, and London: University of Chicago Press.

Benjamin, Walter. 2007. "The Work of Art in the Age of Mechanical Reproduction." In *Illuminations*, edited by Hannah Arendt, translated by Harry Zorn, 217–51. Pimlico. New York: Schocken Books.

Berger, Maurits, and Masha Rademakers. 2015. "Allahoe Akbar! – de jihadisten." *Tijdschrift voor Religie, Recht en Beleid* 6 (1): 5–25.

Berger, Peter L. 1967. *The Sacred Canopy: Elements of a Sociological Theory of Religion*. Garden City, NY: Doubleday.

Berger, Peter L. 1979. *The Heretical Imperative: Contemporary Possibilities of Religious Affirmation*. Garden City, NY: Anchor Press/Doubleday.

Berger, Peter L. 1999. "The Desecularization of the World: A Global Overview." In *The Desecularization of the World: Resurgent Religion and World Politics*, edited by Peter L. Berger, 1–18. Grand Rapids, MI: William B. Eerdmans Publishing.

Berger, Peter L. 2010. "Max Weber Is Alive and Well, and Living in Guatemala: The Protestant Ethic Today." *The Review of Faith & International Affairs* 8 (4): 3–9.

Berger, Peter L. 2014. *The Many Altars of Modernity: Toward a Paradigm for Religion in a Pluralist Age*. Boston, MA, and Berlin: Walter de Gruyter.

Berlin, Isaiah. 2002. *Liberty*. Edited by Henry Hardy. Oxford: Oxford University Press.

Bernts, Ton, and Joantine Berghuijs. 2016. *God in Nederland 1966–2015*. Utrecht: Uitgeverij Ten Have.

Binnendijk, Henk. 2008. *Dichtbij God: de vreugde van het omgaan met Hem*. Kampen: Uitgeverij Voorhoeve.

Bloch, Maurice. 1977. "The Past and the Present in the Present." *Man* 12 (2): 278–92.

Borgman, Erik. 2009. *Overlopen naar de barbaren: het publieke belang van religie en christendom*. Kampen: Klement/Pelckmans.

Bourdieu, Pierre. 1977. *Outline of a Theory of Practice*. Cambridge: Cambridge University Press.

Bourdieu, Pierre. 1990. *The Logic of Practice*. Stanford, CA: Stanford University Press.

Bowen, John R. 2010. *Can Islam Be French? Pluralism and Pragmatism in a Secularist State*. Princeton, NJ, and Oxford: Princeton University Press.

Bowen, John R. 2012a. *A New Anthropology of Islam*. Cambridge: Cambridge University Press.

Bowen, John R. 2012b. *Blaming Islam*. Cambridge, MA and London: MIT.

Bozorgmehr, Medhi, and Philip Kasinitz, eds. 2018. *Growing Up Muslim in Europe and the United States*. Abingdon and New York: Routledge.

Bracke, Sarah. 2004. *Women Resisting Secularisation in an Age of Globalisation: Four Case-Studies within a European Context*. PhD Dissertation, Utrecht University.

Bracke, Sarah. 2008a. "Conjugating the Modern/ Religious, Conceptualizing Female Religious Agency: Contours of a 'Post-Secular' Conjuncture." *Theory, Culture & Society* 25 (6): 51–67.

Bracke, Sarah. 2008b. "'Real' Islam in Kazan: Reconfiguring the Modern, Knowledge and Gender." In *Women and Religion in the West: Challenging Secularization*, edited by Krisin Aune, Sonya Sharma, and Giselle L. Vincett, 183–94. Aldershot and Burlington, VT: Ashgate Publishing.

Braidotti, Rosi, Bolette Blaagaard, Tobijn de Graauw, and Eva Midden, eds. 2014. *Transformations of Religion and the Public Sphere: Postsecular Publics*. New York: Palgrave Macmillan.

Breedveld, Koen, and Van den Broek, Andries. 2002. "De veeleisende samenleving: psychische vermoeidheid in een veranderende sociaal-culturele context." The Hague: Sociaal en Cultureel Planbureau.

Brown, Callum G. 2009. *The Death of Christian Britain: Understanding Secularisation, 1800–2000*. Second edition. London and New York: Routledge.

Brubaker, Rogers. 2004. *Ethnicity without Groups*. Cambridge, MA, and London: Harvard University Press.

Brubaker, Rogers. 2017. "Between Nationalism and Civilizationism: The European Populist Moment in Comparative Perspective." *Ethnic and Racial Studies* 40 (8): 1191–226.

Buijs, Frank J., Froukje Demant, and Atef Hamdy. 2006. *Strijders van eigen bodem: radicale en democratische moslims in Nederland*. Amsterdam: Amsterdam University Press.

Buitelaar, Marjo. 2006. *Islam en het dagelijks leven: religie en cultuur onder Marokkanen*. Amsterdam and Antwerp: Uitgeverij Atlas.

Buitelaar, Marjo. 2008. "Islamisering onder jonge Nederlanders van Marokkaanse afkomst." In *Handboek religie in Nederland: perspecief, overzicht, debat*, edited by Meerten Ter Borg, Erik Borgman, Marjo Buitelaar, Yme Kuiper, and Rob Plum. Zoetermeer: Uitgeverij Meinema/Forum.

Cadge, Wendy, Peggy Levitt, and David Smilde. 2011. "De-centering and Re-centering: Rethinking Concepts and Methods in the Sociological Study of Religion." *Journal for the Scientific Study of Religion* 50 (3): 437–49.

Calhoun, Craig, Mark Juergensmeyer, and Jonathan VanAntwerpen, eds. 2011. *Rethinking Secularism*. Oxford: Oxford University Press.

Calverley, E. E., and I. R. Netton. 2012. "Nafs." In *Encyclopaedia of Islam, Second Edition*, edited by P. Bearman, Th. Bianquis, C. E. Bosworth, E. van Donzel, and W. P. Heinrichs. Brill Online. https://referenceworks.brillonline.com/entries/encyclopaedia-of-islam-2/nafs-COM_0833?s.num=0&s.f.s2_.

Campbell, Colin. 1987. *The Romantic Ethic and the Spirit of Modern Consumerism*. Oxford: Blackwell Publishers.

Candea, Matei. 2018. *Comparison in Anthropology: The Impossible Method*. Cambridge and New York: Cambridge University Press.

Cannell, Fenella. 2006. "Introduction: The Anthropology of Christianity." In *The Anthropology of Christianity*, edited by Fenella Cannell, 1–50. Durham, NC, and London: Duke University Press.

Casanova, José. 1994. *Public Religions in the Modern World*. Chicago, MA, and London: University of Chicago Press.

Castells, Manuel. 2000. *The Rise of the Network Society*. Second edition. Vol. 1. The Information Age: Economy, Society and Culture. Oxford and Malden, MA: Blackwell Publishers.

Castells, Manuel. 2010. *The Power of Identity*. Second edition. Malden, MA: Wiley-Blackwell.

CBS. 2018. "Jaarrapport integratie 2018." https://longreads.cbs.nl/integratie-2018/.

Cesari, Jocelyne. 1998. *Musulmans et républicains: les jeunes, l'Islam et la France*. Brussels: Editions Complexe.

Cesari, Jocelyne. 2003a. "Muslim Minorities in Europe: The Silent Revolution." In *Modernizing Islam: Religion in the Public Sphere in Europe and the Middle East*, edited by John L. Esposito and François Burgat, 251–69. London: Hurst.

Cesari, Jocelyne. 2003b. *When Islam and Democracy Meet: Muslims in Europe and in the United States*. New York: Palgrave Macmillan.

Chua, Liana. 2012. *The Christianity of Culture: Conversion, Ethnic Citizenship, and the Matter of Religion in Malaysian Borneo*. Basingstoke: Palgrave Macmillan.

Clark, Lynn Schofield, ed. 2007. *Religion, Media, and the Marketplace*. New Brunswick, NJ: Rutgers University Press.

Cloïn, Mariëlle, ed. 2013. *Met het oog op de tijd: een blik op de tijdsbesteding van Nederlanders*. The Hague: Sociaal en Cultureel Planbureau.

Coleman, E. Gabriella. 2010. "Ethnographic Approaches to Digital Media." *Annual Review of Anthropology* 39 (1): 487–505.

Coleman, Simon. 2000. *The Globalisation of Charismatic Christianity: Spreading the Gospel of Prosperity*. Cambridge: Cambridge University Press.

Collins-Mayo, Sylvia, and Pink Dandelion. 2010. *Religion and Youth*. Farnham and Burlington, VT: Ashgate Publishing, Ltd.

Connor, Phillip. 2010. "Contexts of Immigrant Receptivity and Immigrant Religious Outcomes: The Case of Muslims in Western Europe." *Ethnic and Racial Studies* 33 (3): 376–403.

Crul, Maurice, Jens Schneider, and Frans Lelie, eds. 2012. *The European Second Generation Compared: Does the Integration Context Matter?* Amsterdam: Amsterdam University Press.

Davie, Grace. 2000. *Religion in Modern Europe: A Memory Mutates.* Oxford: Oxford University Press.

Day, Abby. 2008. "Wilfully Disempowered: A Gendered Response to a 'Fallen World.'" *European Journal of Women's Studies* 15 (3): 261–76.

De Hart, Joep. 2011. *Zwevende gelovigen: oude religie en nieuwe spiritualiteit.* Amsterdam: Uitgeverij Bert Bakker.

De Hart, Joep. 2012. "Reflectie: wat je gelooft dat ben je zelf. Een paar godsdienstsociologische overwegingen." In *Moslim in Nederland 2012*, M. Maliepaard and M. Gijsberts, 169–76. The Hague: Sociaal en Cultureel Planbureau.

De Hart, Joep. 2014. *Geloven binnen en buiten verband: godsdienstige ontwikkelingen in Nederland.* The Hague: Sociaal en Cultureel Planbureau.

De Hart, Joep, and Pepijn Van Houwelingen. 2018. *Christenen in Nederland: kerkelijke deelname en christelijke gelovigheid.* The Hague: Sociaal en Cultureel Planbureau.

De Jong, Jan Dirk. 2008. *Kapot moeilijk: een etnografisch onderzoek naar opvallend delinquent groepsgedrag van "Marokkaanse" jongens.* Amsterdam: Amsterdam University Press.

De Koning, Martijn. 2008. *Zoeken naar een "zuivere" islam: geloofsbeleving en identiteitsvorming van jonge Marokkaans-Nederlandse moslims.* Amsterdam: Bert Bakker.

De Koning, Martijn. 2009. "Moslimjongeren: de salafi-beweging en de vorming van een morele gemeenschap." *Tijdschrift Voor Criminologie* 51 (4): 375–87.

De Koning, Martijn. 2013. "The Moral Maze: Dutch Salafis and the Construction of a Moral Community of the Faithful." *Contemporary Islam* 7 (1): 71–83.

De Koning, Martijn. 2016. "'You Need to Present a Counter-Message': The Racialisation of Dutch Muslims and Anti-Islamophobia Initiatives." *Journal of Muslims in Europe* 5 (2): 170–89.

De Koning, Martijn. 2018. "'I'm a Weak Servant': The Question of Sincerity and the Cultivation of Weakness in the Lives of Dutch Salafi Muslims." In *Straying from the Straight Path: How Senses of Failure Invigorate Lived Religion*, edited by Daan Beekers and David Kloos, 37–53. New York and Oxford: Berghahn.

De Koning, Martijn. 2019. "The Netherlands." In *Yearbook of Muslims in Europe, Vol. 10*, edited by Oliver Scharbrodt, Samim Akgönül, Ahmet Alibašić, Jørgen S. Nielsen, and Egdūnas Racius, 476–92. Leiden and Boston, MA: Brill.

De Koning, Martijn, Joas Wagemakers, and Carmen Becker. 2014. *Salafisme: utopische idealen in een weerbarstige praktijk.* Almere: Parthenon.

De Roest, Henk, and Sake Stoppels. 2007. "Evangelicalisering in de gevestigde kerken." *Praktische Theologie* 34 (2) 163–8.

De Vries, Hent, and Lawrence E. Sullivan, eds. 2006. *Political Theologies: Public Religions in a Post-Secular World*. New York: Fordham University Press.

De Vries, Hent, and Samuel Weber, eds. 2001. *Religion and Media*. Stanford, CA: Stanford University Press.

De Witte, Marleen. 2009. "Modes of Binding, Moments of Bonding: Mediating Divine Touch in Ghanaian Pentecostalism and Traditionalism." In *Aesthetic Formations: Media, Religion, and the Senses*, edited by Birgit Meyer, 183–205. New York: Palgrave.

Decosimo, David. 2018. "For Big Comparison: Why the Arguments against Comparing Entire Religious Traditions Fail." *Religion Compass* 12 (5–6): 1–18.

DeHanas, Daniel Nilsson. 2016. *London Youth, Religion, and Politics: Engagement and Activism from Brixton to Brick Lane*. Oxford: Oxford University Press.

Demant, Froukje. 2005. *De beleving van de islam en de sekseverhoudingen bij Marokkaanse jongeren in Nederland*. Utrecht: Verwey Jonker Instituut.

Den Hertog, G. C. 2005. "Zonde." In *Christelijke Encyclopedie*, edited by George Harinck, Wim Berkelaar, Albert De Vos, and Lodewijk Winkeler, 1921. Kampen: Kok.

Derks, Marco. 2019. *Constructions of Homosexuality and Christian Religion in Contemporary Public Discourses in the Netherlands*. PhD Dissertation, Utrecht University.

Desmond, Matthew. 2006. "Becoming a Firefighter." *Ethnography* 7 (4): 387–421.

Dessing, Nathal M., Nadia Jeldtoft, Jørgen S. Nielsen, and Linda Woodhead, eds. 2013. *Everyday Lived Islam in Europe*. Farnham and Burlington, VT: Ashgate.

Dilger, Hansjörg. 2013. "Religion and the Formation of an Urban Educational Market: Transnational Reform Processes and Social Inequalities in Christian and Muslim Schooling in Dar Es Salaam, Tanzania." *Journal of Religion in Africa* 43 (4): 451–79.

Dilger, Hansjörg, and Dorothea Schulz. 2013. "Politics of Religious Schooling: Christian and Muslim Engagements with Education in Africa: Introduction." *Journal of Religion in Africa* 43 (4): 365–78.

Dorraj, Manochehr. 1999. "The Crisis of Modernity and Religious Revivalism: A Comparative Study of Islamic Fundamentalism, Jewish Fundamentalism and Liberation Theology." *Social Compass* 46 (2): 225–40.

Douwes, Dick, ed. 2001. *Naar een Europese islam? Essays*. Amsterdam: Mets & Schilt.

Duttlinger, Carolin. 2007. "Between Contemplation and Distraction: Configurations of Attention in Walter Benjamin." *German Studies Review* 30 (1): 33–54.

Duyvendak, Jan Willem. 2011. *The Politics of Home: Belonging and Nostalgia in Europe and the United States*. Houndmills and New York: Palgrave Macmillan.

Duyvendak, Jan Willem, Peter Geschiere, and Evelien Tonkens, eds. 2016. *The Culturalization of Citizenship: Belonging and Polarization in a Globalizing World*. London: Palgrave Macmillan.

Eagleton, Terry. 2009. *Reason, Faith, and Revolution: Reflections on the God Debate*. New Haven, CT and London: Yale University Press.

Elisha, Omri. 2011. *Moral Ambition: Mobilization and Social Outreach in Evangelical Megachurches*. Berkeley, CA: University of California Press.

Engelke, Matthew. 2005. "The Early Days of Johane Masowe: Self-Doubt, Uncertainty, and Religious Transformation." *Comparative Studies in Society and History* 47 (4): 781–808.

Engelke, Matthew, and Matt Tomlinson, eds. 2006. *The Limits of Meaning: Case Studies in the Anthropology of Christianity*. Oxford: Berghahn Books.

Eriksen, Thomas Hylland. 2001. *Tyranny of the Moment: Fast and Slow Time in the Information Age*. London and Sterling, VA: Pluto Press.

Esposito, John L. 1994. "Political Islam: Beyond the Green Menace." *Current History* 93: 19–24.

Esposito, John L., ed. 2003. "Nafs." In *The Oxford Dictionary of Islam*, electronic version. Oxford: Oxford University Press. http://www.oxfordreference.com/.

Evans-Pritchard, E. E. 1973. "Some Reminiscences and Reflections on Fieldwork." *Journal of the Anthropological Society of Oxford* 4 (1): 1–12.

Ewing, Katherine P. 1994. "Dreams from a Saint: Anthropological Atheism and the Temptation to Believe." *American Anthropologist* 96 (3): 571–83.

Exalto, John, ed. 2017. *De multiculturele refoschool: het reformatorisch onderwijs en de uitdaging van het pluralisme*. Apeldoorn: Labarum Academic.

Fabian, Johannes. 1983. *Time and the Other: How Anthropology Makes Its Object*. New York: Columbia University Press.

Fadil, Nadia. 2008. *Submitting to God, Submitting to the Self: Secular and Religious Trajectories of Second Generation Maghrebi in Belgium*. PhD Dissertation, Katholieke Universiteit Leuven.

Fadil, Nadia. 2009. "Managing Affects and Sensibilities: The Case of Not-Handshaking and Not-Fasting." *Social Anthropology* 17 (4): 439–54.

Fadil, Nadia. 2013. "Performing the Salat [Islamic Prayers] at Work: Secular and Pious Muslims Negotiating the Contours of the Public in Belgium." *Ethnicities* 13 (6): 729–50.

Fadil, Nadia. 2017. "Recalling the 'Islam of the Parents': Liberal and Secular Muslims Redefining the Contours of Religious Authenticity." *Identities* 24 (1): 82–99.

Fadil, Nadia, and Mayanthi Fernando. 2015. "Rediscovering the 'Everyday' Muslim: Notes on an Anthropological Divide." *HAU* 5 (2): 59–88.

Fadil, Nadia, Francesco Ragazzi, and Martijn De Koning. 2019. *Radicalization in Belgium and the Netherlands: Critical Perspectives on Violence and Security*. London: I.B. Tauris.

Fahy, John. 2020. *Becoming Vaishnava in an Ideal Vedic City*. New York and Oxford: Berghahn.

Fassin, Didier. 2014. "The Ethical Turn in Anthropology: Promises and Uncertainties." *HAU: Journal of Ethnographic Theory* 4 (1): 429–35.

Fischer, Johan. 2008. *Proper Islamic Consumption: Shopping among the Malays in Modern Malaysia*. Copenhagen: NIAS.

Fleischmann, Fenella, and Karen Phalet. 2012. "Integration and Religiosity among the Turkish Second Generation in Europe: A Comparative Analysis across Four Capital Cities." *Ethnic and Racial Studies* 35 (2): 320–41.

Flory, Richard, and Donald Miller. 2008. *Finding Faith: The Spiritual Quest of the Post-Boomer Generation*. New Brunswick, NJ: Rutgers University Press.

Forsey, Martin Gerard. 2010. "Ethnography as Participant Listening." *Ethnography* 11 (4): 558–72.

Foucault, Michel. 1990. *The Care of the Self. The History of Sexuality*, Vol. 3. Translated by Robert Hurley. London: Penguin Books.

Foucault, Michel. 2000. *Ethics: Subjectivity and Truth. Essential Works of Foucault 1954–1984*, Vol. 1. Edited by Paul Rabinow. Translated by Robert Hurley et al. New York: Penguin Books.

Foucault, Michel. 2005. *The Hermeneutics of the Subject: Lectures at the Collège de France 1981–1982*. Edited by Frédéric Gros. Translated by Graham Burchell. New York and Basingstoke: Palgrave Macmillan.

Franks, Myfanwy. 2001. *Women and Revivalism in the West: Choosing Fundamentalism in a Liberal Democracy*. Basingstoke: Palgrave Macmillan.

Fullagar, Simone, Kevin Markwell, and Erica Wilson, eds. 2012. *Slow Tourism: Experiences and Mobilities*. Bristol: Channel View Publications.

Gale, Richard, and Therese O'Toole. 2009. "Young People and Faith Activism: British Muslim Youth, Glocalisation and the Umma." In *Faith in the Public Realm: Controversies, Policies and Practices*, edited by Adam Dinham, Robert Furbey, and Vivien Lowndes, 143–62. Bristol: The Policy Press.

Gardet, L. 2012a. "Al-Ḳaḍāʾ Waʾl-Ḳadar." In *Encyclopaedia of Islam, Second Edition*, edited by P. Bearman, Th. Bianquis, C. E. Bosworth, E. van Donzel, and W. P. Heinrichs. Brill Online. http://referenceworks.brillonline.com/entries/encyclopaedia-of-islam-2/al-kada-wa-l-kadar-COM_0407.

Gardet, L. 2012b. "Ikhtiyār." In *Encyclopaedia of Islam, Second Edition*, edited by P. Bearman, Th. Bianquis, C. E. Bosworth, E. van Donzel, and W. P. Heinrichs. Brill Online. http://referenceworks.brillonline.com/entries/encyclopaedia-of-islam-2/ikhtiyar-SIM_3516.

Gardet, L. 2012c. "Īmān." In *Encyclopaedia of Islam, Second Edition*, edited by P. Bearman, Th. Bianquis, C. E. Bosworth, E. van Donzel, and W. P. Heinrichs. Brill Online. https://referenceworks.brillonline.com/entries/encyclopaedia-of-islam-2/iman-COM_0370

Garner, Steve, and Saher Selod. 2015. "The Racialization of Muslims: Empirical Studies of Islamophobia." *Critical Sociology* 41 (1): 9–19.

Gauthier, François, Tuomas Martikainen, and Linda Woodhead. 2011. "Introduction: Religion et Société de Consummation/Religion in Consumer Society." *Social Compass* 58 (3): 291–301.

Gauthier, François, Tuomas Martikainen, and Linda Woodhead. 2013. "Introduction: Religion in Market Society." In *Religion in the Neoliberal Age: Political Economy and Modes of Governance*, edited by Tuomas Martikainen and François Gauthier, 1–18. Farnham and Burlington, VT: Ashgate.

Geschiere, Peter. 2009. *The Perils of Belonging: Autochthony, Citizenship, and Exclusion in Africa and Europe*. Chicago, IL: University of Chicago Press.

Gilroy, Paul. 2005. *Postcolonial Melancholia*. New York and Chichester: Columbia University Press.
Gingrich, Andre, and Richard Gabriel Fox, eds. 2002. *Anthropology, by Comparison*. London: Routledge.
Giordan, Giuseppe, ed. 2010. *Annual Review of the Sociology of Religion*, Vol. 1: Youth and Religion. Leiden: Brill.
Good, Byron. 1994. *Medicine, Rationality and Experience: An Anthropological Perspective*. Cambridge: Cambridge University Press.
Gracia, Pablo, Lucía Vázquez-Quesada, and Herman G. van de Werfhorst. 2016. "Ethnic Penalties? The Role of Human Capital and Social Origins in Labour Market Outcomes of Second-Generation Moroccans and Turks in the Netherlands." *Journal of Ethnic and Migration Studies* 42 (1): 69–87.
Grundel, Malin, and Mieke Maliepaard. 2012. "Knowing, Understanding and Practising Democratic Citizenship: An Investigation of the Role of Religion among Muslim, Christian and Non-Religious Adolescents." *Ethnic and Racial Studies* 35 (12): 2075–96.
Guhin, Jeffrey. 2016. "Why Worry about Evolution? Boundaries, Practices, and Moral Salience in Sunni and Evangelical High Schools." *Sociological Theory* 34 (2): 151–74.
Gumbel, Nicky. 2006. *Alpha—Questions of Life: An Opportunity to Explore the Meaning of Life*. Eastbourne: Kingsway Communications.
Haegens, Koen. 2012. *Neem de tijd: overleven in de to go-maatschappij*. Amsterdam: Ambo/Anthos Uitgevers.
Hage, Ghassan. 2003. *Against Paranoid Nationalism: Searching for Hope in a Shrinking Society*. Melbourne: Pluto Press Australia.
Hall, Stuart, ed. 1997. *Representation: Cultural Representations and Signifying Practices*. London: Sage.
Hamid, Sadek. 2008. "The Development of British Salafism." *ISIM Review*, no. 21: 10–11.
Hamid, Sadek. 2009. "The Attraction of 'Authentic' Islam: Salafism and British Muslim Youth." In *Global Salafism: Islam's New Religious Movement*, edited by Roel Meijer, 384–403. London: Hurst.
Harding, Susan Friend. 2000. *The Book of Jerry Falwell: Fundamentalist Language and Politics*. Princeton, NJ, and Oxford: Princeton University Press.
Harvey, David. 1989. *The Condition of Postmodernity: An Enquiry into the Origins of Cultural Change*. Oxford and Cambridge, MA: Basil Blackwell.
Haykel, Bernard. 2009. "On the Nature of Salafi Thought and Action." In *Global Salafism: Islam's New Religious Movement*, edited by Roel Meijer, 33–57. New York and Chichester: Columbia University Press.
Haynes, Naomi. 2020. "The Expansive Present: A New Model of Christian Time." *Current Anthropology* 61 (1): 57–76.
Heelas, Paul, and Linda Woodhead. 2005. *The Spiritual Revolution: Why Religion Is Giving Way to Spirituality*. Oxford and Cambridge, MA: Blackwell Publishers (co-authored by B. Seel, B. Szerszynski and K. Tusting).

Hefner, Robert W. 2010. "Religious Resurgence in Contemporary Asia: Southeast Asian Perspectives on Capitalism, the State, and the New Piety." *The Journal of Asian Studies* 69 (4): 1031–47.

Henkel, Heiko. 2005. "'Between Belief and Unbelief Lies the Performance of Salāt': Meaning and Efficacy of a Muslim Ritual." *Journal of the Royal Anthropological Institute* 11 (3): 487–507.

Hepp, Andreas. 2013. *Cultures of Mediatization*. Cambridge and Malden, MA: Polity Press.

Herrera, Linda, and Asef Bayat, eds. 2010. *Being Young and Muslim: New Cultural Politics in the Global South and North*. Oxford: Oxford University Press.

Hervieu-Léger, Danièle. 2000. *Religion as a Chain of Memory*. Translated by Simon Lee. Oxford: Polity Press.

Hervieu-Léger, Danièle. 2006. "In Search of Certainties: The Paradoxes of Religiosity in Societies of High Modernity." *The Hedgehog Review* 8 (1–2): 59–68.

Hirschkind, Charles. 2006. *The Ethical Soundscape: Cassette Sermons and Islamic Counterpublics*. New York: Columbia University Press.

Hockey, Jenny. 2002. "Interviews as Ethnography? Disembodied Social Interaction in Britain." In *British Subjects: An Anthropology of Britiain*, edited by Nigel Rapport, 209–22. Oxford and New York: Berg.

Holmes, Douglas R. 2000. *Integral Europe: Fastcapitalism, Multiculturalism, Neofascism*. Princeton, NJ: Princeton University Press.

Holy, Ladislav, ed. 1987. *Comparative Anthropology*. Oxford: Blackwell.

Hoover, Stewart M. 2006. *Religion in the Media Age*. London and New York: Routledge.

Hopkins, Peter, Elizabeth Olson, Rachel Pain, and Giselle Vincett. 2011. "Mapping Intergenerationalities: The Formation of Youthful Religiosities." *Transactions of the Institute of British Geographers* 36 (2): 314–27.

Houtman, Dick, and Peter Mascini. 2002. "Why Do Churches Become Empty, while New Age Grows? Secularization and Religious Change in the Netherlands." *Journal for the Scientific Study of Religion* 41 (3): 455–73.

Houtman, Dick, Stef Aupers, and Willem de Koster. 2011. *Paradoxes of Individualization: Social Control and Social Conflict in Contemporary Modernity*. Farnham: Ashgate.

Huijnk, Willem. 2018. *De religieuze beleving van moslims in Nederland: diversiteit en verandering in beeld*. The Hague: Sociaal en Cultureel Planbureau.

Ibrahim, Murtala. 2017. "Oral Transmission of the Sacred: Preaching in Christ Embassy and Nasfat in Abuja." *Journal of Religion in Africa* 47 (1): 108–31.

Ivanescu, Carolina. 2010. "Politicised Religion and the Religionisation of Politics." *Culture and Religion* 11 (4): 309–25.

Jacobsen, Christine M. 2011. *Islamic Traditions and Muslim Youth in Norway*. Leiden and Boston, MA: Brill.

Jansen, Mechteld, and Hijme Stoffels, eds. 2008. *A Moving God: Immigrant Churches in the Netherlands*. Münster: Lit Verlag.

Jansen, Yolande. 2011. "Postsecularism, Piety and Fanaticism: Reflections on Jürgen Habermas' and Saba Mahmood's Critiques of Secularism." *Philosophy & Social Criticism* 37 (9): 977–98.

Janson, Marloes. 2013. *Islam, Youth and Modernity in the Gambia: The Tablighi Jama'at*. Cambridge and New York: Cambridge University Press.

Janson, Marloes, and Birgit Meyer. 2016a. "Introduction: Towards a Framework for the Study of Christian-Muslim Encounters in Africa." *Africa* 86 (4): 615–19.

Janson, Marloes, and Birgit Meyer. 2016b. "Special Section. Studying Islam and Christianity in Africa: Moving beyond a Bifurcated Field." *Africa* 86 (4).

Janssen, Jacques, and Maerten Prins. 2000. "The Abstract Image of God: The Case of the Dutch Youth." *Archives de Sciences Sociales des Religions*, no. 109: 31–48.

Jouili, Jeanette S. 2009. "Negotiating Secular Boundaries: Pious Micro-Practices of Muslim Women in French and German Public Spheres." *Social Anthropology* 17 (4): 455–70.

Jouili, Jeanette S. 2015. *Pious Practice and Secular Constraints: Women in the Islamic Revival in Europe*. Stanford, CA: Stanford University Press.

Jouili, Jeanette S., and Schirin Amir-Moazami. 2006. "Knowledge, Empowerment and Religious Authority among Pious Muslim Women in France and Germany." *The Muslim World* 96 (4): 617–42.

Jouili, Jeanette S., and Annelies Moors. 2014. "Introduction: Islamic Sounds and the Politics of Listening." *Anthropological Quarterly* 87 (4): 977–88.

Kamphuis, B. 2005. "Verbond." In *Christelijke encyclopedie*, edited by George Harinck, Wim Berkelaar, Albert De Vos, and Lodewijk Winkeler, 1794–5. Kampen: Kok.

Keane, Webb. 2007. *Christian Moderns: Freedom and Fetish in the Mission Encounter*. Berkeley and Los Angeles: University of California Press.

Kennedy, James C. 1995. *Nieuw Babylon in aanbouw: Nederland in de jaren zestig*. Amsterdam: Boom.

Kennedy, James C., and Markha Valenta. 2006. "Religious Pluralism and the Dutch State: Reflections on the Future of Article 23." In *Geloven in het publieke domein: verkenningen van een dubbele transformatie*, edited by W. B. H. J. van de Donk, A. P. Jonkers, G. J. Kronjee, and R. J. J. M. Plums, 337–51. Amsterdam: Amsterdam University Press/Wetenschappelijke Raad voor het Regeringsbeleid.

Kešić, Josip, and Jan Willem Duyvendak. 2019. "The Nation under Threat: Secularist, Racial and Populist Nativism in the Netherlands." *Patterns of Prejudice* 53 (5): 441–63.

Ketner, Susan. 2008. *Marokkaanse wortels, Nederlandse grond: exploratie, bindingen en identiteitsstrategiën van jongeren van Marokkaanse afkomst*. PhD Dissertation, Rijksuniversiteit Groningen.

Khan, Muhammad Muhsin, trans. 1997. *The Translation of the Meanings of Sahih Al-Bukhari*. Riyadh: Darussalam.

Klaver, Miranda. 2008. "De evangelische beweging." In *Handboek religie in Nederland: perspecief, overzicht, debat*, edited by Meerten Ter Borg, Erik Borgman, Marjo Buitelaar, Yme Kuiper, and Rob Plum, 146–59. Zoetermeer: Uitgeverij Meinema/Forum.

Klaver, Miranda. 2011. *This Is My Desire: A Semiotic Perspective on Conversion in an Evangelical Seeker Church and a Pentecostal Church in the Netherlands*. Amsterdam: Pallas Publications/Amsterdam University Press.

Klingenberg, Maria, and Sjö. Sofia 2019. "Theorizing Religious Socialization: A Critical Assessment." *Religion* 49 (2): 163–78.

Kloos, David. 2018a. *Becoming Better Muslims: Religious Authority and Ethical Improvement in Aceh, Indonesia*. Princeton, NJ, and Oxford: Princeton University Press.

Kloos, David. 2018b. "The Ethics of Not-Praying: Religious Negligence, Life Phase, and Social Status in Aceh, Indonesia." In *Straying from the Straight Path: How Senses of Failure Invigorate Lived Religion*, edited by Daan Beekers and David Kloos, 90–106. Oxford and New York: Berghahn.

Kloos, David, and Daan Beekers. 2018. "Introduction: The Productive Potential of Moral Failure in Lived Islam and Christianity." In *Straying from the Straight Path: How Senses of Failure Invigorate Lived Religion*, edited by Daan Beekers and David Kloos, 1–19. New York and Oxford: Berghahn.

Knibbe, Kim. 2009. "'We Did Not Come Here as Tenants, but as Landlords': Nigerian Pentecostals and the Power of Maps." *African Diaspora* 2 (2): 133–58.

Knibbe, Kim. 2018. "Secularist Understandings of Pentecostal Healing Practices in Amsterdam: Developing an Intersectional and Post-Secularist Sociology of Religion." *Social Compass* 65 (5): 650–66.

Knorr Cetina, Karin. 1999. *Epistemic Cultures: How the Sciences Make Knowledge*. Cambridge, MA, and London: Harvard University Press.

Knott, Kim, Elizabeth Poole, and Teemu Taira. 2014. *Media Portrayals of Religion and the Secular Sacred: Representation and Change*. Farnham and Burlington, VT: Ashgate.

Koopmans, Ruud. 2015. "Religious Fundamentalism and Hostility against Out-Groups: A Comparison of Muslims and Christians in Western Europe." *Journal of Ethnic and Migration Studies* 41 (1): 33–57.

Kracauer, Siegfried. 1995. *The Mass Ornament: Weimar Essays*. Translated by Thomas Y. Levin. Cambridge, MA: Harvard University Press.

Laidlaw, James. 2014. *The Subject of Virtue: An Anthropology of Ethics and Freedom*. New York: Cambridge University Press.

Laidlaw, James, and Jonathan Mair. 2019. "Imperfect Accomplishment: The Fo Guang Shan Short-Term Monastic Retreat and Ethical Pedagogy in Humanistic Buddhism." *Cultural Anthropology* 34 (3): 328–58.

Lambek, Michael, ed. 2010. *Ordinary Ethics: Anthropology, Language, and Action*. NewYork: Fordham University Press.

Landman, Nico. 1992. *Van mat tot minaret: de institutionalisering van de islam in Nederland*. Amsterdam: VU Uitgeverij.

Landman, Nico, and Thijl Sunier. 2014. *Transnational Turkish Islam: Shifting Geographies of Religious Activism and Community Building in Turkey and Europe*. Basingstoke: Palgrave Macmillan.

Lapidus, Ira M. 1984. "Knowledge, Virtue, and Action: The Classical Muslim Conception of Adab and the Nature of Religious Fulfillment in Islam." In *Moral Conduct and Authority: The Place of Adab in South Asian Islam*, edited by Barbara Daly Metcalf, 38–61. Berkeley: University of California Press.

Larkin, Brian. 2014. "Techniques of Inattention: The Mediality of Loudspeakers in Nigeria." *Anthropological Quarterly* 87 (4): 989–1015.

Larkin, Brian, and Birgit Meyer. 2006. "Pentecostalism, Islam and Culture: New Religious Movements in West Africa." In *Themes in West Africa's History*, edited by E. K. Akyeampong, 286–312. Oxford: James Currey.

Lauzière, Henri. 2016. *The Making of Salafism: Islamic Reform in the Twentieth Century*. New York and Chichester: Columbia University Press.

Leach, Edmund R. 1964. *Political Systems of Highland Burma: A Study of Kachin Social Structure*. London: The Athlone Press [originally published in 1954].

Lebner, Ashley B. 2015. "The Anthropology of Secularity beyond Secularism." *Religion and Society* 6 (1): 62–74.

Liberatore, Giulia. 2013. "Doubt as a Double-Edged Sword: Unanswerable Questions and Practical Solutions among Newly Practising Somali Women in London." In *Ethnographies of Doubt: Faith and Uncertainty in Contemporary Societies*, edited by Mathijs Pelkmans, 225–50. London: I.B. Tauris.

Liberatore, Giulia. 2017. *Somali, Muslim, British: Striving in Securitized Britain*. London: Bloomsbury.

Lovink, Geert. 2013. "The Aesthetics of Dispersed Attention: An Interview with German Media Theorist Petra Löffler." *NECSUS: European Journal of Media Studies* 2 (2): 545–55.

Luckmann, Thomas. 1967. *Invisible Religion: The Problem of Religion in Modern Society*. New York and London: The Macmillan Company/Collier-Macmillan.

Luhrmann, Tanya M. 2004. "Metakinesis: How God Becomes Intimate in Contemporary U.S. Christianity." *American Anthropologist* 106 (3): 518–28.

Luhrmann, Tanya M. 2007. "How Do You Learn to Know That It Is God Who Speaks?" In *Learning Religion: Anthropological Approaches*, edited by David Berliner and Ramon Sarró, 83–102. New York: Berghahn.

Luhrmann, Tanya M. 2012a. "A Hyperreal God and Modern Belief: Toward an Anthropological Theory of Mind." *Current Anthropology* 53 (4): 371–95.

Luhrmann, Tanya M. 2012b. *When God Talks Back: Understanding the American Evangelical Relationship with God*. New York and Toronto: Alfred A. Knopf.

Lury, Celia. 2011. *Consumer Culture*. Second edition. Cambridge and Malden, MA: Polity Press.

Lynch, Gordon, and Jolyon Mitchell, eds. 2012. *Religion, Media and Culture: A Reader*. London and New York: Routledge.

Mahmood, Saba. 2001. "Rehearsed Spontaneity and the Conventionality of Ritual: Disciplines of Ṣalat." *American Ethnologist* 28 (4): 827–53.

Mahmood, Saba. 2005. *Politics of Piety: The Islamic Revival and the Feminist Subject*. Princeton, NJ, and Oxford: Princeton University Press.

Mahmood, Saba. 2012. "Preface to the 2012 Edition." In *Politics of Piety: The Islamic Revival and the Feminist Subject*. Princeton, NJ, and Oxford: Princeton University Press.

Mahmood, Saba. 2016. *Religious Difference in a Secular Age: A Minority Report*. Princeton, NJ, and Oxford: Princeton University Press.

Maliepaard, Mieke, and Mérove Gijsberts. 2012. *Moslim in Nederland 2012*. The Hague: Sociaal en Cultureel Planbureau.

Mandaville, Peter G. 2001. *Transnational Muslim Politics: Reimagining the Umma*. London: Routledge.

Marsden, Magnus. 2005. *Living Islam: Muslim Religious Experience in Pakistan's North-West Frontier*. Cambridge: Cambridge University Press.

Marsden, Magnus, and Konstantinos Retsikas. 2013. "Introduction." In *Articulating Islam: Anthropological Approaches to Muslim Worlds*, edited by Magnus Marsden and Konstantinos Retsikas, 1–31. Dordrecht: Springer.

Marshall, Ruth. 2009. *Political Spiritualities: The Pentecostal Revolution in Nigeria*. Chicago, IL and London: University of Chicago Press.

Martikainen, Tuomas, and François Gauthier, eds. 2013. *Religion in the Neoliberal Age: Political Economy and Modes of Governance*. Farnham and Burlington, VT: Ashgate.

Martin, David. 1990. *Tongues of Fire: The Explosion of Protestantism in Latin America*. Oxford and Cambridge, MA: Basis Blackwell.

Martin, David. 2001. *Pentecostalism: The World Their Parish*. Oxford: Wiley-Blackwell.

Marzouki, Nadia, Duncan McDonnell, and Olivier Roy, eds. 2016. *Saving the People: How Populists Hijack Religion*. London: Hurst.

Mattingly, Cheryl, and Jason Throop. 2018. "The Anthropology of Ethics and Morality." *Annual Review of Anthropology* 47 (1): 475–92.

Maudet, Marion. 2017. "Religion and Sexuality in France from the 1970s to the 2000s: Changes in Practices and Attachment to the Heterosexual Family." Translated by James Tovey. *Population* 72 (4): 671–96.

Mayblin, Maya, and Diego Malara. 2018. "Introduction: Lenience in Systems of Religious Meaning and Practice." *Social Analysis* 62 (3): 1–20.

Mazower, Mark. 1999. *Dark Continent: Europe's Twentieth Century*. London: Penguin.

McDonald, Kevin. 2006. *Global Movements: Action and Culture*. Malden, MA: Blackwell Publishing.

McDougall, Debra. 2009. "Christianity, Relationality and the Material Limits of Individualism: Reflections on Robbins's Becoming Sinners." *The Asia Pacific Journal of Anthropology* 10 (1): 1–19.

McGrath, Alister. 1996. *Beyond the Quiet Time: Practical Evangelical Spirituality*. Grand Rapids, MI: Baker Books.

McGuire, Meredith B. 2008. *Lived Religion: Faith and Practice in Everyday Life*. Oxford: Oxford University Press.

McLeod, Hugh. 1997. *Religion and the People of Western Europe, 1789–1989*. Oxford: Oxford University Press.

Meer, Nasar, and Tariq Modood. 2019. "Islamophobia as the Racialisation of Muslims." In *The Routledge International Handbook of Islamophobia*, edited by Irene Zempi and Imran Awan, 18–31. Abingdon and New York: Routledge.

Meijer, Roel. 2009. "Introduction." In *Global Salafism: Islam's New Religious Movement*, edited by Roel Meijer, 1–32. New York and Chichester: Columbia University Press.

Mepschen, Paul, Jan Willem Duyvendak, and Evelien H. Tonkens. 2010. "Sexual Politics, Orientalism and Multicultural Citizenship in the Netherlands." *Sociology* 44 (5): 962–79.

Metcalf, Barbara Daly, ed. 1984. *Moral Conduct and Authority: The Place of Adab in South Asian Islam*. Berkeley: University of California Press.

Meyer, Birgit. 2006. "Impossible Representations: Pentecostalism, Vision, and Video Technology in Ghana." In *Religion, Media, and the Public Sphere*, edited by Birgit Meyer and Annelies Moors, 290–312. Bloomington: Indiana University Press.

Meyer, Birgit. ed. 2009. *Aesthetic Formations: Media, Religion, and the Senses*. New York: Palgrave Macmillan.

Meyer, Birgit. 2010. "The Indispensability of Form." *The Immanent Frame* (blog). November 10, http://blogs.ssrc.org/tif/2010/11/10/indispensability-of-form/.

Meyer, Birgit. 2012. "Mediation and the Genesis of Presence. Towards a Material Approach to Religion." Inaugural lecture. Utrecht: Utrecht University.

Meyer, Birgit. 2015. *Sensational Movies: Video, Vision, and Christianity in Ghana*. Oakland: University of California Press.

Meyer, Birgit. 2016. "Towards a Joint Framework for the Study of Christians and Muslims in Africa: Response to J. D. Y. Peel." *Africa* 86 (4): 628–32.

Meyer, Birgit. 2019. "Recycling the Christian Past: The Heritagization of Christianity and National Identity in the Netherlands." In *Cultures, Citizenship and Human Rights*, edited by Rosemarie Buikema, Antoine Buyse, and Antonius C. G. M. Robben, 64–88. Abingdon and New York: Routledge.

Miller, Donald E. 1997. *Reinventing American Protestantism: Christianity in the New Millennium*. Berkeley and Los Angeles: University of California Press.

Mittermaier, Amira. 2011. *Dreams That Matter: Egyptian Landscapes of the Imagination*. Berkeley: University of California Press.

Moors, Annelies. 2009. "The Dutch and the Face-veil: The Politics of Discomfort." *Social Anthropology* 17 (4): 393–408.

Morgan, David. 1998. *Visual Piety: A History and Theory of Popular Religious Images*. Berkeley: University of California Press.

Morgan, David, ed. 2008. *Key Words in Religion, Media and Culture*. New York and London: Routledge.

Muehlebach, Andrea, and Nitzan Shoshan. 2012. "Introduction." *Anthropological Quarterly* 85 (2): 317–43.

Muis, J. 2005. "Verzoening." In *Christelijke encyclopedie*, edited by George Harinck, Wim Berkelaar, Albert De Vos, and Lodewijk Winkeler, 1806. Kampen: Kok.

Mullet, Etienne, and Fabiola Azar. 2009. "Apologies, Repentance, and Forgiveness: A Muslim–Christian Comparison." *The International Journal for the Psychology of Religion* 19 (4): 275–85.

Nagra, Baljit. 2011. "'Our Faith Was Also Hijacked by Those People': Reclaiming Muslim Identity in Canada in a Post-9/11 Era." *Journal of Ethnic and Migration Studies* 37 (3): 425–41.

Niewöhner, Jörg, and Thomas Scheffer. 2010. "Introduction. Thickening Comparison: On the Multiple Facets of Comparability." In *Thick Comparison: Reviving the Ethnographic Aspiration*, edited by Thomas Scheffer and Jörg Niewöhner, 1–15. Leiden: Brill.

Nolte, Insa, Olukoya Ogen, and Rebecca Jones. 2017. *Beyond Religious Tolerance: Muslim, Christian and Traditionalist Encounters in an African Town*. Rochester, NY: James Currey.

North, Paul. 2012. *The Problem of Distraction*. Stanford, CA: Stanford University Press.

Nussbaum, Martha C. 2012. *The New Religious Intolerance: Overcoming the Politics of Fear in an Anxious Age*. Cambridge, MA: Belknap Press.

Nyhagen, Line, and Beatrice Halsaa. 2016. *Religion, Gender and Citizenship: Women of Faith, Gender Equality and Feminism*. New York: Palgrave Macmillan.

Olsson, Susanne. 2017. "Shia as Internal Others: A Salafi Rejection of the 'Rejecters.'" *Islam and Christian—Muslim Relations* 28 (4): 409–30.

Oosterbaan, Martijn. 2017. *Transmitting the Spirit: Religious Conversion, Media, and Urban Violence in Brazil*. University Park: The Pennsylvania State University Press.

Orsi, Robert A. 2005. *Between Heaven and Earth: The Religious Worlds People Make and the Scholars Who Study Them*. Princeton, NJ and Oxford: Princeton University Press.

Osella, Filippo, and Benjamin Soares, eds. 2010. *Islam, Politics, Anthropology*. Malden, MA: Wiley-Blackwell.

Peel, J. D. Y. 2015. *Christianity, Islam, and Orisa-Religion: Three Traditions in Comparison and Interaction*. Oakland: University of California Press.

Pelkmans, Mathijs. 2013. "Outline for an Ethnography of Doubt." In *Ethnographies of Doubt: Faith and Uncertainty in Contemporary Societies*, edited by Mathijs Pelkmans, 1–42. London: I.B. Tauris.

Peter, Frank. 2006. "Individualization and Religious Authority in Western European Islam." *Islam and Christian-Muslim Relations* 17 (1): 105–18.

Petrini, Carlo. 2003. *Slow Food: The Case for Taste*. New York and Chichester: Columbia University Press.

Pons, Anneke, ed. 2014. *Biblebelt online: bevindelijk gereformeerden en nieuwe media*. Apeldoorn: Labarum Academic.

Portes, Alejandro, and Rubén G. Rumbaut. 2001. *Legacies: The Story of the Immigrant Second Generation*. Berkeley and Los Angeles: University of California Press.

Poulson, Stephen, and Colin Campbell. 2010. "Isomorphism, Institutional Parochialism, and the Sociology of Religion." *The American Sociologist* 41: 31–47.

Rath, Jan. 1991. *Minorisering, de sociale constructie van "etnische minderheden."* Amsterdam: Sua.

Reinhardt, Bruno. 2017. "Praying until Jesus Returns: Commitment and Prayerfulness among Charismatic Christians in Ghana." *Religion* 47 (1): 51–72.

Righart, Hans. 2004. *De wereldwijde jaren zestig: Groot-Britannië, Nederland, de Verenigde Staten*. Hilversum: Uitgeverij Verloren.

Robben, Antonius C. G. M., and Jeffrey A. Sluka. 2007. *Ethnographic Fieldwork: An Anthropological Reader*. Malden, MA: Blackwell Publishing.

Robbins, Joel. 2003. "What Is a Christian? Notes toward an Anthropology of Christianity." *Religion* 33 (3): 191–9.

Robbins, Joel. 2004. *Becoming Sinners: Christianity and Moral Torment in a Papua New Guinea Society*. Berkeley: University of California Press.

Robbins, Joel. 2007. "Continuity Thinking and the Problem of Christian Culture: Belief, Time, and the Anthropology of Christianity." *Current Anthropology* 48 (1): 5–38.

Robbins, Joel. 2013. "Beyond the Suffering Subject: Toward an Anthropology of the Good." *Journal of the Royal Anthropological Institute* 19 (3): 447–462.

Robbins, Joel, Bambi B. Schieffelin, and Vilaça. Aparecida 2014. "Evangelical Conversion and the Transformation of the Self in Amazonia and Melanesia: Christianity and the Revival of Anthropological Comparison." *Comparative Studies in Society and History* 56 (3): 559–90.

Robson, J. 2012. "Hadīth." In *Encyclopaedia of Islam, Second Edition*, edited by P. Bearman, Th. Bianquis, C.E. Bosworth, E. van Donzel, and W.P. Heinrichs. Brill Online. https://referenceworks.brillonline.com/entries/encyclopaedia-of-islam-2/hadith-COM_0248?s.num=0&s.f.s2.

Roeland, Johan. 2009. *Selfation: Dutch Evangelical Youth between Subjectivization and Subjection*. Amsterdam: Pallas Publications/Amsterdam University Press.

Roeland, Johan, Stef Aupers, Dick Houtman, Martijn de Koning, and Ineke Noomen. 2010. "The Quest for Religious Purity in New Age, Evangelicalism and Islam: Religious Renditions of Dutch Youth and the Luckmann Legacy." In *Annual Review of the Sociology of Religion*, Vol. 1: Youth and Religion, edited by Giuseppe Giordan, 289–306. Leiden: Brill.

Roex, Ineke. 2013. *Leven als de profeet in Nederland: over de salafi-beweging en democratie*. PhD Dissertation, University of Amsterdam.

Roex, Ineke, Sjef Van Stiphout, and Jean Tillie. 2010. *Salafisme in Nederland: aard, omvang en dreiging*. Amsterdam: IMES-Institute for Migration and Ethnic Studies, University of Amsterdam.

Roof, Wade Clark. 2001. *Spiritual Marketplace: Baby Boomers and the Remaking of American Religion*. Princeton, NJ: Princeton University Press.

Rose, Nikolas. 1999. *Powers of Freedom: Reframing Political Thought*. Cambridge: Cambridge University Press.

Roy, Olivier. 2004. *Globalized Islam: The Search for a New Ummah*. London: Hurst.

Roy, Olivier. 2013. *Holy Ignorance: When Religion and Culture Part Ways*. Translated by Ros Schwartz. Oxford: Oxford University Press.

Rudnyckyj, Daromir. 2011. *Spiritual Economies: Islam, Globalization, and the Afterlife of Development*. New York: Cornell University Press.

Runia, K. 2005. "Genade & genadeleer." In *Christelijke encyclopedie*, edited by George Harinck, Wim Berkelaar, Albert De Vos, and Lodewijk Winkeler, 624–6. Kampen: Kok.

Rutsky, R. L. 2002. "Pop-Up Theory: Distraction and Consumption in the Age of Meta-Information." *Journal of Visual Culture* 1 (3): 279–94.

Saeed, Abdullah, Mahmoud M. Ayoub, and Vincent J. Cornell. 2005. "Qur'ān." In *Encyclopedia of Religion*, edited by Lindsay Jones, Second edition, 7561–74. Detroit, MI: Thomson Gale.

Said, Edward W. 1995. *Orientalism*. London: Penguin Books [first published in 1978].

Sanneh, Lamin. 1996. *Piety and Power: Muslims and Christians in West Africa*. Maryknoll, NY: Orbis Books.

Scheffer, Thomas, and Jörg Niewöhner, eds. 2010. *Thick Comparison: Reviving the Ethnographic Aspiration*. Leiden: Brill.

Schielke, Samuli. 2010. "Second Thoughts about the Anthropology of Islam, or How to Make Sense of Grand Schemes in Everyday Life." *ZMO Working Papers* 2.

Schielke, Samuli. 2015. *Egypt in the Future Tense: Hope, Frustration, and Ambivalence before and after 2011*. Bloomington, IN: Indiana University Press.

Schiffauer, Werner. 1988. "Migration and Religiousness." In *The New Islamic Presence in Europe*, edited by T. Gerholm and Y. Lithman, 146–59. London: Mansell.

Schinkel, Willem. 2012. *De nieuwe democratie: naar andere vormen van politiek*. Amsterdam: De Bezige Bij.

Schlatmann, Annemeik. 2016. *Sji'i Muslim Youth in the Netherlands: Negotiating Sji'i Fatwas and Rituals in the Dutch Context*. PhD Dissertation, Utrecht University.

Schmidt, Garbi. 2002. "Dialectics of Authenticity: Examples of Ethnification of Islam among Young Muslims in Sweden and the United States." *The Muslim World* 92 (1–2): 1–17.

Schulz, Dorothea Elisabeth. 2012. *Muslims and New Media in West Africa: Pathways to God*. Bloomington: Indiana University Press.

Scott, Michael W. 2005. "'I Was Like Abraham': Notes on the Anthropology of Christianity from the Solomon Islands." *Ethnos* 70 (1): 101–25.

Sennett, Richard. 1998. *The Corrosion of Character: The Personal Consequences of Work in the New Capitalism*. New York and London: Norton.

Shibley, Mark A. 1996. *Resurgent Evangelicalism in the United States: Mapping Cultural Change since 1970*. Columbia, SC: University of South Carolina Press.

Shibley, Mark A. 1998. "Contemporary Evangelicals: Born-Again and World Affirming." *The Annals of the American Academy of Political and Social Science* 558 (1): 67–87.

Simmel, Georg. 1950. *The Sociology of Georg Simmel*. Edited and translated by Kurt H. Wolff. New York: The Free Press.

Simon, Gregory M. 2009. "The Soul Freed of Cares? Islamic Prayer, Subjectivity, and the Contradictions of Moral Selfhood in Minangkabau, Indonesia." *American Ethnologist* 36 (2): 258–75.

Simon, Gregory M. 2014. *Caged in on the Outside: Moral Subjectivity, Selfhood, and Islam in Minangkabau, Indonesia*. Honolulu, HI: University of Hawai'i Press.

Smit, Regien. 2012. *More Than Conquerors: Space, Time and Power in Two Lusophone Pentecostal Migrant Churches in Rotterdam*. PhD Dissertation, Vrije Universiteit Amsterdam.

Smith, Christian, and Patricia Snell. 2009. *Souls in Transition: The Religious and Spiritual Lives of Emerging Adults*. Oxford: Oxford University Press.

Smith, Wilfred Cantwell. 1977. *Belief and History*. Charlottesville: University Press of Virginia.

Smith, Wilfred Cantwell. 1979. *Faith and Belief*. Princeton, NJ: Princeton University Press.

Soares, Benjamin, ed. 2006. *Muslim-Christian Encounters in Africa*. Leiden: Brill.

Stoffels, Hijme. 1990. *Wandelen in het licht: waarden, geloofsovertuigingen en sociale posities van Nederlandse evangelischen*. Kampen: Kok.

Stoffels, Hijme. 1995. *Als een briesende leeuw: orthodox-protestanten in de slag met de tijdgeest*. Kampen: Uitgeverij Kok.

Stolow, Jeremy. 2012. *Deus in Machina: Religion, Technology, and the Things in Between*. New York: Fordham University Press.

Strhan, Anna. 2015. *Aliens and Strangers? The Struggle for Coherence in the Everyday Lives of Evangelicals*. Oxford: Oxford University Press.

Sunier, Thijl. 2010. "Islam in the Netherlands: A Nation despite Religious Communities?" In *Religious Newcomers and the Nation State: Political Culture and Organized Religion in France and the Netherlands*, edited by Erik Sengers and Thijl Sunier, 115–30. Delft: Eburon.

Sunier, Thijl. 2011. "The Making of Muslim Youth Cultures in Europe." In *Mediating Faiths: Religion and Socio-Cultural Change in the Twenty-First Century*, edited by Michael Bailey and Guy Redden, 147–59. Aldershot and Burlington, VT: Ashgate Publishing.

Sunier, Thijl. 2014. "Domesticating Islam: Exploring Academic Knowledge Production on Islam and Muslims in European Societies." *Ethnic and Racial Studies* 37 (6): 1138–55.

Tamimi Arab, Pooyan. 2012. "(Dis)Entangling Culturalism, Nativism, Racism." *Krisis* 2012 (2): 68–74.

Tamimi Arab, Pooyan. 2017. *Amplifying Islam in the European Soundscape: Religious Pluralism and Secularism in the Netherlands*. New York: Bloomsbury.

Taylor, Charles. 1991. *The Ethics of Authenticity*. Cambridge, MA, and London: Harvard University Press.

Taylor, Charles. 2002. *Varieties of Religion Today: William James Revisited*. Cambridge, MA, and London: Harvard University Press.

Taylor, Charles. 2007. *A Secular Age*. Cambridge, MA, and London: Harvard University Press.

Ter Borg, Meerten, Erik Borgman, Marjo Buitelaar, Yme Kuiper, and Rob Plum, eds. 2008. *Handboek religie in Nederland: perspectief, overzicht, debat*. Zoetermeer: Uitgeverij Meinema/Forum.

Ter Laan, Nina. 2016. *Dissonant Voices: Islam-Inspired Music in Morocco and the Politics of Religious Sentiments.* PhD Dissertation, Radboud University Nijmegen.

Ter Laan, Nina. forthcoming. "'They Have No Taste in Morocco.' Home-Making Practices among Dutch-Speaking *Muhajirat* in Morocco." *Contemporary Islam.*

Tillich, Paul. 1959. *Theology of Culture.* Edited by Robert C. Kimball. Oxford: Oxford University Press.

Trilling, Lionel. 1971. *Sincerity and Authenticity.* Cambridge, MA: Harvard University Press.

Uitermark, Justus, and Jan Willem Duyvendak. 2008. "Civilising the City: Populism and Revanchist Urbanism in Rotterdam." *Urban Studies* 45 (7): 1485–1503.

Van Bruinessen, Martin, and Stefano Allievi, eds. 2011. *Producing Islamic Knowledge: Transmission and Dissemination in Western Europe.* London and New York: Routledge.

Van Dam, Peter. 2011. *Staat van verzuiling: over een Nederlandse mythe.* Amsterdam: Wereldbibliotheek.

Van Dam, Peter, and Paul Van Trigt. 2015. "Religious Regimes: Rethinking the Societal Role of Religion in Post-War Europe." *Contemporary European History* 24 (2): 213–32.

Van de Kamp, Linda. 2016. *Violent Conversion: Brazilian Pentecostalism and Urban Women in Mozambique.* Suffolk and Rochester, NY: James Currey.

Van de Port, Mattijs. 2011. *Ecstatic Encounters: Bahian Candomblé and the Quest for the Really Real.* Amsterdam: Amsterdam University Press.

Van den Hemel, Ernst. 2014. "(Pro)Claiming Tradition: The 'Judeo-Christian' Roots of Dutch Society and the Rise of Conservative Nationalism." In *Transformations of Religion and the Public Sphere: Postsecular Publics,* edited by Rosi Braidotti, Bolette Blaagaard, Tobijn de Graauw, and Eva Midden, 53–76. New York: Palgrave Macmillan.

Van der Stoep, Jan. 2007. "Binnenstebuiten en andersom: verinnerlijking en vormgeving van de ervaring." In *Alles wat je hart begeert?: christelijke oriëntatie in een op beleving gerichte cultuur,* edited by Jan Van der Stoep, Roel Kuiper, and Timon Ramaker, 171–90. Amsterdam: Buijten & Schipperheijn Motief.

Van der Veer, Peter. 2006. "Pim Fortuyn, Theo van Gogh, and the Politics of Tolerance in the Netherlands." *Public Culture* 18 (1): 111–24.

Van der Veer, Peter. 2016. *The Value of Comparison.* Durham, NC: Duke University Press.

Van Dijk-Groeneboer, Monique, ed. 2010. *Handboek jongeren en religie: katholieke, protestantse en islamitische jongeren in Nederland.* Almere: Parthenon.

Van Dijk-Groeneboer, Monique, Martijn De Koning, Joris Kregting, and Johan Roeland. 2010. "Ze geloven het wel." In *Handboek jongeren en religie: katholieke, protestantse en islamitische jongeren in Nederland,* edited by Monique Van Dijk-Groeneboer, 25–88. Almere: Parthenon.

Van Es, Margaretha A. 2016. *Stereotypes and Self-Representations of Women with a Muslim Background: The Stigma of Being Oppressed.* New York: Palgrave Macmillan.

Van Es, Margaretha A. 2018. "Muslims Denouncing Violent Extremism: Competing Essentialisms of Islam in Dutch Public Debate." *Journal of Muslims in Europe* 7 (2): 146–66.

Van Es, Margaretha A. 2019. "Muslim Women as "Ambassadors" of Islam: Breaking Stereotypes in Everyday Life." *Identities* 26 (4): 375–92.

Van Geest, P. 2005. "Augustinus." In *Christelijke encyclopedie*, edited by George Harinck, Wim Berkelaar, Albert De Vos, and Lodewijk Winkeler, 119. Kampen: Kok.

Van Harskamp, Anton. 2000. *Het nieuw-religieuze verlangen*. Kampen: Uitgeverij Kok.

Van Harskamp, Anton. 2008. "Existential Insecurity and New Religiosity: An Essay on Some Religion-Making Characteristics of Modernity." *Social Compass* 55 (1): 9–19.

Van Harskamp, Anton. 2010. "Van secularisering, seculariteit en sacralisering… En van wat de theologie te doen staat." *Tijdschrift voor theologie* 50 (3): 304–21.

Van Harskamp, Anton. 2014. "Epilogue: Studying Religion as Our Intimate Stranger." In *Methods for the Study of Religious Change: From Religious Studies to Worldview Studies*, edited by André Droogers and Anton Van Harskamp, 180–7. Sheffield and Bristol, CT: Equinox.

Van Nieuwkerk, Karin, Mark LeVine, and Martin Stokes, eds. 2016. *Islam and Popular Culture*. Austin: University of Texas Press.

Van Rooden, Peter. 1996. *Religieuze regimes: over godsdienst en maatschappij in Nederland 1570–1990*. Amsterdam: Bert Bakker.

Van Rooden, Peter. 2010. "The Strange Death of Dutch Christendom." In *Secularisation in the Christian World*, edited by Callum G. Brown and Michael Snape, 175–95. Farnham and Burlington, VT: Ashgate Publishing.

Vásquez, Manuel A., and Marie F. Marquardt. 2003. *Globalizing the Sacred: Religion across the Americas*. New Brunswick, NJ, and London: Rutgers University Press.

Vellenga, Sipco, and Kees De Groot. 2019. "Securitization, Islamic Chaplaincy, and the Issue of (de)Radicalization of Muslim Detainees in Dutch Prisons." *Social Compass* 66 (2): 224–37.

Versteeg, Peter G.A. 2010. *The Ethnography of a Dutch Pentecostal Church: Vineyard Utrecht and the International Charismatic Movement*. Lewiston, NY: Edwin Mellen Press.

Vincett, Giselle, Elizabeth Olson, Peter Hopkins, and Rachel Pain. 2012. "Young People and Performance Christianity in Scotland." *Journal of Contemporary Religion* 27 (2): 275–90.

Vincett, Giselle, Sonya Sharma, and Kristin Aune. 2008. "Introduction: Women, Religion and Secularization: One Size Does Not Fit All." In *Women and Religion in the West: Challenging Secularization*, edited by Krisin Aune, Sonya Sharma, and Giselle L. Vincett, 1–19. Aldershot and Burlington, VT: Ashgate Publishing.

Wagemakers, Joas. 2016. *Salafism in Jordan: Political Islam in a Quietist Community*. Cambridge: Cambridge University Press.

Waldring, Ismintha, Maurice Crul, and Halleh Ghorashi. 2014. "The Fine Art of Boundary Sensitivity: Successful Second Generation Turks and Moroccans in the Netherlands." *New Diversities* 14 (1): 71–87.

Wallis, Roy, and Steve Bruce. 1992. "Secularization: The Orthodox Model." In *Religion and Modernization: Sociologists and Historians Debate the Secularization Thesis*, edited by Steve Bruce, 8–30. Oxford: Clarendon Press.

Weber, Max. 1978. *Economy and Society: An Outline of Interpretive Sociology*, Vol. 1. Edited by Guenther Roth and Claus Wittich. Translated by Ephraim Fischoff et al. Berkeley: University of California Press.

Weber, Max. 2003. *The Protestant Ethic and the Spirit of Capitalism*. Translated by Talcott Parsons. Mineola, NY: Courier Dover Publications.

Weber, Samuel. 1996. "Mass Mediauras; or, Art, Aura, and Media in the Work of Walter Benjamin." In *Walter Benjamin: Theoretical Questions*, edited by David S. Ferris, 24–49. Stanford, CA: Stanford University Press.

Wekker, Gloria. 2016. *White Innocence: Paradoxes of Colonialism and Race*. Durham, NC: Duke University Press.

Wiktorowicz, Quintan. 2006. "Anatomy of the Salafi Movement." *Studies in Conflict and Terrorism* 29 (3): 207–39.

Winkeler, Lodewijk. 2004. *Stromingen in katholiek Nederland*. Kampen: Uitgeverij Kok.

Woodhead, Linda, and Paul Heelas, eds. 2000. *Religion in Modern Times: An Interpretive Anthology*. Oxford and Malden, MA: Blackwell.

Yanow, Dvora, and Marleen Van der Haar. 2013. "People Out of Place: Allochthony and Autochthony in the Netherlands' Identity Discourse—Metaphors and Categories in Action." *Journal of International Relations and Development* 16 (2): 227–61.

Yip, Andrew Kam-Tuck, and Sarah-Jane Page. 2013. *Religious and Sexual Identities: A Multi-Faith Exploration of Young Adults*. Farnham: Ashgate.

Yukich, Grace. 2018. "Muslim American Activism in the Age of Trump". *Sociology of Religion* 79 (2): 220–47.

Zigon, Jarrett. 2007. "Moral Breakdown and the Ethical Demand: A Theoretical Framework for an Anthropology of Moralities". *Anthropological Theory* 7 (2): 131–50.

Zulfikar, Yavuz Fahir. 2012. "Do Muslims Believe More in Protestant Work Ethic than Christians? Comparison of People with Different Religious Background Living in the US". *Journal of Business Ethics* 105 (4): 489–502.

Index

acceleration 19, 32, 122, 124, 133–7, 143, 144, 148, 160, 176, 178, 179, 195 n.6
adhan (call to prayer) 129, 196 n.10
Adorno, Theodor W. 160
affective experience 117, 138
Africa 17, 36, 59
Agger, Ben 135–6, 144, 195 n.2, 195 n.6
Ahmadis 187 n.6
Alevis 187 n.6
Ali B. 88–9
allochthonous 13, 14
ambivalence 21, 22, 33, 66, 115, 137, 143, 149, 151, 152, 155, 156, 193 n.13
Ammerman, Nancy Tatom 22, 97, 99
anthropology
    of Christianity 3, 4, 15–18, 192 n.12
    of ethics 66, 191 n.1
    of Islam 3, 15–18, 22, 23, 38, 39, 67, 192 n.12
    of religion 3, 21, 22
Aquinas, Thomas 71
articulation 23, 24, 67, 91, 177
Asad, Talal 112, 178, 189 n.4
    on ritual (or religious practice) 38, 119, 124, 149, 163
    on secularism 19, 192 n.12
    on social conditions of religious practice 23
authenticity 8, 18, 31, 61, 64, 66–9, 73, 74, 80–3, 91, 175, 178, 192 n.12
    ethics of 18, 31, 61, 64, 66–9, 80–3, 91, 175
autochthony 13, 14
autonomy 13, 67, 82, 91, 192 n.12

Baudet, Thierry 12
Baumann, Gerd 16, 193 n.4
Becker, Howard 190 n.12
belief 2, 8, 14, 19, 32, 38, 41, 42, 56, 78, 97, 102, 103, 108–12, 114, 116, 118, 119, 176
    distinction between faith and 38

Benjamin, Walter 160, 161
Berger, Peter L. 19, 109, 116–18, 123, 194 n.12
Bible 1, 24–5, 53, 54, 56, 59, 60, 63, 69, 70, 72, 87, 89, 90, 95, 103, 121, 124, 130–3, 140–2, 148, 149, 157, 158, 162–4, 174, 191 n.20
Bible Belt 9, 25
Binnendijk, Henk 158, 159
Bourdieu, Pierre 56, 62, 118
burqa (face veil) 150, 195 n.2

Calvinism 5, 7–9, 14, 28, 52, 59, 63, 86, 89, 90, 123, 124, 157, 183, 190 n.17, 191 n.23
capitalism 18–20, 23, 24, 32, 33, 72, 122, 123, 135–7, 139, 143, 144, 160, 176–8, 182, 184, 195 n.4
    consumer 19, 20, 32, 178
    fast 18, 20, 32, 122–4, 135, 136, 139, 143–5, 176–8, 195 n.6
    high 4, 19, 135, 160, 178, 182, 185
"care of the self" (Foucault) 83
Catholics 4, 7, 9, 25, 110, 187 n.1
Charismatic (Christianity) 59, 84, 164
Christelijke Hogeschool Ede 24
Christianity
    anthropology of 3, 4, 15–18, 192 n.12
    institutionalized 4, 7, 8, 184
church
    doctrines 58–9
    migrant 9
    PKN 7, 26, 53, 54, 56, 57, 60, 61, 94, 101, 103, 190 n.17
    reformed 7, 26, 53, 57, 90, 101, 121, 190 n.17. *See also* Protestant churches
community
    contemporary forms of 97, 98
    and conviction 97, 106–7, 117, 193 n.4
    new settings of 98–9
    participation 99, 100, 116, 118, 119

comparison 3–4, 6, 15–18, 24, 29, 31, 36, 63, 81, 94, 118, 163, 174, 184, 185, 188 n.10, 193 n.5
consumer capitalism 19, 20, 32, 178
consumerism 6, 123, 136, 150
conviction 26, 30, 32, 40, 58, 62, 80, 81, 90, 96, 97, 103, 104, 106, 107, 110, 111, 114–17, 119, 121, 127, 157, 176, 177, 183, 193 n.15
covenant 58, 191 n.23
cultural pluralism 18, 97. *See also* pluralism
cultural revolution 12–13

Day of Judgment 85, 86, 168
deprivatization 99
devil 150, 157, 159. *See also* Satan
discourses on religion 6, 11–14
discrimination 10, 29, 48, 49
"discursive tradition" (Asad) 23, 81
distraction 22, 32, 147–50, 152, 154, 159–62, 165–8, 170, 171, 176, 178, 179
doubt 23, 32, 33, 49, 63, 94, 97, 102, 104, 105, 107, 108, 112–21, 162, 176, 177, 179, 194 n.11
and pluralism 108–11

Eagleton, Terry 71
emotion 39, 47, 55, 58, 68, 84, 89, 124, 127, 138, 174, 188 n.11
entertainment 32, 134, 136, 151, 158, 160, 161, 175, 178
Erasmus University Rotterdam 25, 40, 71, 94, 126, 138
ethics
  anthropology of 66, 191 n.1
  of authenticity 18, 31, 61, 64, 66–9, 80–3, 91, 175
  of capitalism 24, 123, 143
  of submission 31, 66–9, 81–3, 91
"ethnic minorities" 5, 11
Europe 2–6, 8, 12, 17, 18, 20, 44, 48, 51, 69, 81, 82, 98, 123, 130, 173, 174, 181, 182, 184, 188 n.11, 193 n.3
  Christians in 1–3, 5, 6, 17, 18, 66, 69, 81, 97, 98, 174, 184
  Muslims in 1–3, 5, 6, 17, 18, 20, 37, 44, 48, 66, 69, 81, 82, 96–8, 130, 174, 180–2, 184, 189 n.6, 189 n.8, 193 n.3, 196 n.9

evangelicalism 28, 58–64, 82, 155, 182, 191 n.24
  churches affiliated with 60, 61
  in the Netherlands 60–1
  and revivalism 17, 29, 36, 50, 55, 64
  in the United States 99, 109, 136, 155, 157
Evangelische Omroep 60, 147
Evans-Pritchard, E. E. 15, 30, 31
exceptionalism (with regard to Islam) 173, 179–85
exclusion 48, 49

Facebook 150, 151, 155, 158, 160, 161
Fadil, Nadia 22, 44, 82, 192 n.12
failure 22, 108, 115, 130, 133, 134
faith 5, 19, 28, 31, 35–8, 61, 70, 72, 73, 87, 89–91, 95, 97, 99, 100, 109, 112–16, 120–2, 127–34, 142, 147–9, 151, 152, 154–62, 166–71, 174–9, 181, 183, 185, 191 n.20
  affirmation of 101–8
  Christian 8, 23, 52–8, 84, 113, 121, 132
  conscious 31, 35, 61
  distinction between belief and 38
  Islamic 28, 31, 35, 37–41, 61, 79–81, 115, 116, 120, 122, 148, 161, 174. *See also* iman
  "living" 38, 52–7, 59
  nourishment of 162–5
  personal 35, 53, 58, 87, 100, 124, 142, 161, 165, 175, 193 n.14
  as a relationship with God 163–4
  revivalist 36, 64
  sincerity of 79–81
family 1, 29, 39, 40, 49, 52, 54, 57, 62, 63, 88, 101, 103, 104, 121, 129, 135, 136, 139
fast capitalism 18, 20, 32, 122–4, 135, 136, 139, 143–5, 176–8, 195 n.6
fasting 10, 40, 43, 114. *See also* Ramadan
first generation (of migrants) 11, 189 n.8
Fortuyn, Pim 12
Foucault, Michel 66, 67, 82, 83, 192 n.12
fragmentation 23, 32, 136, 170
freedom 4, 13, 65, 66, 69, 79, 82, 91, 180
  and free will 77–9
  and fulfillment 72–4
  "negative" (Berlin) 78
  personal 65, 72, 79, 91

Index

free will 65, 77–9, 85, 192 n.9
fundamentalism 6, 12, 18, 35, 179

geloof (faith) 37–8. *See also* faith; *iman*
Gereformeerde Kerken vrijgemaakt 53, 54, 57, 58, 190 n.17, 191 n.21
God
    and prayer 124–5
    closeness to 38, 63, 64, 75, 124–5, 144, 162–8, 171, 174, 177, 178, 184
    distractions from 149, 154, 157–62
    mercy of 38, 70, 86
    submission to 74–7
    will of 65, 69–73, 75, 78, 79, 82, 85, 90, 91, 112, 165, 176
good deeds 86, 87
"groupism" (Brubaker) 21
Gülen movement 25, 87, 129, 137, 188 n.16
Gumbel, Nicky 72

habituation 152, 153, 158, 170
habitus 158
    primary 56, 62
    specific 62, 118
hadith 50, 75, 86, 88, 89, 93, 96, 127, 151, 190 n.16, 193 n.1
Hagoort, Henk 71–3
halal 10, 42, 123
Hall, Stuart 23–4
Harvey, David 135, 195 n.2
Heelas, Paul 68, 82
Hervieu-Léger, Danièle 117, 118
high capitalism 4, 19, 135, 160, 178, 182, 185
hijab (Islamic veil) 11, 40, 41, 65, 75
Hirschkind, Charles 138, 169, 195 n.5
Hirsi Ali, Ayaan 12
Hizmet. *See* Gülen movement
Holy Spirit 59, 132
Hoover, Stewart M. 66, 148–9

identity 7, 9, 13, 14, 17, 20, 21, 35, 49, 70, 72, 74, 94, 142, 180, 182, 183, 187 n.8. *See also* "reactive identification" (Nagra)
    formation 2
    national 4, 14
    politics 3
ihsan (perfection) 93, 127

iman (faith) 37, 38, 40, 104–6, 108, 115, 138, 139, 149, 150, 152, 154, 165–8, 179, 189 n.3, 194 n.11, 196 n.9. *See also* faith
    "low" 115
imperfection 22, 66, 70, 76, 83–7, 91, 121, 125, 133, 145, 154, 185
Indonesia 9, 24, 123, 154, 187 n.5
"integration" 2, 3, 11, 12, 18, 47, 173, 180, 182, 185, 196 n.6
internet 11, 41, 42, 51, 97, 98, 104, 134, 135, 147, 150, 151, 155, 158–60, 169, 194 n.7, 196 n.7
    as used for religious purposes 151, 155
Islam
    anthropology of 3, 15–18, 22, 23, 38, 39, 67, 192 n.12
    debates on 12–13, 47–9, 180, 195 n.2
    institutionalization of 9
    politicization of 47–9
    "true" 42–4
Islamic State in Iraq and al-Sham (ISIS) 12, 51, 181, 190 n.14
Islamophobia 11–14, 183

Jesus Christ 57–9, 72, 73, 79, 84, 87, 90, 94, 95, 114, 125, 164
jihad 52, 181, 190 n.15
jihad an-nafs (battle against the self) 76, 85
jihadi-Salafism 51–2
Jouili, Jeanette S. 100, 180, 189 n.6, 194 n.1

Keane, Webb 3, 81, 119, 192 n.11
Kloos, David 22, 153–4
Kracauer, Siegfried 160, 161
Kuyper, Abraham 7

Lapidus, Ira M. 76
Leach, Edmund R. 16
liberal-secularism 4, 39
Liberatore, Giulia 81, 115, 193 n.13
"living" faith 38, 52–7, 59
Luckmann, Thomas 68, 99
Luhrmann, Tanya M. 23, 55, 109, 111, 115

madhhab (school of Islamic law) 39
Mahmood, Saba 38–9, 67, 69, 119, 149, 192 n.12
marginalization 30, 170, 175, 184

mass media 4, 32, 120, 148, 154–7, 160, 162, 165, 169, 170, 176
mass-mediated popular culture 32, 148, 154–60, 165, 176, 178
materialism 136, 155
media technologies 148, 149, 151, 154, 155, 167, 169, 170
"methodical sanctification" (Weber) 85
Meyer, Birgit 35–6, 119, 156, 169, 189 n.1
migration studies 2, 5, 9, 29, 65, 187 n.4, 187 n.8
minority studies 2, 3, 5, 8, 14, 17, 54, 94, 129, 173, 184, 185
modern media 18, 123, 134, 136, 148, 149, 159, 160, 167, 185
moral ambivalence 22, 66, 143, 193 n.13
moral coherence 22
morality 14, 20, 111
"moral registers" (Schielke) 82
Moroccan-Dutch 9–11, 13, 29, 44, 187 n.8, 189 n.5
movies 149, 151, 152, 154–7, 159, 169, 170, 183
music 5, 42, 54, 57, 60, 75, 147–9, 151–9, 161, 162, 169, 170, 190 n.17, 191 n.18, 196 n.5
Muslim preachers 46–7, 78, 189 n.7

nafs (self) 76, 85, 125, 150, 192 n.7
nativism 32–3
new media 6, 136, 151, 154, 155, 158
nine-eleven "(9/11)" 12, 48, 49, 181

opbouwen (edify) 162, 191 n.20
Opwekking (evangelical organization and festival) 25, 60, 84, 89
"othering" 1–2, 180

Paul (the Apostle) 70, 85–6
peace (as an emotional state) 39, 63, 122, 124, 132, 137–41, 143, 158. See also *rust* (peace)
pedagogy 32, 46, 47, 52, 97, 107, 108, 115, 118, 121, 176, 179, 180
Pentecostalism 9, 14, 21, 26, 36, 59, 68, 89, 90, 123, 131, 151, 156, 169, 190 n.17
piety 6, 20–5, 28, 32, 33, 39, 43, 45, 48, 50, 51, 67, 69, 83, 85, 86, 88, 92, 100, 107, 119, 133, 151, 154, 168, 169, 177, 180, 184, 188 n.12
  as conceptualized in the anthropology of Islam 3, 38–9
  negative connotations of 180
  as precarious 174–9, 184
  in relation to capitalist ethics 143
  in relation to everyday life 22
  in relation to "faith" 39
  as situated 21
"pillarization" 7–8, 110
pluralism 18, 19, 23, 97, 116, 178, 194 n.12
  Charles Taylor on 23, 108–11
  doubt and 108–11
  Peter Berger on 19, 116, 194 n.12
  as a trait of secular culture 19, 108–9
popular culture 1, 4, 6, 59, 99, 136
  as a source of attraction and distraction 32, 148–62, 165, 169–70, 175–6, 178, 185
post-Fordism 20, 135, 195 n.2
post-secular 188 n.11
prayer 10, 39, 40, 43, 45, 54, 60, 70, 74, 80, 89, 90, 94, 96, 98, 101, 104, 113, 115, 121, 122, 124–31, 133, 134, 137–45, 149, 150, 153, 163–8, 170, 176, 180, 194 n.1, 196 n.10
precarious piety 174–9, 184
privatization 68, 97, 99, 107
Prophet Muhammad 30, 41, 50, 74, 86, 93, 167
Protestant Church in the Netherlands (PKN) 26, 53, 54, 57, 101, 103, 190 n.17
Protestant churches
  mainline 52, 53, 56, 60, 61, 94
  orthodox 53, 190 n.17
  strictly orthodox 101, 121, 157, 190 n.17. See also church
Protestant nation 7
Protestantism (or Protestant Christianity) 5, 24, 31, 36, 57, 59, 60, 70, 71, 86, 155, 174, 192 n.12
"public church" 7

"quiet time" 140, 144
Quran 39, 43, 46, 65, 74, 75, 78, 93, 126, 138, 151, 152, 158, 159, 168, 181
  recitation of 30, 39, 47, 96, 127, 149, 150, 165, 167, 168, 170

racialization 14
radicalization 12, 33, 181, 182
Ramadan 10, 39, 43, 104, 113, 167. *See also* fasting
"reactive identification" (Nagra) 48, 190 n.12
redemption (in Christianity) 58, 70, 73, 79, 84, 85, 125, 164, 174, 191 n.23
Reformed church 7, 26, 53, 57, 90, 101, 103, 121, 190 n.17
relativism 15, 97, 108, 109, 112-14, 176, 178
religious minorities 1, 184, 185
religious pedagogy 32, 46, 50, 97, 107, 115, 118, 121, 176, 179, 180
revivalism (religious) 5-6, 17, 19, 28, 29, 31, 35-7, 50, 61-4, 66, 91, 98, 173-6, 180, 188 n.12, 195 n.4
  Christian 55-6, 59-61
  Islamic 21, 44, 48, 50, 127, 180
Robbins, Joel 3
Roeland, Johan 81, 82, 99, 191 n.26, 192 n.12
Rose, Nikolas 192 n.12
Rotterdam 24, 25
Roy, Olivier 17-18, 35, 98, 192 n.3
rust (peace) 124, 137, 138, 140, 141. *See also* peace

al-salaf al-salih ("the pious forefathers") 50
Salafism 5, 12, 46, 60-4, 74, 75, 80, 127, 154, 179, 181-2
  anxieties about 12, 181, 182
  distinction between purists, politicos and jihadis 190 n.15
  and ISIS 12, 51, 181
  mosques oriented toward 10, 11, 25, 45, 52, 105, 181
  in the Netherlands 51-2, 194 n.7
  and revivalism 28, 29, 35, 50, 61, 175
  self-identification with 52, 190 n.16
  and violent extremism 52, 181
salat (Islamic prayer) 39, 40, 124-30, 137-40, 144, 194 n.1. *See also* prayer
salvation 70, 71, 83, 85-7, 125, 133
Satan 76, 115. *See also* devil
Schielke, Samuli 27, 195 n.4
second generation (of migrants) 11, 18, 29, 194 n.14

secular 2-6, 13, 17-19, 23, 26, 31-3, 59, 63, 82, 108, 110, 111, 115-18, 130, 141, 148, 149, 155, 162, 169, 173, 175-8, 180, 182-5, 188 n.11, 196 n.10
  approaches to 18-20
secularism 3, 188 n.11, 192 n.12
  and liberalism 39, 82, 192-3 n.12
  as a mode of governance (or regulation) 18, 19, 178, 192 n.12
  Talal Asad on 19, 192-3 n.12
secularist discourses 13
secularity 4, 18-20, 23, 31, 39, 111, 177
  and capitalism 20
  Charles Taylor on 19, 23, 108-9, 111
  as lived reality 19-20
  and pluralism 19, 108-9
secularization 2, 3, 18-20, 99, 109, 144, 173
security (as a policy concern) 12, 33
self-cultivation 39, 67, 68, 81, 119, 133
self-expression 8, 68, 110
self-fulfillment 3, 68, 69, 71-4, 77, 79, 82, 143, 159
self-improvement 50, 71, 83-7, 91, 92, 108, 115, 127
self-realization 8, 65, 68, 71, 82, 91, 175
self-reflection 35, 87-91, 110, 165, 179
self-vigilance 83, 87-92
senses 89, 159, 161
sexuality 1, 4, 13, 14, 17, 58, 72, 76, 77, 84, 150, 152, 154-7, 159, 166, 167, 180, 183, 196 n.6
Shi'is 52, 187 n.6
shirk (idolatry) 50, 86
Simmel, Georg 160
sincerity 31, 66, 67, 79-81, 83, 86, 88, 91, 104, 108, 174-6, 192 n.11
skepticism 23, 177, 178
Smith, Christian 99, 100, 119, 136, 189 n.4, 194 n.8
Smith, Wilfred Cantwell 38
socialists 7
sociality 54, 97-100
socialization 44, 56, 59, 95, 109, 118, 193 n.3
social media 148, 155, 169
social networks 37, 38, 115
social religious settings 55, 88, 95-100, 104, 107, 155

socio-economic position 10
sociology of religion 2, 68, 97, 99, 109, 194 n.15
spiritual experience 39, 63, 64, 100, 118, 174
spirituality 8, 39, 43, 55, 59, 63, 64, 68, 76, 81, 100, 118, 125, 145, 174, 175
stereotypes 1, 6, 14, 48, 63, 173, 181
stilgezet worden (being brought to a standstill) 142
"*stille tijd*" 140. *See also* "quiet time"
Strhan, Anna 107, 136, 183–4
subjective turn 67, 68, 192 n.12
subjectivity 21, 56, 66, 69, 82, 91, 188 n.11
subjectivization 68, 81
submission 64–9, 73, 76, 79, 92, 134, 175
  ethics of 31, 66–9, 81–3, 91
Sunna 41, 50, 52, 190 n.16
Sunnism (or Sunni Islam) 5, 9, 31, 36, 39, 50, 138, 174

tawhid (unity of God) 50, 112
Taylor, Charles 19, 23, 67, 68, 108–11, 177
  on authenticity 8, 67, 68, 83
  on pluralism 23, 108–11
  on the relation between individuality and community 118
  on secularity 19, 23, 111, 177
television 8, 42, 110, 131, 134, 140, 142, 147–9, 151, 155–9, 161, 169
The Hague 24–6, 74, 154
time 84, 104, 105, 122, 133–6, 143–5, 167, 168, 195 n.3
  and capitalist ethics 123
  and "care of the self" (Foucault) 83
  for (Christian) prayer and bible reading 130–3, 163, 165
  and Christian worship 140–2
  and high capitalism (or post-Fordism) 135–7, 143

leisure 110, 113
politics of 13
and *salat* (Islamic prayer) 45, 124, 137–9, 165–6, 176
for *salat* (Islamic prayer) 126–30
and the use of modern media or popular culture 155, 158, 160, 162
for worship practices 32, 70, 121–2, 133, 142–5, 170, 178
trans-denominational approach 53, 57–9
Trilling, Lionel 81
Turkish-Dutch 9–11, 13, 29, 30, 51, 187 n.8

uncertainty 22, 32, 80, 86, 107, 109, 111, 115, 117
university 1, 24, 25, 27, 45, 46, 54, 55, 93, 95, 101, 104, 105, 113, 116, 122, 129, 136, 141, 142, 150, 153, 167, 168

Van Gogh, Theo 12, 51
Van Harskamp, Anton 66, 191 n.24, 191 n.26
Van Rooden, Peter 7–8, 110, 194 n.13
Verdonk, Rita 12
vigilance. *See* self-vigilance
vreemdelingschap (being a stranger) 157
vroomheid (piety) 39. *See also* piety

Weber, Max 85, 86, 123, 155
Wilders, Geert 12, 116
Woodhead, Linda 68, 82
work (as in having a job) 16, 29, 128, 130, 134, 141, 175
worship music (or worship songs) 5, 25, 30, 57, 60, 61, 94, 97, 155, 190 n.17

Zerstreuung (distraction) 160–1. *See also* distraction

www.ingramcontent.com/pod-product-compliance
Lightning Source LLC
Chambersburg PA
CBHW072230290426
44111CB00012B/2039